COMMUNICATIONS
IN THE
RURAL THIRD WORLD

COMMUNICATIONS IN THE RURAL THIRD WORLD

The Role of Information in Development

edited by
Emile G. McAnany

PRAEGER

PRAEGER SPECIAL STUDIES • PRAEGER SCIENTIFIC

Library of Congress Cataloging in Publication Data
Main entry under title:

Communications in the rural third world.

Bibliography: p.
Includes index.
1. Underdeveloped areas--Communication.
2. Communication in rural development. I. McAnany,
Emile G.
HN980.C66   301.16'09172'4   79-21406
ISBN 0-03-052986-7

Published in 1980 by Praeger Publishers
CBS Educational and Professional Publishing
A Division of CBS, Inc.
521 Fifth Avenue, New York, New York 10017 U.S.A.

0123456789   038   987654321

Printed in the United States of America

ACKNOWLEDGMENTS

It is difficult to acknowledge all the help that went into the creation of this volume, but one place to start is the institution where it had its beginning, the Institute for Communication Research, Stanford University. Among the many people who were in some way responsible for the research reported here, Robert Hornik, now at the Annenberg School of Communication, University of Pennsylvania, was of key importance. As co-investigator with me on the work in Guatemala and close adviser of authors Eduardo Contreras and Jeremiah O'Sullivan, he deserves much of the credit for rigor and thoroughness. Others then at the institute, less involved but helpful at different stages, were Peter Spain, John Mayo, Kathy Graham, and Liz Vincent. Everett Rogers provided advice for one of the authors, Larry Shore, and funding to see to the final preparation of this volume. Former students and researchers who contributed to research for the Ivory Coast project were Mireille Etaix, Pierre Seya, Faustin Yao, and Joseph Yao. Special thanks are due to many generous collaborators in the Ivory Coast and Guatemala, too numerous to mention by name.

I wish to thank the generous collaboration of all of the authors included here in helping me to prepare this volume. Special support was provided by a New Jersey foundation in working on this writing project, and I would like to thank Rosemary Ellmer for arranging this support.

Santa Cruz, California

v

CONTENTS

Chapter

PART I

INFORMATION IN RURAL DEVELOPMENT: GENERAL SOCIAL ISSUES

LIST OF TABLES AND FIGURES

OVERVIEW

Emile G. McAnany

We do not need to be reminded that the majority of humankind live in the rural villages of low-income countries and that the lot of this vast majority is one of relative and absolute poverty. World hunger has haunted the conscience of the affluent industrialized nations; so have the specters of population, disease, and illiteracy. During the development decade of the 1970s, a "new" approach was declared (as, perhaps inevitably, at the beginning of each decade), one concentrating not on the old paradigm of rapid industrialization and urbanization of low-income countries but on agricultural improvement, rural services to the poor, and greater participation of the majority in their own development. As we approach a new decade, we may expect even newer paradigms and approaches, but perhaps this is an appropriate time to review some of the consequences of the recent development credos of the 1970s.

The past decade has manifested not only new paradigms for development but also an increasing concern about the role that communication technology plays in the modern society of all nations (UNESCO 1978a). International concern has focused on how increasingly sophisticated technology provides us not only with increasing information and communication opportunities but also with problems about what kind of social impact television may be having on our children and our society, or what kind of cultural impact the export of communications products may have on other countries. All communication indexes are up, even in low-income countries and even, it seems, in remote villages of those countries. No village seems so remote that radio, at least, does not reach it. The attitudes toward this communication expansion range from optimistic to cautious to negative, depending on one's value perspectives and the evidence to which one is exposed. Some see it as an opportunity for change in the stagnant sectors of their societies; others see it as simply a more refined tool for penetration of the dominant power holders in society; still others, as a two-edged sword that can produce change of a beneficial nature, provided the conditions for this change are available in the society. Whatever the perspective, there is a general agreement that communication and its content have taken on an increasingly important role in modern—also called postmodern or information—society.

The concern about information's role in rural development is not new to this decade. The United Nations Educational, Scientific and Cultural Organization (UNESCO), for example, has from the early

1950s devoted a large portion of its budget and efforts to mass media and development. There have been any number of projects using the mass media for education, agriculture, family planning, and even for health and nutrition in low-income countries. What is new in the present decade is, perhaps, the definition of the problem—reaching and improving the lot of the rural poor. This change of the target audience has had pronounced impacts on a number of development efforts, including communications. In this latter field, we have changed the kinds of outcomes that we expect from communication. A great deal of communication for rural development was defined previously within the paradigm of the diffusion of innovations, admirably summarized at the beginning of the decade by Rogers and Shoemaker (1971). The shortcomings of this approach were several. Although it measured elements of social structure, it drew no policy implications from the consistent finding that "progressive" farmers (that is, those already relatively better off in a rural environment) were the ones who were the early adopters. The innovations that were being diffused were often created in a high-technology country like the United States and were not appropriate to the areas where they were being introduced. Outcome measures often were not focused on the economic impact of adoption and continuation but simply on the adoption behavior itself. A number of diffusionists are beginning to revise their own paradigm (Rogers 1976; Röling, Ascroft, and Chege 1976).

Given the new focus upon the poor majority, information's and communication's role had to be reexamined in terms of equity (who benefits from information) and productivity (what impact information has on agricultural productivity, health, and income, as well as on knowledge, attitudes, and behavior of rural people). The research brought together in this book is an attempt to see the problem from this new perspective. If the conclusions seem to be pessimistic, the problem is that we are only beginning to discover the real characteristics of the situation of the rural poor, including their communication behavior and its consequences. Social and political structures enter into the formation of the problems of rural poor, and the problems cannot be solved by ignoring this reality. We do believe that there is a solution and that communication/information has an important if modest role to play, but the necessary condition of this role will be some changes in the environment other than the addition of information. We do not offer solutions in this analysis but, rather, concentrate on how social structure enters into the difficulty of reaching the rural poor and of changing, to any significant extent, their situation.

A brief historical note will place this work in some perspective in the communication field, especially that area now referred to as development communication. This latter is sometimes defined as the study of how to apply various kinds of communication technology and techniques to the solution of different social problems of developing countries.

The work of this volume was largely generated by a group at the Institute for Communication Research, Stanford University, while the editor was a member of the faculty in the early and mid-1970s. With the exception of Ashby and Pachico, all of the authors were members, at one time or another, of a research group at the institute.

Historically, this was an important period for communication research as it applied to development, and even the term development communication became popular during this time. The institute was given institutional support by the Agency for International Development in the form of a 211d grant to continue and to expand the study of communication's role in development that had begun in the late 1960s with a number of field studies in communication's role in education. This early research had developed some directions to be pursued and suggested other questions about communication that were as yet unexplored.

In two field studies in El Salvador and Mexico from 1968 to 1973, members of the institute studied the effectiveness of television in two school systems (Mayo, Hornik, and McAnany 1976; Mayo, McAnany, and Klees 1975). Questions concerning learning as well as costs of the technology were pursued in these investigations, and a number of answers were provided—especially in the first study, which spanned four years of fieldwork and emerged with a detailed assessment of how a technology such as television affects an entire school system. This period marked a beginning of an important change in some research questions and methodologies to which members of the group had been exposed up to this point. Working with economists, educators, and development planners prompted many new questions and demanded some changes in directions for the communication researchers.

Besides changes due to work in multidisciplinary teams, another change emerged at this time that bore as much relation to value as it did to scientific method. While working on the effectiveness of communication in the formal school system, the questions were raised and examined: Who among students benefit most (or at all) from the school system? and What kind of difference in the distribution of the schooling benefits does communication technology make? The answers indicated that with television in Mexico and El Salvador the opportunity of access was broadened and that the learning gaps were probably not widened among the different social groups enrolled. But the question about those groups that were not enrolled or those who dropped out early was left largely unanswered.

Over the period of approximately four years (1974-78), the work of the institute continued to examine the problems of effectiveness, cost, and equity—equity becoming increasingly important as a criterion variable. Several new questions were raised and studied in field settings. The first was whether communication could achieve some of its proved effectiveness in the area of <u>nonformal education</u> (however broadly that term was to be defined). The second was whether communication could have any significant beneficial impact on the poorest segments of society—the usually illiterate mass of persons living on subsistence and small, cash-crop farms. Two new projects were undertaken in Guatemala and the Ivory Coast, under the direction of R. Hornik and myself, in the former, and of solely my direction, in the latter. This book represents an attempt, through this research, to provide some answers to these questions.

There are no final answers in the subsequent chapters, but some new evidence is presented concerning the role of communication in bringing information and education to the rural poor. There are some clarifications that seem to emerge about the limits of information in transforming the situation of poverty in rural areas. The policy questions that are being asked by many people interested in change among the rural poor are those concerned with social and economic services to this population. This focus has made communication researchers review their own research about delivery of information to this audience and to pay special attention to three important areas of the problem: selection, outcomes, and causal attribution of change to information.

For questions of equity, it is of obvious relevance to know who it is that chooses to participate in communication programs. Lenglet, in his chapter, has given special attention to this question of who the target audience is supposed to be and who it is in actuality. Reviewing research on development in general, it seems plausible that information resources, like many other resources in a society, will be distributed in such a way that they benefit those already higher in the social structure. This question was not given major attention in communication studies before the early part of this decade (Tichenor, Donahue, and Olive 1970) and remained largely unexamined in the diffusion tradition. Shore has reviewed, in his chapter, some of the research on development and has reanalyzed data from two large diffusion projects of the 1960s to see whether information follows other patterns of social structure. Focus on exclusively rural areas does not alleviate the problem of selection, because differences between urban and rural areas are not the only important distinctions to be made. The rural populace is highly differentiated and we must ask whether within the rural audience there is a difference of listening audiences (subsistence, small cash-crop, and large farmers, for example). Shore, Lenglet, O'Sullivan, and Contreras bring a great deal of evidence to bear on this question.

The outcomes that communication research focuses upon vary widely according to the theoretical and policy orientation that guide it. Development communication has attempted to explore the application of communication principles and techniques in the areas of such practical outcomes as education, health, nutrition, family planning, and agriculture. This means, primarily, learning outcomes in education and training but runs the gamut from learning, attitudes, and behavior to outcome status in health, nutrition, and agriculture. The measures of outcome typical of previous development communication research often stopped at questions of simple exposure to a message (as Shore indicates in his chapter, it is not an unimportant question in itself) or change in knowledge and attitude and, sometimes, behavior (as in much of the diffusion literature). But few studies were able to go beyond, to whether communication had any influence on outcome status and what particular path this influence took. O'Sullivan and Contreras describe studies that attempted to trace the economic outcomes of information on farmers' productivity and income. Ashby and her associates, in their chapter, provide a great deal of detail concerning the thinking behind such studies. Lenglet indicates that measures of outcomes among large rural audiences are not easy to come by and that the open audience for development communication messages may be more important than the organized audience that meets regularly and discusses these messages.

The final unanswered question, which the field research reported here attempted to unravel in a modest way, concerned the causal role of information in the change process itself. As Contreras points out, the role of communication in an explanatory model of rural change is much more complex than previous research has indicated. At a certain time in the 1960s, it seemed that it was a simple thing to harness communication for change and development. As our views of development changed, our optimism about the role of communication also changed and grew more complex, if not more pessimistic. As Ashby and her associates point out, there are at least two distinct views and approaches to development among economists, as well as among educators and communicators. Marxist and neoclassical approaches in economics are paralleled by similar approaches in other fields. Historical factors are a serious consideration in social research in trying to understand how the rural poor became the poor and how their situation is maintained. Contreras has attempted to model information's influence on innovation adoption and other outcomes, and O'Sullivan has tried to ascertain what influences the productivity and income of Guatemalan Highland farmers. Neither has arrived at final and satisfying models of information's role; but their attempts have enlarged our set of questions and made us more cautious about the role that information and communication can be expected to play in rural development.

Despite the apparent downgrading of communication in the process of development, there is a clear benefit from this exercise. Communication may be assigned its proper role in development, and we can expect favorable outcomes when the conditions of change are better understood. As I point out in my chapter, there is a necessity to combine both a political and technical analysis of the problem of the rural poor if information is to have a positive role in change. Communication can operate in a political situation where equity considerations are primary among government priorities and where material resources, as well as information, are available. It also can operate in a situation where there is a minimum of other resources that are provided to the poor. In the first case, we can expect information to have a significant contribution to make if the communication system is well planned; in the second, the expectations are lowered and the ratio of change is such that, although with careful planning some positive results may take place, the benefits may not exceed the costs. It is here that someone must make decisions about whether, and how, to invest in better communication and information for the rural poor.

PART I

INFORMATION IN RURAL DEVELOPMENT: GENERAL SOCIAL ISSUES

1

THE ROLE OF INFORMATION IN COMMUNICATING WITH THE RURAL POOR: SOME REFLECTIONS

Emile G. McAnany

INTRODUCTION

During the past several years the nonaligned nations have held several symposia concerning the flow of information among different countries of the world. They confirmed, not surprisingly, that they were informationally,* as well as economically, dependent upon advanced countries—especially the United States. To promote a new economic order, they agreed, first, to take control of their information systems, both to stem the tide of one-sided news, cultural programs, and other kinds of information coming from advanced capitalist countries and to turn their information resources internally toward promoting the social and economic welfare of their own people, especially the masses of poor people in rural areas (for example, Ma Ekonzo and Basri 1976).

Not many years before, the U.S. Congress had directed the Department of State (U.S., Congress 1975) to create a priority in foreign assistance for the poorest countries and the poor majority in these

---

*Information in the context of international declarations is not a clear concept. But, in addition to the obvious cultural messages of radio, television, and film entertainment, national spokespersons seem also to include information relevant to solving problems in agriculture, health, nutrition, and the like; it is in this sense that this chapter understands it. There is, in addition, important proprietary, technological information that business and industrial concerns control, but, unfortunately, this seems rarely alluded to in the context of such international information meetings.

countries. A similar priority was proposed in 1973 by Robert Mc-
Namara of the World Bank, the development assistance loans of
which reached a record of nearly $9 billion in 1978 (World Bank 1978).
A significant amount of money from the World Bank has been spent on
rural development to help raise productivity of small farmers and to
meet basic human needs for food, shelter, education, and health services.

One point of convergence among both nonaligned countries and
international aid agencies is a growing belief in the importance of information, education, and communication (IEC) to promote goals of
increased material welfare and improved social services for the rural
poor of low-income countries. It is not enough to create more schools
or even adult, nonformal education schemes if the immediate needs
of people for information in their everyday lives are not met by access to this information through some kind of communication system.

Given this increased interest in an IEC approach by countries
and development aid agencies, a careful examination must be made
of some basic assumptions of this approach and the evidence on which
it rests. A later section of this chapter will examine the information
environment of the rural poor, the constraints facing the contribution
of IEC projects, the evidence for their effectiveness, and, finally,
some recommendations for policy development in the area.

SOME BASIC ASSUMPTIONS
ABOUT INFORMATION'S ROLE

In The Design of Rural Development (1975), World Bank economist Uma Lele designates a number of key areas where improvement
would impact on the productivity and income of farmers—the backbone
of most Third World countries. These are agricultural extension,
local farmer participation, credit, marketing, social services, project administration, and training. If these areas are analyzed carefully, in each activity is found an information component that is assumed by the author but is hardly touched upon in the text. In extension, for example, the agent is basically the source of new information. In most of the Third World, these agents are in such short supply that they reach only a fraction of the farmers, yet there may be
other ways, such as mass media, of diffusing the same information
to a much larger portion of the target population. Local participation, when it is a built-in goal of a project, can be promoted by both
interpersonal and mediated communication. It also depends upon a
feedback mechanism, so that information flows in both directions.
Credit is obviously a resource; but it is also often an underused service in rural areas, because the poor, isolated farmers may not know

about it. Information about the availability of credit could change
this. Marketing depends, in an intimate way, on information, and if
the communication system is strictly a proprietary one, its benefits
go to those who control it. A more open market-information system,
on radio perhaps, would help to promote equity. Social services in
rural areas are a mix of material resources and information, whether
they are concerned with adult education, health, family planning, nutrition, or community development. Administration of rural services
also heavily depends on communication. For example, a two-way
communication system, often missing entirely in rural areas, could
keep field personnel in touch with central project leaders. Finally,
training is obviously a largely information-based activity.

What this brief exercise is meant to illustrate is that almost
every activity considered vital to rural development is information
related or information dependent in some way. The argument for
paying increased attention to this aspect of rural development should
not be taken to mean that communication can be substituted completely
for other resources but only that a better mix of material and information resources can achieve a better result, perhaps at less cost.

There are a number of assumptions about information's role
that need to be carefully examined within the context of the new approach, alluded to above, in which governments are placing more emphasis on mobilizing national information resources for national development goals, especially regarding the poor, rural majority. The
author will identify and discuss briefly some of the more important
assumptions in the following paragraph.

Equity

There are two assumptions about the equity properties of information that need careful scrutiny in a Third World context. The first
characteristic of information that seems to promote equity is that,
unlike material resources, information (or education) is not a zero-
sum phenomenon. Giving it to others does not take it away from another. But information that has any potential for economic impact is
assimilated immediately into the prevailing economic structure. Information concerning manufacturing processes, or even management
know-how, is proprietary and sold to Third World customers like any
other commodity (Goulet 1977; Oettinger 1977). Information, if not
"owned" by someone, is often available to those in power to serve
their own economic interests. Third World government officials can
use their knowledge of international aid to help direct these resources
to areas of the country where they own or can acquire property. Information too widely diffused can lose its economic value, just as too

many primary school degrees can devalue the education investment of many Third World people.

The second assumption about equity that needs to be questioned is that public information with potential value reaches everyone. The rural poor are isolated from such public information that could be useful, by a series of filters that makes reaching them more difficult than reaching other groups. Thus, they are often physically isolated, illiterate, perhaps speaking the dominant language poorly if at all, without a radio, and suspicious of information coming from a government long exploitative, or at least negligent, of their needs. (Further exploration of this assumption is made by Shore in the following chapter.)

Cost Efficiency

It is assumed, often correctly so, that technologies such as radio or print can provide massive public information in substitution, for example, of human information carriers, such as social service agents. Thus, insofar as radio can substitute for or complement the work of an agricultural extension agent, it can reach more people at a lower cost than the agent alone. What needs careful review, however, is whether it is the information that is lacking to most small farmers or the resources needed to put the information into practice (Grunig 1971).

Feasibility

Governments often assume that a plan on paper can be translated directly and easily into action, with all of the promised benefits of increased information and education, through the media. This overlooks the historical record of the success/failure rate of such projects and does not take seriously the constraints to implementation (to be discussed below) that limit impact. Thus, planners often point to a few examples of relative success without carefully specifying the particular factors in these cases that may have contributed to the success (McAnany 1978b).

Change Model

There is often an assumption that the problems of the rural poor are of a technical, rather than political, nature and that with sufficient care in planning and resource input they can be resolved on a technical level. Unless all the structural limitations are considered within the political context of their origin and continuation, the role of information and its impact will be judged only as a technical matter. Examples of information used to mobilize masses of the rural poor in Tanzania (Hall 1978) or Cuba (Fagen 1969), for example, can be found that are heavily political in their contents, yet practical in their outcomes for health or adult literacy. One fundamental assumption in any program is the extent to which the government is willing to make political choices to bring about this change (for example, land tenure policies that are highly controversial in nature). All of this argues for the dual nature of the problem as being both political and technical.

Change Rates

There are always constraints, both internal and external, to a project that limit the impact of information or education to a maximum of potential change possible in the given environment. The ratio of maximum change is often unspecified in projects for the rural poor or based on unfounded positive assumptions. Thus, for example, more information, training, and credit for small farmers with only one or two acres of land may have a maximum of, say, a 6 percent increase in income, even if everything works perfectly in a project to help these farmers. Because they already may be working at almost maximum efficiency on their small plots of land, they cannot significantly change their productivity nor their income without major changes either in land tenure or cropping patterns and market structures. The question here is not whether some, but how much, change is possible. There is an additional question of whether a little change may not be counterproductive by delaying recognition of the need for more fundamental structural change.

Unless these assumptions are carefully examined, there is a danger of misleading people with the promise of significant benefits from investing in information for the rural poor. This danger holds even for those countries in the Third World that have managed to gain control of their national information system and have turned off much of the "free flow" of information from outside.

THE INFORMATION ENVIRONMENT
OF THE RURAL POOR

If the postindustrial society in the most advanced nations is being referred to as an information society in which information replaces energy as the basic economic component (Parker 1976), by contrast, the least developed sectors of the Third World are those least rich in the kind of information likely to have direct economic impact. We know very little about the information environment of the rural poor of the Third World.* Our knowledge is often fragmented, according to the disciplinary interests of those researching the question.

There is a good deal of research in the area of agricultural economics and economic anthropology concerning how small farmers or others involved in rural marketing get information and make decisions (for example, Myren 1970); there is an extensive literature on the diffusion of innovations among farmers and other Third World groups (Rogers and Shoemaker 1971); and there are studies, among anthropologists especially, of how traditional communication systems work through such channels as plays, mimes, and town criers. Some sociologists and political scientists, studying the media's role in the Third World, find that consumerist messages from commercial media are more powerful to persuade the poor to purchase Coca Cola or powdered milk than to adopt more positive nutritional behaviors (Wells 1972; Beltran 1976b).

There is, however, very little good descriptive evidence of the comprehensive information environment of the rural poor, nor even a good description of the process of the penetration of the mass media into rural areas. We know, for example, even from national statistics (UNESCO 1978b), that both radio and television have grown exponentially over the last two decades in all Third World countries. Partial evidence also permits us to assume that some of this growth, especially in radio, has taken place in rural areas. But there is only scattered empirical evidence concerning the exposure of rural audiences (see Shore in Chapter 2), what the content of the media messages are (Seya and Yao 1977), and how they might affect the quality of users' lives (Contreras 1979; and in Chapter 5).

To pursue an examination of the role of information for improving the quality of life of the rural poor, a hypothetical taxonomy of the information environment in which they live must be proposed.

Among the interpersonal forms of communication through which rural people will be likely to receive and give information are the family and neighborhood, markets and washing areas, and festival gatherings for the village. Institutional networks would involve the church or religious network, the administrative structure, the politi-

---

*Our knowledge of the information environment of the poor in the United States is much better researched, although the practical solutions to the knowledge gaps, even for the relatively media-rich U.S. poor, have not yet been forthcoming (Dervin 1978).

cal party, the school, police or army, and such government service agencies as agricultural extension, health, and family planning—among others that might operate in the village.

For the mediated forms of mass communication, there are radio, film, posters, printed materials (such as newspapers and pamphlets), and television. Among the person-to-person media there are the telephone, telex or telegraph, and mail systems.

There are two sets of questions concerning these forms of communicating information in the rural environment: What functions do the various kinds of media perform in different rural environments? and How widespread are the various communication structures? There is no empirical evidence to make any useful generalizations about either of the questions, so the form information takes in rural environments must be speculative, for the most part.

On the interpersonal level, the communication of a variety of information can be traced through social networks. The role of networks in the study of communication is increasingly recognized by scholars (Rogers 1977). A number of social networks—such as neighborhoods, traditional markets, and wandering merchants or performers—are part of the traditional structure of rural communications and still function, for the most part, as they always have. They serve as communication networks for the kinds of content that usually flow in each neighborhood, such as news and gossip, cultural information reinforcing traditional values, and price information on local goods. Although such networks, as well as folk media, could be used to transmit other kinds of development information, no successful formula has yet been devised to tap into this potentially rich resource on a large scale.

The social and political institutions typically serving rural areas have important communication functions to perform. Usually, the information serves to promote the continuation of the structures of society (one thinks of such institutions as schools, churches, armies, and political administrations in many rural areas). However, there are some types of information that directly benefit people—as, for example, information to farmers concerning available credit or to rural women concerning health or nutritional practices.

The mass medium that one is most likely to encounter among poor rural people is radio. There may be a few printed materials, such as the Bible or the Koran and perhaps a pamphlet or two. It is unlikely that newspapers come regularly to the isolated village, at least to more than a few households; nor is it likely that there is a cinema, television, posters, telegraph, or telephone available (although some form of mail service may bring letters to local officials).

Looking at the hypothetical rural information environment, then, one can conclude that probably there are not many channels functioning to bring development information to rural people. There are a number of traditional networks, but these function for traditional purposes. Modern media, with the exception of radio, are almost nonexistent. This leads analysts to one of several strategies in efforts to help the rural poor: (1) an attempt to use traditional media and networks to introduce new information and behavioral change; (2) an attempt to place more information agents in the service institutions of agriculture, health, education, and community development; and/or (3) an attempt to increase the availability of information through radio or other mass media, if they can be more widely and equitably distributed.*

CONSTRAINTS ON AN INFORMATION/COMMUNICATION APPROACH

The problems or constraints that face attempts to improve the economic and social levels of the rural poor are numerous. Only a few of the more general ones can be alluded to here.

Political Constraints

One very good indicator of a government's priority for a social program is the size of the budget it allocates to the effort. The rural poor are not often high on anyone's priority list, but when they are, they are so numerous that projects, which are often pilot programs, have little impact on the overall problem. They are, by definition, that proportion (whatever the percentage one wishes to choose—30, 50, 70, or 90 percent) of the population that is the hardest to reach and has the least education, the worst health conditions, the least cash income, and the least number of material resources, such as land. This immediately makes it not only much more difficult to communicate with the rural poor but also—though politicians often do not wish to recognize it—much more costly. For most governments, the first problem encountered in serving the rural poor is the dilemma of cost. Communication projects for these people may promise to save money, but often these costs are based upon comparisons with delivering in-

*The use of two-way systems, such as telephones and two-way radio, have only begun to be tried in some places. The cost of access to such channels has been an obstacle to widespread use previously; it remains to be seen whether the benefits of two-way communication can justify the costs (Parker 1978).

formation to urban audiences or the highly motivated rural elite, not to the hard-to-reach mass of rural people.

The second problem is knowing how much difference information can make on the structural constraints of rural areas. Agricultural knowledge, as has been mentioned, may not be able to make any significant impact on the productivity of very small farm holdings, already at almost a maximum of efficiency (Daines 1975; O'Sullivan 1978b). Another structural problem related to land tenure is the increasing number of landless laborers in rural areas. For them much information concerning agriculture may be useless. They are not needed on very small farms, where the owner and family do the work; and they cannot be absorbed into larger farms, where investment is in more technology rather than more labor. Even if they are not pushed toward the city, the usual kind of agricultural information is irrelevant because any increased productivity that may result from applying new knowledge will go to their employer, not to themselves.

The third problem is that of the credibility of the source of information. If the poor are at the bottom of the social system, they will have a built-in bias against information from a government source, unless that government has taken some clear steps to improve their situation. The danger that the poor may see in government information is that it can be self-serving and political and may simply be a device to substitute words for concrete actions in helping rural people.

These first three constraints suggest that the approach to a "solution" to the problem of the rural poor is a political one, rooted in the history of the country and the structures that continue to support the status quo; however, the political solution is not the only aspect of importance, and a look at the technical constraints must be considered as well. How much of a technical solution is possible within a given set of political constraints is what has been referred to above under the assumption of the change ratio, How much room for maneuver is there in a situation?

Technical Constraints

If it is correct to assume that the government is willing to invest a reasonable amount of money in rural areas, but is unable or unwilling to make basic structural changes, there are some technical constraints that can hinder even the relative amount of change possible. These constraints are primarily internal to the project and concern the efficiency and effectiveness of its operation, whereas the constraints discussed above are external and concern not the short-term objectives but the longer-term goals of projects.

At the level of planning, development communication projects often ignore the most elementary principles in defining their goals as based on the objective needs of the people. Moreover, the goals are often unrealistic in their ambitions. There are often a series of empirical assumptions underlying the ultimate goal of a project for which there is little empirical evidence. Thus, a radio project in agriculture may assume that the rural poor own sufficient radios to listen in great numbers to radio messages, that most people speak the language of broadcast well enough to receive the messages, or that the information, once applied, can lead to increased productivity regardless of the land size of most of the farms in the area. With careful planning, many of these assumptions can be checked before going ahead with implementation, but such planning research is frequently not done.

Lack of significant leadership within a project may be an important constraint hindering both planning and implementation. One project in Guatemala, which lost its original leader, failed for two years to clearly decide on the objectives it wished to pursue. In contrast, the success of Columbia's Acción Cultural Popular (ACPO) radio project during the 30 years of its existence is in large part due to the leadership of its founder.

At the institutional level, communication projects often cut across a number of rival bureaucracies—such as broadcasting, education, agriculture, and health, to mention only the most common. Attempts to get coordination have not worked well in rural education in projects in Brazil and Guatemala (McAnany and Oliveira, forthcoming; O'Sullivan 1977) and in the Ivory Coast (Lenglet 1976). It seems easier to define goals narrowly under the jurisdiction of one institution than to broaden the scope of rural communication and risk the problems caused by shared responsibility and bureaucratic rivalries. Yet, the integrated approach to rural development could have important benefits if institutional constraints could be overcome. Some small, self-contained private groups often can achieve a more integrated approach, although on a more limited scale (White 1976).

Carefully planned and executed teaching/learning strategies that have had success in formal schooling have not had comparable development for rural adults in the less formal learning areas of agriculture, health, nutrition, and the like. There are questions of sequential versus nonsequential programming, organized versus open audiences, motivational versus didactic approaches, and active versus passive response modes of reception that all need testing among rural adult audiences.

How best to organize the audience for reception and follow-up action is both an obvious need, in most cases, and a basic constraint. Esman (1974) sees the organization of small farmers into cooperative groups as an essential element in successfully helping them to increase their agricultural productivity. But organizing the rural poor runs into the technical problems of creating a structure, where none has existed, and financing it, as well as winning the trust and loyalty of persons long suspicious of external agencies. But there is a major political problem, as well, of organizing a group—the rural majority —that is usually very sensitive. There is a fear of widespread mobilization of the rural poor. Elliot (1974) speaks of the difficulty that creating animation groups in the rural Ivory Coast caused the government, and of their eventual elimination.

Many rural projects are constrained by a lack not only of leadership but also of trained persons in such areas as educational planning and broadcast production and evaluation. This is in part due to the general scarcity of trained persons for any kind of rural development project and, in part, to the specialized skills in broadcasting and communications that are demanded in this case. Once people have received some training in these areas, they often are hired away by the private sector or other government agencies. It is also clear that unless people are personally committed to the work, they are less likely to want to stay in rural, rather than urban-oriented, projects.

The bureaucratic constraint is a significant one for the administration of rural projects and may account for a large part of the inefficiency and failure that is reported in the literature of rural development projects. How this might be avoided or improved has no easy answers. The size of the project may be one aspect of the problem, but commitment to a set of common goals may be a significant element as well. Such commitment is rare across government bureaucratic structures.

A final constraint is one already touched upon above but worth mentioning separately; this concerns the participation of rural people in projects directed toward them. There are a number of policy statements by lending institutions, as well as by politicians from Third World governments, concerning participation of rural people in their own development. There are many meanings and degrees of participation and ways to measure it, but the basic starting point concerns who and how many of the target audience take part in the project. Many rural projects simply have reached too few of the right people to have made any significant impact on the problems of the rural poor. Self-selection is the problem with most projects of this kind. Where information is available, those who are most likely to take advantage of it are the relatively better off. This phenomenon is clear in communication projects where information or education may be freely available to all, but taken advantage of by few; the result is a widening of a knowledge gap among different social classes. The same thing happens in other kinds of interventions where services or other public goods are offered, as in the adoption of innovations (Röling, Ascroft, and Chege 1976). Unless some way is found to overcome the structural bias against participation of the rural poor, by some carefully planned strategy to diminish the self-selection bias, the result of programs for the rural poor will be not only unsuccessful but often even counterproductive, making the poor relatively worse off than before.

A good deal of space has been devoted to constraints, here, because the topic is focused on poverty, which is the underlying constraint in the situation. Also, a balanced emphasis on the constraint side of the picture will help keep the effectiveness side, which follows, in proper perspective.

IMPACT OF INFORMATION:
POTENTIAL AND REAL

Education is sometimes thought of as training in how to process a wider spectrum of information. One problem with simply making more information available in rural areas is that the rural poor are generally illiterate or without much formal education, and their ability to take advantage of new information may be limited. With the spread of the nonprint mass media, such as radio and television, however, information can be made more accessible in verbal and audiovisual-based messages, instead of those coded in printed language.

A second consideration is the possibility of substituting mass media for expensive extension agents in rural areas. Agricultural productivity, for example, could be significantly improved by the regular visits of an extension agent to farmers; but when the agent can visit only a small fraction of the potential clientele, as often happens, radio might provide the information more widely. In health or nutrition education, information vital for preventive medicine may be substituted for health educators, who are in chronic short supply. The same analysis can be made for nutrition, education, and community development.

As a support to field agents, information in the form of non-formal didactic messages, appropriately organized and presented, can supplement a poorly trained group leader or field agent. This is especially true in educational programs where a teacher's skills may be limited yet the teacher can guide the students in a form of self-education that can be quite effective.

These two strategies of substitution for development agents or support of development agents with added media messages are important to consider seriously because their successful application could mean a substantial saving in the cost, as well as in the improved effectiveness, of rural projects.

It must be asked what evidence there is, or might be developed, to test the validity of either of the two strategies of substitution or supplementation suggested above. In agricultural productivity, we find in Lockheed, Jamison, and Lau (forthcoming) and Ashby et al. (1977) evidence that there is a consistent, although small, positive relationship between education and agricultural productivity. The same is true, to a lesser degree, for information, extension agent visits, and some forms of nonformal education (for example, literacy). If projects can massively provide appropriate agricultural information via radio to a significant number of rural listeners, then some benefits may accrue from this exposure. Some evidence for this appears in a rural project in Guatemala (Academy for Educational Development 1978).

In the field of health care, health and nutrition education, and family planning, there is much less evidence, although the potential would seem greater than for agriculture. This is true because health practices may be adopted without as many resource inputs as in agriculture, where results depend not just on practice but resources (credit) to buy fertilizers, seeds, pesticides, tools, and the like. White (1977), for example, found that in a group of Honduran villages that received health and agricultural information from a local radio station, the health practices were employed significantly more often than were the agricultural practices—presumably, as the author believes, because it cost little or nothing to adopt the health practices.

Nutrition and environment education (concerning latrines, water supply, and the like) are two high-potential areas where slight improvements would have much wider consequences on the quality of life than may appear. Improved nutrition practice may have an indirect but significant impact on size, mortality, and cognitive growth of children, while improved water and latrinization can help improve health, as well as raise agricultural productivity and the level of employment. Hall (1978) provides a case study of a massive mobilization of almost two million rural people in Tanzania for a public health radio campaign, the short-term benefits of which included an estimated 750,000 latrines built. Experimental efforts to use radio spot announcements in several Third World countries (that is, Ecuador, the Philippines, and Nicaragua) to get mothers to adopt simple nutritional practices also seem to have had some success (Cooke and Romweber 1977).

Finally, in the area of nonformal education for agriculture, health, literacy, and the like, we come closer to a relatively information-weighted practice. There have been a number of efforts to use low-cost communication technologies, especially radio, in the education of rural people (Spain, Jamison, and McAnany 1977; Jamison and McAnany 1978). There are several examples in the Dominican Republic (White 1976), Nicaragua (Suppes, Searle, and Friend 1979), and Tanzania (Hall 1978) where results have been encouraging.

Some examples of rural projects have been mentioned that have had success in providing better information to rural areas, but there is a need to review the circumstances of each project carefully and to estimate the potential impact it has for improving the lives of the rural poor. The structural context is something that enters into the outcome of any communication strategy and considerably modifies the potential benefit of most projects. For example, Spain (1977) argues that even if we could educate rural children in Mexico to finish primary school, the rural environment would not provide employment for those graduates. The positive impact of education and information on agricultural productivity may be considerably lessened when we look at traditional subsistence farms separately and not lump together large and middle-sized farms with very small plots. Mexican researchers found that in a second trial of the impact of their version of "Sesame Street" in rural Mexico, there was no replication of the positive findings among the poor of Mexico City (Diaz-Guerrero et al. 1976). Grunig (1971) found—among Colombian peasants—that although information can help an individual adapt to a changing situation, "it can do little to change the situation." The small subsistence farmers may not lack for information but often cannot use it in any productive way because of structural constraints such as land size or lack of credit (as the cases in Chapters 3 through 5 indicate). The principle for planning information strategies that pay off for the poor seems to be a careful estimate of the ratio for potential change in the target area of each project.

POLICY ALTERNATIVES FOR INFORMATION'S ROLE

There are, as have been pointed out above, two ways to analyze the problems of the rural poor—a political analysis of the factors that have caused and continue to help keep the poor "in their place" and an analysis of the problem that looks for a technical solution to the situation. In neither case is the author satisfied with the solution offered in isolation from the other. It has been suggested that both kinds of analysis be made and that, ultimately, the problem demands an integrated solution, both political and technical. Thus, for countries that, politically, have made serious choices to put equity into practice, the technical analysis may be a help in carrying out such a development goal more effectively. Tanzania, for example, has tried to further the benefits of its equity principle for the rural masses through radio mobilization campaigns. For those countries that do not put priority on equity, there may be some benefit for the rural poor in a careful technical approach to an information strategy. Thus, at given historical moments even status quo-oriented governments may allow their own agencies or private groups to promote programs that try to mobilize rural people for development. But contents of the campaign may make political differences, so that a rural health and nutrition education campaign might clash less with vested interests in rural areas than an agricultural campaign that may quickly arrive at the fundamental necessity for land reform.

There are two sets of policy recommendations that must be briefly mentioned in this context—those that help ensure IEC projects of benefiting the right people in rural areas (that is, the poor, not the relatively better-off farmers) and those that ensure IEC projects of achieving a more effective outcome, regardless of selection.

At the political and administrative level should be placed certain preconditions for the planning of IEC projects:

1. There should be a serious political commitment of the government to improve the conditions of the rural poor (an important but not exclusive measure is the budget commitment).

2. The project should not be a pilot project but involve enough people so that it will be more difficult, if the project succeeds, for a future government to cut it off.

3. There should be a clear-cut mechanism for involving the target audience itself (participation in planning, implementation, definition of needs, and sharing in benefits).

4. There should be an integrated approach covering several areas of rural need (for example, health education, agricultural practice, nutrition education, environmental hygiene) so that a broader participation of rural people is encouraged.

All of these provisions are applicable to governments that have sought political and technical solutions to rural poverty and those that seek only a technical solution. At the technical planning level, there are several recommendations to be made:

1. There should be an analysis of different substantive areas for rural change projects (for example, health and nutrition, agriculture, literacy, small industry, and the like) in which the physical resource/information trade-off is most clear.

2. There should be a careful task analysis within those areas that hold the most promise for an information substitution or supplementation strategy to see what part may benefit most from informa-

tion (for example, in health, information may help more in reducing infant diarrhea than river blindness).

3. There should be a study of the self-selection mechanisms of rural audiences and a subsequent monitoring of the information/resource delivery to assure the project planners that not only the right people are selected but also that they continue to receive the services.

4. There should be a policy study to decide whether investment in a greater number of smaller, private projects or in fewer, large-scale government projects in rural development would be more beneficial.

5. There should be an evaluation not only of the shorter- but also of the longer-term benefits of IEC projects for their impact on rural equity.

Currently, there is much attention being given to the question of a new international economic order and to a new information world order. If Third World countries succeed in freeing their communication systems from undue influence and control by metropolitan countries, they face the vital stage of transforming their communication infrastructure into a system that will, in turn, help to create a better economic base for their people. A major task that confronts most countries is to try to equalize the difference between their urban and rural populations. The role that information might play in this task of helping rural people to lead more productive, healthy lives depends not only on political decisions concerning the struggle to eliminate structural blocks to growth but also on a decision to use their own information resources in the most appropriate way in that struggle.

2

MASS MEDIA FOR DEVELOPMENT: A REEXAMINATION OF ACCESS, EXPOSURE, AND IMPACT

Larry Shore

INTRODUCTION

The purpose of this chapter is to examine the distribution and stratification of mass media in rural areas in developing countries. Particular attention will be focused on the composition of the audiences for the different mass media and how the social stratification of rural audiences affects issues of access, exposure, content, understanding, and utilization of the mass media. On a general level, this chapter should be seen within the context of recent concerns with equity in rural development.

The chapter is divided into five sections: a discussion of some key theoretical issues relevant to an understanding of the information environment of rural populations; a suggested model/framework within which to examine the issues and research literature in media access and exposure; a summary of that research literature; a presentation of findings of a reanalysis of media access, and especially exposure, studies in two countries, rural India and rural Nigeria; and conclusions.

DEVELOPMENT COMMUNICATION: THEORETICAL APPROACHES

Inherent in theories and applications of mass media for development in underdeveloped countries has been the assumption that information made available via the mass media can and does make a difference in promoting change. Rooted very firmly in an idealistic conception of social change and theories of development based on the experiences of the Western industrialized countries, development communication theorists have often assumed that communication/information was an independent variable in the development process. Consequently, it was believed that exposure to mass media messages would be a powerful enough force to generate the changes necessary for development.

One of the conceptual problems with such theories was the level at which change was envisaged. The locus of control for change was centered within the individual. What was needed was to change the attitudes, values, and aspirations of the individuals in the population; from that would result the benefits of modernization with which such change was identified. The problem with development, then, lay in the individual who was ignorant and traditional. Exposure to new ways of thinking, through the mass media, could remedy the problem (Lerner 1958). This individual-blame view of the problem of underdevelopment failed to set the information environment of the rural population firmly within the larger political and economic structures of the particular country. The external and internal structures of domination, and the structural constraints on the potential of information, were largely ignored. More recently, a number of writers have tried to right the balance by placing more emphasis on structural, rather than individual, factors:

> The tendency to equate communication problems with problems in disseminating technical information has led many . . . to virtually ignore social and institutional structures in promoting development. This is even the case in areas where field workers and educators realize that information alone cannot change social conditions. [Felstehausen 1968]

These structural constraints severely limit the importance of information in rural development:

> Skillful communication can change a peasant's perceptions of his situation but it cannot, acting alone, change that situation very much. It can help a farmer to see opportunities he ignores, but if few opportunities exist, information will not create them. [Brown and Kearl 1967]

Whether in the empathy part of Lerner's (1958) paradigm, the "need achievement" of McClelland (1961), the externally induced diffusion of innovation of Rogers (1969), or the other "modern" attributes suggested by Schramm (1964), Pye (1963), and Inkeles and Smith (1974), the problems and objectives for development were defined, operationalized, and measured with the largely individual psychological characteristics that are assumed in the modernization theory of the times. The problem is both conceptual and practical—conceptual insofar as one tries to assign the cause of underdevelopment (the individual and/or the social context), practical insofar as the assignment of cause in the model leads to quite different policy decisions in using communications for development.

In recent years, the assumptions and biases of earlier development communication theory have been the object of much criticism and reformulation (Beltran 1976a; Golding 1974; Grunig 1971; McAnany 1978a; Rogers 1976). What is apparent from these authors, and from the results of research in rural development over the past two decades, is the need to consider communication not as a simple independent variable but as both a dependent and an independent variable in a complex set of relationships with social, economic, and political structures and processes. Communication is more realistically an auxiliary variable subject to the constraints of the rest of the social system.

The criticisms do not seek to negate the importance of change at the individual level nor the importance of communication and information in rural development but, rather, to set it within a larger context. What seems important for the present, in contrast to earlier optimism, is not to be totally pessimistic about the role of communication under present structural conditions but to see the need for a clear understanding of what the prior limitations are and what conditions need to exist for communication to contribute to equitable rural development. It is a question not only of defining what communication can accomplish under present restrictive conditions but also of discovering how communication can be used to change these conditions. If structural changes are forthcoming, and some "action space" results, then communication and information might have a vital role to play in coordinating, informing, and mobilizing the rural masses. Mass media would certainly have a part in this function.

This chapter, therefore, will attempt to place communication in rural areas within the larger social structure by examining the relationship between socioeconomic factors and the distribution and use of mass media in rural areas. More specifically, this study will focus on the question of equal or differential access and exposure of different sectors of the rural population to information from various sources, especially the mass media, and the consequences of such differences.

The research that exists in the area of access and exposure to mass media in rural areas is quite fragmented and, at times, conflicting. One of the problems in understanding the conclusions of the research done in different countries is the important differences that exist among developing countries themselves. Generalizing the findings in different countries—and, even in some cases, in different geographical areas of a single country—becomes very difficult. Nevertheless, trends in the number of mass media available in certain world regions are available and help us to understand the continued growth, although not the distribution, of these media.

In general, two types of data exist on access and exposure: macro data, usually on a continental level, of the number of radio and television sets, daily newspaper copies, cinema seats, and the like per 1, 000 of the population and micro data on specific countries and specific areas within countries. The best example of the first type of macro data is that of the United Nations Educational, Scientific and Cultural Organization (UNESCO). The second type of data will be reviewed later in this chapter. For many years, UNESCO has provided the valuable service of annually gathering data on overall trends. For example, Table 2.1 shows a rapid spread of the mass media over a decade, particularly of radio. Although this type of data is useful as a starting point, the limitations are clear. A growth of 400 percent in television sets in Africa still meant that there was only one for every 250 people, far short of the relative saturation in the United States and Europe. It also ignores the vital question of the concentration and distribution of the mass media across the population within different nations. It is quite clear that unless there is information on the degree of equality of the distribution of mass media, it is impossible to make a valid judgment on its penetration and impact on the lives of different sectors of the population in developing countries. The criticism of this index approach is similar to criticisms of using gross national product and per capita income as measures of economic development without considering the different distribution patterns among the population. UNESCO has also suggested minimum levels for mass media availability in different continents, that is, the number of each mass media that ought to be available per 100 inhabitants. An unstated assumption is that if an area of the world reaches these minimum levels, as was the case for Latin America in 1971 (Beltran 1971), then a satisfactory level of mass media development has occurred. Once again these guidelines have their uses and their limitations.

Undoubtedly, there has been a rapid quantitative diffusion of mass media in developing countries over the last two decades. Radio, in particular—since the appearance of transistors—has expanded dramatically in almost every area of the world, and it is the most widespread of the mass media in rural areas (McAnany 1973). The press has also reached advanced levels, particularly in Latin America (Frapier 1969). Although the number of television sets and television stations has increased substantially in many developing countries, the evidence suggests that television is available primarily for urban elite audiences (Nordenstreng and Varis 1973).

When considering the concentration and distribution of mass media in rural areas, the primary concern is with radio and, to a

TABLE 2.1

Comparisons of Media Development
(units per 1,000 persons)

Region	Radio Receivers	Television Receivers	Daily Newspaper Copies	Cinema Seats
Africa				
1963	32	>1	10	6
1973	54	4	14	4
Percent change	+69	+400	+40	-33
Asia				
1963	12	>1	17	8
1973	41	4	20	6
Percent change	+242	+400	+18	-25
Latin America				
1963	104	22	73	34
1973	171	68	62	22
Percent change	+64	+209	-15	-35

Source: Adapted from Schramm (1976b).

lesser degree, newspapers—which, supposedly, have substantially
penetrated rural areas. The key issue of debate among scholars concerned with the role of communication in rural development is whether
the rapid expansion of media has penetrated deeply into the lives of
rural people and brought consequent benefits or whether the penetration has been uneven and irrelevant in its contents, particularly for
the poorer sectors of the rural population that have not benefited from
this expansion. The latter position questions how the increase in
mass media has been distributed and suggests that, even if there is
reasonably widespread access and exposure, the suitability and usefulness of the messages cannot be assumed.

Beltran (1974), representing this more skeptical view, has argued that the evidence thus far does not indicate that most mass media even reach the rural masses:

As a rule, the distribution of these messages in Latin America is uneven within groups of countries, within each country, and within each of the cities. Research has found urban

concentration of mass media messages to be particularly
high in the larger cities, especially in the cases of television and the press; concentration is appreciably less acute
for radio and somewhat less acute for the cinema. For the
most part, mass media do not reach the masses in rural
Latin America. Communication in this region is but one
more privilege enjoyed by the ruling elite. Within each
city, a minority of the population has far more access to
mass media messages than the majority. And within rural
areas, even smaller minorities have the privilege of access
to these messages.

Finally, one may ask whether the various media, such as radio,
television, and the press, fulfill the same or different functions. If
they fulfill the same function, then one medium—say, radio—may do
as well for rural people as a variety of media do for urban people.
There are a number of studies that need to be reviewed, but, first,
a model or framework for considering the role of media in rural development will be presented.

RURAL MEDIA FOR DEVELOPMENT:
A PROGRESSIVE MODEL

Almost all earlier research concerning access and exposure
to media in rural areas failed to distinguish clearly among access,
exposure, content, information outcomes, and social outcomes.
To understand better the process of information's spread and effects,
a simple model of the relationships among the different variables is
presented in Figure 2.1.
This model may be called "progressive" because the progress
from outer to inner circles is usually in stages. It suggests that in
the process of different kinds of information diffusing to rural people
through the mass media, a series of stages needs to be distinguished.
These are represented by concentric circles that begin with access of
the population to media, a stage that one cannot assume for all rural
people, even for a widespread medium such as radio. This model
also suggests that in order to obtain a genuine understanding of the
role of the mass media in rural areas, all the components of the model
have to be considered within general social structures of the society
in question.* Beginning from the outermost circle, each stage as-

———————————

*Social context is not indicated in the graphic model, because it
is a central concern of this chapter and pervades each stage.

FIGURE 2.1

A Progressive Model for Mass Media Impact

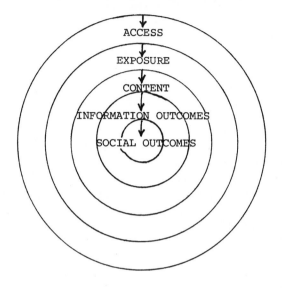

Source: Compiled by the author.

sumes the presence of the previous one in order to have an impact. Thus, access is both logically and temporally prior to exposure, and reception of certain kinds of mass media content assumes exposure. One cannot assume, for example, that <u>potential</u> access to a mass medium will necessarily imply exposure for a group or an individual, nor can one assume that exposure will necessarily lead to content appropriate to a particular audience. In short, each stage is a necessary, but not sufficient, condition for achieving the next stage.

A brief explication of the five stages may help to clarify how the model works. This will be followed with a review of relevant research to see how far the model has been tested.

Access and exposure are so closely linked in most research that it is necessary to explicate the vital differences between them. Access is a necessary, but not sufficient, condition for exposure. <u>Access</u> generally refers to the essential physical potential for exposure— the situation where there is a newspaper, radio, television, or other mass medium within reasonable range of the potential audience. In some cases in rural areas, this might be an individual's access to a private radio, but it can also be a situation of a shared radio or a newspaper read by a number of people. In most rural areas, access is primarily to radio and print.

Various constraints beyond just physical distance might limit access. In the case of radio, this might involve set cost and maintenance factors as well as the quality of signal received in a particular rural area. Access to print is limited by availability as well as literacy levels.

The above definition of access seems automatically to be limiting access to the reception of messages; it is important also to consider a broader view of access to include access to the production and distribution of messages. In a society such as the United States, where penetration for most mass media is almost 100 percent, access quite clearly cannot be defined purely in terms of physical access to the reception of mass media. In developing countries, where the mass media have not penetrated as deeply, it is natural to first consider reception questions. Nevertheless, researchers should be careful not to repeat the same top-down and passive receiver view of mass media prevalent in earlier research. Access to active participation in creation of media messages should also be considered. Although this kind of access might only be feasible on a small scale, it has important implications for the decentralization of the mass media, bottom-up change, and local development goals. For the purposes of this chapter, access is viewed in terms of the first, more limited, view of access to a passive reception mode. The broader view of access to media in a more active capacity should be the object of future research in developing countries (Jouet 1977; O'Sullivan and Kaplun, forthcoming).

Exposure is more complicated than access because it deals not only with whether a person is within physical range of the particular mass medium but also whether a person is actually exposed to the message. Exposure is hearing, seeing, reading, or, more generally, experiencing, with at least a minimal amount of interest, the mass media message. This exposure might occur at an individual or group level.

Many studies, although possibly distinguishing between access and exposure, do not go further in examining questions of message content of the different media. The content of a radio program or a newspaper usually is designed with a particular audience in mind. In some cases, content that was designed for a broad audience might be understood and utilized to different degrees by different sectors of the audience. Content can be broken down in various ways: information, entertainment programs, music, news, sports, and the like —in the case of radio, for example. These categories can obviously be broken down further into subtypes and production sources. An important distinction should also be made between commercial programming and purposive, social change programming. The audience and kinds of programs might be very different in these two types of programming structure. Distinctions have also been made between implicit and explicit content (for example, the difference between the explicit message of an advertisement on radio to buy a certain product and the implicit message for rural people that such a purchase is more "modern," and thus better).

Following from these prior stages, the next step of the model is that concerning the information outcomes, viewed as the cognitive, affective, or attitudinal impact of exposure to mass media messages. In terms of information programs, it examines what has been learned as a result of exposure. It naturally is closely connected to some of the issues concerning content mentioned above. Questions of what has been learned are more difficult in the case of entertainment programs. These outcomes need not only be from a single exposure but also from exposure over a period of time.

The final stage of the model is the social outcome, defined as any social change resulting from exposure to mass media. The concept incorporates both shorter- and longer-term outcomes—from actions taken and operations improved to a betterment in the quality of peoples' lives that are the results of actions taken. Final outcome measures include changes in levels of agricultural productivity and improvement in levels of health care, nutrition, and the like. This final stage of the model is important in relation to the issues raised in the beginning of this chapter concerning the role of information in rural development, and whether information really makes a difference.

The question of social change and the role of information in this process is also related to the classic debate between those who argue that individual change comes first in the process and those who argue that structural change must occur first for other changes, such as attitudes of individuals, to be possible. The author will avoid getting immersed in this debate by suggesting the adoption of a dialectical view of the process—where the individual is not glorified to the extent of ignoring the social structure and where the social structure is not seen in a rigid, deterministic manner that ignores the ongoing humanizing praxis of the individual.

One aspect of the model presented above, which has not been discussed but which needs to be considered, is that of feedback loops. The review of literature and secondary analysis of access/exposure data will not be able to include feedback, but it should be kept in mind as important for the whole model.*

---

*Feedback is especially critical in purposive uses of communication for development, which are not discussed extensively in this chapter.

REVIEW OF RESEARCH ON
THE MASS MEDIA MODEL

Any literature review of such a broad area cannot hope to be all-inclusive. The author's objective is to provide a starting point for considering the components of the model suggested above. Further research should fill in the relevant gaps. It should also be remembered that data on access and exposure and the other components of the model are, in most cases, area specific. General trends are, at best, seen on a continental level. Ideally, there would be data that could be broken down in detail according to class, socioeconomic status, age, sex, ethnic groups, language groups, regions, and continents.

There are a number of problems facing a thorough review of literature relevant to media access and exposure, as well as for other components of the model. First, research is often not focused on one aspect of the model but on several. Nevertheless, it is useful to report the research under separate components. Second, there appears to be an imbalance in the amount of research from different regions of the world. (Most research on access and exposure available to the author comes from Latin America.) Third, some mass media have received more attention than others, especially in rural areas. Radio has received more attention (Jamison and McAnany 1978; Spain, Jamison, and McAnany 1977) than other media in recent years. Fourth, much of the microresearch that has been done in different countries is simply not available to most scholars but remains in technical reports in the offices of sponsoring agencies. As a consequence, this review is not meant to be exhaustive—merely suggestive of how a sample of research fits the model.

Access

For Latin America, the research suggests that the distribution of mass media follows the pattern of steep stratification that characterizes the socioeconomic structure prevailing in the region: higher levels of income, education, and status are strongly associated with higher levels of access to mass media messages (Beltran 1974). There is also a high degree of concentration of the mass media in the cities, especially the larger ones. Lower-class urbanites and rural peasants have as low a level of access to communication as is their access to food, shelter, and education. This concentration is particularly true for newspapers and television. There is modest access to film in some nonurban areas, and radio has the highest access level in rural areas (Beltran 1971). The stratification and concentration that exist in terms of the rural-urban dichotomy also occur within each area. Within rural areas, a small percentage of the peasants have substantially higher access levels than the masses. Garcia (1966), studying the press in Columbia and Mexico, found a heavy concentration of newspapers in urban areas. Mattelart (1970) found a definite stratification of access to, and use of, mass media among urban workers, slum dwellers, and farmers in Chile. He also found the greatest disparity among people for access to television. Other studies that point to the concentration and stratification of mass media access in rural areas are those of Blair (1960) and Bostian and Oliveira (1965) in Brazil, and of Ruanova (1958) and Myren (1964) in Mexico.

Moving away from Latin America, different access data are found. In Thailand, Story and Story (1969) found very low access to radio in rural areas. In contrast, however, Polpatanarithi (1970) found very high access to radio in rural India. Spain (1971) found high levels of access to radio in the southern Philippines, and Seya and Yao (1977) found relatively high levels of access to radio in the rural Ivory Coast, despite great language diversity. One of the major studies on rural access and exposure is that of Frey (1966) in Turkey. He found clear evidence (as is the case in almost all other studies) that, at least on a gross level, access to radio was greater than to any other media. He also found that access to one medium correlated significantly and positively with access to other media.

Two tentative conclusions emerge from this brief survey: first, there is great variation from area to area in the amount of access to media in rural areas; second, whatever the access, whether heavy or light, its general pattern follows the pattern of social structures in the country studied.

Exposure

In Latin America, the exposure research seems to support the stratification view suggested by Beltran (1974). Mejia (1971) in Peru and Canizales and Myren (1967) in Mexico confirm the view that mass media exposure is stratified between urban and rural areas and within rural areas themselves. Taking one extreme of the spectrum, Deutchmann, McNelly, and Ellingworth (1961) found that the mass media exposure of subelites (professionals and technicians) in 11 Latin American countries equaled—and, in some cases, exceeded—the exposure of similar samples in the United States.

Physical factors—such as lack of roads, distance from urban areas, and lack of electricity—undoubtedly contribute to the skewed distribution of some of the mass media in rural areas. Nevertheless, Diaz-Bordenave (1964) in Pernambuco, Brazil, and Gutierrez Sanchez

TABLE 2.2

Cross-Cultural Studies of Mass Media Exposure
(in percent)

Mass Media Exposure	Turkey	Venezuela	Colombia	Laos	Kenya	Egypt	Jordan
Newspaper							
Daily	4	6	—	3	1	—	—
Weekly	20	28	60	—	8	—	—
Never	52	43	—	48	83	—	—
Illiterate	72	53	62	—	60	—	—
Radio							
Daily	19	61	60	9	8	42	—
Weekly	43	85	45	—	38	—	—
Never	36	1	—	41	34	—	42
Cinema							
Past year	27	38	68	—	38	—	25
Never	56	17	32	—	62	—	75

Sources: Frey (1966). References to individual studies are included in the Bibliography. They are Frey (1966) for Turkey, Silva et al. (1964) for Venezuela, Rogers (1964) for Colombia, and Lerner (1958) for Egypt and Jordan.

and McNamara (1968) in Colombia found that despite the relative proximity of peasants to urbanized areas, exposure to the mass media was very low. This suggests that despite the relative availability of mass media, exposure was low, perhaps because, among other things, peasants did not find the content very useful.

There is a large source of data from the family planning literature on the use of media to reach clients, often in rural areas. Radio was the first source of information for family planning in Korea, Taiwan, Kenya, Honduras, and Iran in studies reported by Sweeney (1977). There is some doubt, however, whether exposure to large-scale family planning programs are comparable to exposure to other kinds of media programs. Many governments and international agencies have given special emphasis to such programs, minimizing other social services. Also, it is clear that family planning has not reached those rural poor who are without access to the mass media.

Frey (1966) concludes from his study in Turkey that although total exposure figures were not very high, this did not preclude the impact of the mass media on rural life. Frey's data, together with two other studies in Turkey by Kiray (1964) and Sewell (1964), indicate an increase in mass media exposure that accompanies rural-to-urban migration. Frey also provides a comparison with exposure studies in other countries (Table 2.2). Although these studies are somewhat dated, they provide a useful cross-cultural comparison for the time. As was true of the previous data on access, one finds it difficult to draw generalizations from Frey's data. Respondents in these seven studies were not alike, nor were they all selected in ways that satisfy all the requirements of random selection. Frey's conclusion from this comparison is tentative: "The mass media would seem to be generally capable of reaching an impressive sector of the peasantry, though one can be sure that another and perhaps somewhat larger sector will not be reached at all" (Frey 1966).

Content

That the mass media are unequally distributed across the population is in itself a negative factor characteristic of underdevelopment. However, even if this were eliminated—or, at the minimum, improved—there is still reason to be concerned with the content of the messages. As Beltran (1971) points out, the fact that access increases and mass media messages reach progressively wider sectors of the population does not automatically guarantee the contribution of these messages to development. A substantial amount of research, particularly in Latin America, has been done on the content of newspapers, less on the content of television, and the least on the content of radio.

For newspapers, Diaz Rangel (1967) and Simmons, Kent, and Misgra (1968) suggest that consistently less space is devoted to information relevant for development than to that for sports, entertainment, and such socially negative news as crime. In general, trivial information substantially dominates the content over information relevant for development. Gutierrez Sanchez and McNamara (1968), Gutierrez Sanchez (1966), and De Vries and Echevarría (1967) all found that the content of the mass media did not hold much use for peasants in Colombia, as it met more the needs of large farmers than those of the peasants. Cordera (1973) found a similar lack of information in the daily newspapers of Costa Rica concerning agriculture, the major activity of the country. Roca (1969) suggests from a study in Peru that the press in Latin America is deliberately oriented against social change for peasants and is at the service of the large landowning elites. Other studies suggest that, even where substantive information is available, the language of most newspapers, including agricultural newspapers, is beyond the understanding of the peasants or does not correspond to their culture (Beltran 1971).

Studies on the content of radio show that preference for the trivial or non-development-oriented subjects was even more considerable than for the press, and the content of radio was alien to most peasants (for example, Pasquali 1963; Felstehausen 1968).

Some of the most interesting research concerning content has been done for television. Salazar (1962) and Pasquali (1967), in Venezuela, found a high percentage of violent programs and stereotypical plots and characters showing middle-class individuals and U.S. nationals in a positive light and lower-class people in a negative light. Rincon (1968), also in Venezuela, studied the content of television and radio serials and argues that the stereotypes in the content falsify reality and pervert the average taste of the masses. Marques de Melo (1969), in his study of television soap operas in São Paulo, Brazil, suggests an evasion-inducing mechanism in operation for audiences of these programs. A Colombian researcher, Bibliowicz (1973), suggests that the content of soap operas reinforces the perceptions of class immutability. In a study that looks more at effects than only at content, Colomina de Rivera (1968) interviewed housewives in Maracaibo, Venezuela. She found that a large percentage of the housewives believed that the problems presented in soap operas were identical to theirs and that the solutions offered could help solve their own problems.

Although more work beyond just content analysis needs to be done in this area, the tentative results give much reason for concern for the contribution of this type of mass media content to development objectives and the attainment of greater social equity.

In concluding this section, the distinction between commercial programming and purposive (development communication) programming must be recalled, as well as the consequences on access, exposure, and content. The impact of these two types of program content on rural development might be very different. Further research might study the differential impact of commercial and development programming on rural audiences and further specify the model to see what effect sources with different orientations might have. A more refined content analysis that distinguishes between latent and overt content and looks at ideological as well as cognitive message content would help to improve the knowledge concerning the effects of content on both thought and action.

Information and Social Outcomes

The most important factors in the mass media model outlined earlier in this chapter are the outcomes—especially the social outcomes. Information outcomes are the cognitive, affective, and attitudinal consequences of the audience access and exposure to, and comprehension of, the media content. The previous review of research has indicated that even when lower socioeconomic groups have sufficient levels of access and exposure, the irrelevance of content will lower levels of exposure in a kind of self-regulating fashion. Research concerning the communication effects on the gap in knowledge among different social groups (Ticheonor, Donahue, and Oline 1970; Shingi and Mody 1976) suggests that one reason why some people learn more than others from the media is the self-selective nature of the audience. Although all groups may have access, those that are better off are more likely to take advantage of the information available. Thus, although there might be general potential exposure, the real exposure between poorer and better-off members of the audience will differ, and the audience with better education and higher social status will expose themselves more and gain more from the information. Only where relevance of the content is specifically geared to lower socioeconomic groups through appropriate feedback mechanisms,* and information appropriate to their needs is developed, will this knowledge gap possibly be halted or reversed. Even this might be of limited value if the underlying unequal distribution of not only information but also of resources is not taken into consideration.

Too often, in planning development communication projects, it is assumed that there will be an impact if people would only attend to the message. But, as Grunig (1971) points out in his study of Colombian peasants, the important question may not be whether appropriate information is lacking but whether resources needed to put

---

*In only mentioning this feedback (or feedforward), the author does not intend to slight the great theoretical and practical importance it has.

the information into practice are available. Research (O'Sullivan 1978a) has shown that agricultural information may not be able to make any significant impact on productivity when it is applied where the farmer is already operating at maximum efficiency on a very limited landholding.

Nevertheless, within structural constraints, there is some evidence that under certain circumstances communication and education can contribute to social outcomes. Lockheed, Jamison, and Lau (forthcoming) cite evidence that there is a consistent, although small, positive relationship between education and agricultural productivity. The Basic Village Education project in Guatemala (Academy for Economic Development 1978) also showed that adoption of new agricultural practices was one social benefit that was related to exposure to a special agricultural radio program. Different information might also have possibilities for positive social outcomes in different aspects of peoples' lives. For example, White (1977) found that Honduran villagers exposed to development radio messages adopted health practices significantly more often than they did agricultural practices. The author believes that this is because the adoption of health practices was helped by existing women's organizations in the rural areas and that these practices did not demand added resources, whereas agricultural practices were constrained by lack of credit and land.

Hall and Dodds (1977) cite evidence of social outcomes, such as latrines built, in a massive public health program in rural Tanzania. Other positive results have been found in experimental use of radio spots: to get mothers to adopt nutritional practices, in Nicaragua and the Philippines (Cooke and Romweber 1977), and to increase the use of contraceptives, in Colombia, Costa Rica, and the Dominican Republic (Sweeney 1977).

To summarize, there is a twofold problem in the outcome area. First, the general mass media are not found to promote positive social outcomes to any large extent. This may not be surprising when one recalls the limited exposure of many poor audiences to media and the overwhelmingly irrelevant messages. Still, the poor may use what media are available as best they can in trying to substitute for extension agents or other sources of information. Second, when the media are used purposively for development communication projects, there are some indications that they can promote some change; but, even here, under favorable circumstances, constraints limit the impact to modest positive outcomes in some but not all cases.

FACTORS AFFECTING MEDIA EXPOSURE:
TWO CASES IN INDIA AND NIGERIA

To test some of these contentions—in particular, the relationship between socioeconomic factors and the distribution of media ex-

posure—data from two studies in rural India and Nigeria were reanalyzed.* These data came from a large three-nation study of diffusion
of innovations done in the mid-1960s (Rogers, Ascroft, and Röling
1970). Although the analysis here deals primarily with mass media
exposure, it should be considered within the larger framework of the
model. Further examination of outcomes in similar circumstances
are reported by Contreras in Chapter 5. The following hypotheses
were generated for testing some of the relationships that have been
examined above:

1. There is a positive correlation between mass media exposure and socioeconomic factors (that is, higher socioeconomic status
[SES] groups will have greater exposure).
2. This positive relation will differentiate between lower and
higher SES groups for all media.
3. Mass media exposure does not intervene between socioeconomic factors and the knowledge and adoption of health and agricultural innovations.

The India Case Study

Background

Data for the study were gathered in eight Indian villages in 1967
(N = 680). Three of the villages were in Andhra Pradesh (N = 210),
two in Maharashtra (N = 246), and three in West Bengal (N = 224).
Villages were chosen so as to be in the same or contiguous blocks
within states. All of the farmers who were interviewed in each village
were those who cultivated 2.5 acres of land or more and were 50
years of age or younger. The media behavior of the very poorest
sector of farmers (those with less than 2.5 acres) are therefore not
included in the study. In most cases, the respondent was head of the
household.

For the first two hypotheses, the dependent variable was mass
media exposure, measured separately for radio, newspaper, and
film. A combined mass media exposure variable was also used in
some cases. For the third hypothesis, where mass media exposure
was tested as an intervening variable, the dependent variables were
knowledge of health innovations, knowledge of agricultural innovations,
trial adoption of health innovations, and trial adoption of agricultural
innovations. These variables were created by a combined index of

---

*For a more complete report of both cases, see Shore (1978).

FIGURE 2.2

Mass Media Exposure Model for India

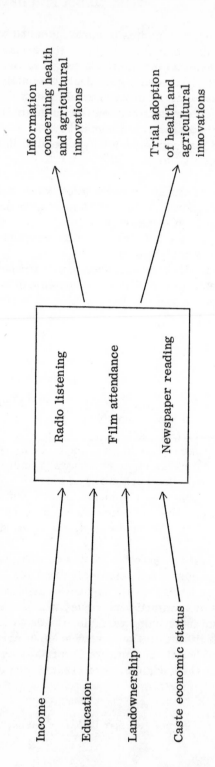

Source: Compiled by the author.

knowledge and trial adoption of eight different health and agricultural innovations.

For the independent variable, rather than combining four different socioeconomic measures into a single SES index, it was decided to keep them separate as proxies for SES so that the consistency of the findings could be tested across the different measures. The four variables were education, landownership, income (measured by the payment of the panchayat, or village council tax), and economic status (measured by a caste economic status ranking).

To compare the exposure of different groups on the socioeconomic hierarchy, the independent variables were divided in the following way:

1. Education. This included farmers with no education, those with some, and those who had completed primary education; farmers with some high school and those who were high school graduates; and farmers with some college and those who were college graduates.

2. Landownership. This variable was divided in two different ways: first, farmers with less than 5 acres and those with more and, second, farmers who did not own any land, those who owned 1 to 5 acres, those who owned 5 to 20 acres, and those who owned more than 20 acres.

3. Income. This included low-income farmers who paid zero to Rs5 in tax, middle-income farmers who paid Rs6 to Rs15 in tax, and high-income farmers who paid more than Rs15 in tax.

4. Economic status. This variable was divided into three parts, for low-, medium-, and high-economic status. Because of the different castes in different villages, and of the differing statuses of the farmers among the eight villages, these divisions were approximated. This variable is therefore not as reliable a measure as the other three socioeconomic variables.

To visualize the organization of the analysis better, the relationships are outlined in Figure 2.2.

Results

The general audience for the mass media showed radio, at 76 percent, to be the most commonly attended medium. Film was next, with 66 percent of the audience, and newspaper last, with 32 percent. Although there was little difference among SES groups (low, medium, and high on the three indicators of land, income, and economic caste) in radio listening and film attendance, the audience for newspapers was consistently from the higher SES groups.

The general positive relationship between higher SES standing and greater exposure to media is sustained by the evidence shown in

TABLE 2.3

Bivariate Relationships between Socioeconomic Variables and
Mass Media Exposure, India
(zero-order correlations with exposure; N = 680)

SES Variables	Listen to Radio	Exposed to Film	Read a Newspaper
Income	0.27	0.21	0.32
Landownership	0.17	0.10	0.35
Education	0.25	0.23	0.50
Caste economic status	0.16	0.13	0.31

Note: All figures are significantly different from zero at the
1 percent level.

Source: Compiled by the author.

Table 2.3. The correlations reported here are significantly different
from zero and indicate that, in general, the higher an individual is on
one of the SES indicators, the more likely the exposure to the three
media. Newspaper exposure suggests the strongest elite bias. Significant correlations were also found for the SES variables with a combined media index; however, when compared with previous correlations of separate media, the relationship of education to the index is
stronger than for separate media, while income is considerably lower.
These four SES variables quite likely act not only as independent
variables but also as intervening ones. To test this, partial correlations were computed, but the only noticeable reductions in the correlations occurred when controlling for education with landownership
and income as the independent variables. The correlations are reduced most for newspaper reading, indicating that education has a
stronger intervening effect for this medium than for radio and film.
In the previous paragraph, the general relationship between high
SES and high media exposure was demonstrated. An examination of
distinct SES groups and their exposure to the three mass media un-
covers the same trends. Landownership, for example, was used as
the predictor variable in comparing small and large farmers. The
results (Table 2.4) showed statistically significant differences for the
two groups. When the same variable was divided into four groups of
farmers, there were similar findings. Newspaper reading is again
shown to be the most unequally distributed medium across the various
social strata. Trends similar to those for landownership are evident

TABLE 2.4

Crosstabulation of Landownership and Mass Media Exposure, India

Landownership (acres)	Radio Listening		Film Exposure		Newspaper Reading	
	Number	Percent	Number	Percent	Number	Percent
Less than five (N = 405)	281	69	249	62	79	19
More than five (N = 275)	241	88	202	74	138	50
Total (N = 680)	522		451		217	
Chi square	29.58*		9.98		69.52*	

*Significantly different from zero at the 1 percent level.

Source: Compiled by the author.

for the other three variables of education, income, and economic status. The same trend is present when a combined mass media index is used. These results indicate a clear pattern of bias in mass media exposure among the Indian farmers of the sample. As one moves up the social hierarchy, however it is measured, exposure to media increases.

To assess the role of mass media information in certain social outcomes, mass media exposure was tested as an intervening variable between socioeconomic factors and knowledge about, and the trial adoption of, health and agricultural innovations to see whether mass media significantly affected the direct relationship between SES and adoption of innovations. Four composite indexes were used for the innovation variables of knowledge and trial for both health and agricultural innovations. The results suggest that except, in some cases, for newspaper exposure the information received from the mass media did not play an intervening role in the knowledge that farmers had concerning the innovations or whether they decided to try the innovation. This is the case for both health and agricultural innovations.

These results are supported when mass media channels and other channels of information are compared. The data suggest that change agents were the most important source of information concerning innovations and their adoption. When asked how they came to know about various agricultural innovations, 8.6 percent of the farmers indicated the mass media, whereas 52 percent replied that they heard through a change agent or other interpersonal channel. The mass media were used most for information about the district headquarters. To compare change agents as a channel of information with the partial correlations controlling for mass media exposure, similar partial correlations were computed that controlled for change agent contact. The results indicate that change agents are a much more important channel of information for farmers than are mass media. The high correlation of change agent contact with newspaper reading helps to explain our earlier finding that newspaper exposure is the only mass media that has some intervening effects on innovation knowledge and adoption. Farmers from higher socioeconomic groups are more likely to have both more contact with change agents as well as greater exposure to newspapers, but no causal implications can be drawn.

Summary

The findings of this small test of our model show that there is a stratified relationship between socioeconomic factors and exposure to the three mass media. Radio was the most equally distributed across socioeconomic groups, whereas exposure to newspapers has

the greatest socioeconomic bias. Of the four socioeconomic variables, only education acted as somewhat of an intervening variable.*
Radio and film exposure played a negligible role in knowledge and
trial adoption of health and agricultural innovations. Newspaper reading, in some cases, played an intervening role between landownership, education, and the innovation variables, but this was highly correlated with change agent contact and was not clearly differentiated
from the latter because of the analytic level of the study.

It should be remembered that the respondents in this study did
not include the smallest farmers, who cultivated less than 2.5 acres.
If these people were included in the study, it is quite probable that
the stratification of mass media exposure across the socioeconomic
hierarchy would be even more exaggerated.

The Nigerian Case Study

Background

Data were gathered from 1,142 individuals in 18 villages in the
eastern region of Nigeria in 1966. Of the 18 villages, 4 were inhabited
by Ibibio speakers (N = 245), and 14 were Ibo (N = 897). The two
tribes were selected because they formed 80 percent of the population
of the eastern region. Eligible respondents were males 20 years or
older who professed agriculture to be their main source of income.
All eligible respondents in a village were listed, and a random sample
of about 65 respondents were selected for interview in each village.

For the first two hypotheses, the dependent variable was mass
media exposure, measured separately for radio, newspaper, and film
exposure. For the third hypothesis, the dependent variables were a
combined index of the adoption of four health innovations, a combined
index of information about 13 agricultural innovations, and a combined
index of the adoption of 14 agricultural innovations. Two independent
variables were used: education and number of laborers hired per day.
To compare the exposure of different socioeconomic groups, the independent variables were divided as follows:

1. Education. This included farmers with no education; those
with some primary education; and those with completed primary,
secondary, and college education.

2. Hired labor. This was broken down into farmers who did
all their own work and did not hire other labor, those who hired one
to three laborers, and those who hired four or more laborers.

---

*For more discussion of this, see Chapter 6. Also see Jamison
and Lau (1978) for a favorable view of education in farm productivity.

In order to visualize better the organization of the analysis, the relationships are outlined in Figure 2.3.

FIGURE 2.3

Mass Media Exposure Model for Nigeria

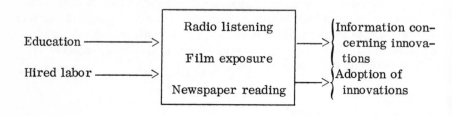

Source: Compiled by the author.

Results

The results of the analysis of the media exposure data, as with the Indian data, will be presented primarily under the three hypotheses after first giving some brief descriptive data on audience size and characteristics. Media exposure of rural people in the Nigerian sample was similar in pattern to Indian findings. Radio had the largest audience, with 41 percent; film was next, with 35 percent; and newspapers least, with 21 percent. There were two kinds of socioeconomic descriptors that characterized the Nigerian farmers in the sample: (1) an educational division among those with no education (58 percent), some primary (33 percent), and those finishing primary or more (9 percent) and (2) a measure of socioeconomic status among those farmers who hired no extra labor (41 percent), those who hired one to three workers (28 percent), and those who hired four or more (31 percent). Relating these characteristics to mass media exposure, one finds a fairly similar media exposure pattern to that of India. The next step is to see to what extent findings similar to those of the Indian case study emerge for the three hypotheses with the Nigerian data.

The test of the first prediction was made by correlating exposure to the three media with the two variables of education and hiring farm help. Table 2.5 provides the results of the analysis and shows a general confirmation of the hypotheses. Education as a predictor of media exposure is better than hired labor. Exposure to newspapers has the strongest correlation with education.

TABLE 2.5

Bivariate Relationships between Socioeconomic Variables and
Mass Media Exposure, Nigeria
(zero-order correlations with exposure)

SES Variables	Listen to Radio	Exposed to Film	Read a Newspaper
Education	0.27	0.18	0.39
Hired labor	0.13	0.10	0.14

Note: Figures are significantly different from zero at the 1 percent level.

Source: Compiled by the author.

The second hypothesis examines the different exposure levels for different socioeconomic groups. For the education variable, there were consistent differences among groups for media exposure, higher education groups being significantly more exposed to all media than lower groups. However, at the medium exposure levels for radio listening and film attendance, there is very little difference between the exposure levels of different socioeconomic groups. As in India, newspaper exposure reflects the greatest elite bias. Radio ownership data (a test of access, not exposure) showed similar sharp stratification according to educational differences, with the 57 percent of the sample with no education owning only 4 percent of the radios.

For the hired labor variable, similar trends were evident, although to a much lesser degree and especially so with regard to newspaper exposure, where differences were greatest among education groups but least among the different groups hiring labor.

As in the Indian case study, mass media exposure was tested as an intervening variable between socioeconomic factors and knowledge and adoption of health and agricultural innovations. As with the Indian data, change agent contact was also tested for what intervening role it might play between SES characteristics and innovative knowledge and behavior. The results suggest, as do those of India, that the mass media by and large do not play an intervening role, but, unlike the Indian results, the Nigerian change agent does not seem to play an important intervening role either.

Summary

Although the Nigerian findings are similar to those of India and demonstrate that the stratification of media exposure follows that of other factors, such as education and economic resources, there are a few differences. Newspapers did not seem to be as highly related to innovation nor to change agent visits. The economic factor of hired labor did not distinguish as well the difference among different groups for exposure to the media.

CONCLUSIONS AND IMPLICATIONS

This chapter has been concerned with the general question of concentration and stratification of mass media in developing countries and, in particular, with questions of access and exposure in rural areas. Although it is impossible to generalize across different social contexts represented by the studies cited, certain general conclusions emerge from our data analysis and the other research literature in this area.

As the model given earlier suggests, questions of access and exposure and the impact of mass media on equitable rural development cannot be considered in isolation from each other, nor can one component of the model be assumed from the other. To have a detailed understanding of the communication environment of rural populations, one needs to consider the role of each of the components of the model in the overall process of media use and social change. It is hoped that other research will fill in many details of these components, as the other chapters in this book begin to do.

In general, the data indicate quite clearly the inequality in the distribution of mass media in developing countries. This stratification of distribution occurs not only between urban and rural areas, as much previous evidence attests, but, more important, the present analysis shows that there is an important imbalance within rural areas themselves. Television is the mass media with the greatest elite bias in most developing countries, and radio is the most generally available. However, even radio is quite unequally distributed across the social strata. When one also considers questions of content and the usefulness of mass-mediated information, it is not inappropriate to conclude that the majority of rural people in underdeveloped countries live in a state of "undercommunication." The evidence suggests that despite the rapid expansion of radio to almost all areas of the world in the last two decades, great inequalities still exist that hinder the potential use of mass media in development.

The distribution of mass media and of development information availability in rural areas mirrors the unequal distribution of other resources. Even where mass media are widely available, serious reservations remain concerning the contribution of the information to a more equitable rural development. This is particularly the case with commercially oriented mass media in rural areas.

Certain implications emerge concerning future research, development communications theory, and the implementation of mass media projects. Information is not an independent variable in the development process but is dependent upon other factors in the larger political and economic context of a particular society. Information must be considered in relation to these other variables and structural constraints. This view is not to suggest that information is unimportant in development but, rather, that one should examine what prior limitations exist and what preconditions are necessary for information to make a difference.

Clearly, one needs to go beyond individual-blame theories of underdevelopment or, put another way, to avoid an inappropriate amount of attention being placed on individual change variables in the development process. Greater emphasis should be placed on systemic and structural variables. One should not overcompensate for previous important omissions by focusing only on structural variables but, rather, should consider structural and individual variables in a dialectical relationship. This balance is essential for examining questions of stratification and equity in rural development, as well as the information it might provide in how to reach different audiences in the rural population, in the hope that, at least marginally, information can play a role in improving the lives of rural people.

PART II

INFORMATION WITHIN STRUCTURAL CONSTRAINTS: THREE CASE STUDIES

3

THE IVORY COAST: WHO BENEFITS FROM EDUCATION/INFORMATION IN RURAL TELEVISION?

Frans Lenglet

INTRODUCTION

Among Third World countries, the last decade has seen an up-surge of interest in development communication and education proj-ects that are particularly meant to reach the so-called underprivileged social groups. International organizations and governments, as well as universities, are promoting the idea and practice that one of the ways to solve development problems is to reach the poor and the il-literate with education and information, especially in the rural areas. The lack of basic literacy skills and knowledge about health care, nu-trition, and agricultural production is thought to be one of the main ob-stacles to development. It is assumed that reaching the "education poor" or "information poor" with functional and relevant information will help to eradicate the phenomenon of underdevelopment, which is characterized by poor health, low agricultural productivity, unem-ployment, rural exodus, overpopulation, and inequities in the distri-bution of wealth and power.

There are many common assumptions underlying these educa-tion and communication programs that remain untested. Too often, the internal and external effects (or lack thereof) of these programs are not analyzed. The immediate impact in terms of knowledge gains, innovation adoption, or awareness increase are far too often assumed, instead of assessed. The external or longer-term effects of these

Part of this article is based on Frans Lenglet, "Out-of-School Educational Television in the Ivory Coast: Its Effectiveness in Rural Development" (Ph.D. diss., Stanford University, 1978).

programs in terms of increased economic output or redistribution of income are usually not tested at all. Therefore, it remains unclear who actually benefits from such information and education schemes as agricultural extension projects, literacy campaigns, or radio farm forums. It is often uncertain whether these programs reach the target group they are supposed to serve, or which socioeconomic groups they reach at all.

The question remains, Who benefits from these information and education programs? Is it possible that among those who are exposed to these programs only small numbers of people derive a benefit, or that the real benefits are reaped by the program managers or other outside groups?

These questions will be addressed mainly on the basis of two and a half years of field research in the Ivory Coast.* There the author was involved in evaluating an out-of-school, or nonformal, education system that—with the use of television and especially set up for rural adults—started operating in 1973.

TARGET GROUPS IN SOME RECENT CASES

Insufficient knowledge of the actual audiences and the effects of communication and education programs is gradually stimulating more research in evaluating the workings of these programs. Recent field research across the Third World demonstrates that, in many instances, the intended target group—the people who are supposed to be the prime beneficiaries of these programs—is not reached. That is, the target groups are either not reached at all or only a smaller segment of the groups is actually exposed to the "message." This often means that within the target group some categories profit disproportionately from the advice given and the information dispensed. Six examples of this type of research are briefly reviewed below.

Satellite Instructional Television Experiment (SITE)

First, there was the large-scale SITE experiment in India in 1975/76. The experiment brought education and development information to community viewing centers in 2,400 villages by means of a television broadcast satellite (ATS-6). Through permanent monitoring and evaluation studies, it was found that children, not adults, were the most regular television viewers; that among adult viewers,

---

*The project evaluation is summarized in Grant et al. (1978).

the small farmers attended much more regularly than the large farmers; and, especially, that the landless laborers were very much interested in the television programs. At the same time, some knowledge gain took place, but a limited number of prescriptions given by the television could be followed or implemented by the small farmer. Many of the agricultural practices proposed required either individual purchasing power or inputs, such as fertilizer, and an infrastructure, such as roads and markets. By definition, these are not present among small farmers and landless laborers.

New Delhi

A second case, also in India, studied the audience and effects of television programs, broadcast from New Delhi, aimed at teleclub farmers. On the one hand, it was found that agricultural television—with a content that large farmers already understand—can close, rather than widen, the gap that exists between the amount of knowledge the small farmers possess and that of the large farmers. This should be considered an illustration of the potential "positive" effects of information and communication. However, on the other hand:

> Those farmers with higher education, higher reading ability, greater exposure to other media, and higher standards of living attend the programs more frequently than those with less education, less reading ability, limited exposure to other media, and a lower standard of living. [Shingi and Mody 1976, p. 94]

These two findings confirm that the highest attendance is among those who have access to other sources of information; they also indicate that, with proper management (for example, formative evaluation), special efforts to reach the people with limited access to other information sources can succeed.

Kenya

Because so many agricultural extension projects cater mainly to the richer farmers, and because these farmers always profit much more from new agricultural methods and knowledge than farmers and laborers without the same resources, an unconventional extension project took place in Kenya several years ago. The initiators of the experiment argued:

> The net effect of the diffusion of diffusion research tenets,
> themselves based on observations of current practices, has
> been to re-inforce, condone and systemise current prac-
> tice. That practice is to provide intensive services to a
> handful of innovative, wealthy, large, educated and infor-
> mation seeking farmers and to expect that the effect of
> these services will reach other farmers by autonomous
> diffusion processes. [Röling, Ascroft, and Chege 1974,
> p. 5]

To counter this empirical reality, the project experimented with a
new strategy to promote the adoption of productivity-increasing agricultural innovations, especially among the less progressive farmers.
     Evaluation of the first experiment dealing with hybrid maize
showed that almost all selected farmers could be recruited for the
course but that the majority of those recruited were progressive farmers, although the intention was precisely to reach the less progressive farmers. Thus, even when a conscious effort is made to reach
the less progressive farmer with agricultural information and to exclude the more progressive farmer, it does not always work.

Thailand

     A fourth study deals with the Mobile Trade Training School
(MTTS) in Thailand, which was originally aimed at revitalizing and
stimulating rural development through both light industry and agriculture. The MTTS was to provide skill training to unskilled and unemployed youth and to adults who had little or no opportunity to continue
their schooling (Papagiannis 1977). More than ten years after its in-
ception, the goals of the MTTS were redefined because, in the course
of time, the composition of the participants had changed and fairly
large numbers of participants were urban and employed—rather than
rural youth who needed improved skills for rural development.
     This is another case in which the original goal of the project
was not met and where, to a large extent, others than the intended
beneficiaries profited from the training offered. What had been set
out as rural skills training developed into urban upgrading and consumption education.

Colombia

     The Acción Cultural Popular (ACPO) project in Colombia is
well known for its use of mass media in reaching large numbers of

rural people with information and education. Evaluation research findings strongly suggest, however, that,

> Only those Colombian farmers who already had a minimal economic basis of their own were able to utilize the knowledge they had gained from the ACPO programs in order to improve their livelihood and fulfill some of their raised aspirations. [Chu, Rahim, and Kincaid 1976, p. 413]

Data also indicate that the ACPO program achieved success in raising the level of literacy and knowledge among only about 5 percent of the potential rural audience. "This small section of people has not yet shown any active sign of initiation or leadership in educating and mobilizing others," conclude Schramm and Lerner (1976, p. 159).

UNESCO Literacy Program

The last example is the United Nations Educational, Scientific and Cultural Organization (UNESCO) World Experimental Literacy Programme. In general, its results have been rather meager, especially considering the enormous amount of resources and effort that went into it (UNESCO 1976). The experimental program was intended to be confined to young illiterate adults between the ages of 15 and 29, and its objective was "the selective, intensive approach to functional literacy." In 1973 Blaug (1973) made the following remark:

> An interim evaluation report from one country (Iran) suggests that even carefully designed experiments quickly acquire all the familiar features of mass campaigns, attracting women and children rather than men, for social rather than for economic motives, and in no direct relationship to productive work in farms or factories. [P. 56]

Thus, the common observation in all six of these rural education and communication projects is that the intended target group is not reached, but only a segment thereof. The people who are assumed to need this education and information are often not reached, while others who are not the prime target population benefit from it. The only exception is the teleclubs project of New Delhi, although a disproportionate number of large farmers was found among the television viewers.

ASSUMPTIONS OF EDUCATION/
INFORMATION PROJECTS

The foregoing observations, which are based on solid evidence, cannot simply be explained as inefficiencies of the education/information programs themselves. They are too persistent for that, and they are recurring too often and in very different settings. One cannot argue that they are unfortunate errors that can be immediately corrected by more preparatory research and better planning. Yet, it seems that this is the most common position taken by development communication and nonformal education advocates. They say that by improving the planning of these projects, by increasing the relevance of the pedagogical and information materials, and by improving the software and message delivery systems, the programs will be better geared to the interests of the various target groups, will reach larger numbers of participants, and will have larger effects on living conditions, productivity, and other quality-of-life factors. Without doubt, such reasoning is necessary when planning an education/information program. However, it seems to belong at the end, rather than the beginning, of the analysis of the problem of who participates and who benefits from these programs. It is the author's contention that education and development communication programs begin by being placed in their larger societal context. Communication and information programs should be analyzed in their immediate relationships with the various institutional sectors of the society in which they operate and with the different agencies that deal with similar audiences and problems. But these programs should also be studied from the perspective of the overall socioeconomic and political strategy of the country in which they operate.

The reasons why certain target group segments are not reached, or why certain socioeconomic groups profit more from these programs than others, should not and cannot immediately be explained by the internal workings of the programs (that is, their software, organization, and the like), although these internal aspects may be important in explaining the learning outcomes and other short-term impacts. The basic explanation must be found in the nature of the role such programs play in the socioeconomic and political context of the country.

Special rural education and information programs do not operate in a social vacuum. Much as ordinary formal schooling, these programs are, on the one hand, the result of tensions and contradictions within the larger socioeconomic system; on the other, they exert influence on this system, either directly through their participants or indirectly through their institutional relationships with the system. More precisely, education and information programs in rural areas of Third World countries must be seen from the perspective of state intervention in these areas. This intervention is political, economic, and ideological in character and can to a large extent be equated with what is commonly called "rural development" (Goussault 1976). State intervention cannot be dissociated from global capitalist development, in which developing countries—particularly their rural areas—are the producers and suppliers of raw materials and labor. Capitalist intrusion into these areas—and this is not a recent phenomenon—affects the traditional modes of production as well as the social formations. Thus, there is an immediate link between the resulting socioeconomic stratification and the participants and beneficiaries of education/information programs.

The traditional modes of production and social stratification systems in developing countries are undergoing rapid and fundamental changes. In many instances the public and explicit objective of education/information programs is to accelerate and accompany these change processes by creating "modern" values, beliefs, and allegiances, as well as by transferring new skills and cognitive knowledge (Inkeles and Smith 1974). At the same time, these programs are also meant to alleviate the problems this rapid socioeconomic transformation is causing. The programs are supposed to cater to the socially underprivileged groups in rural society by improving their living conditions through the distribution of the fruits of economic progress to all segments of society. This latter goal, especially, is not reached. Many of the education/information programs do not reach the population they are supposed to serve, and real impact in terms of awareness, learning, and behavior change is often very limited. But even if there is real impact, it is unclear how the learning, awareness, and action effects of these programs are translated into national productivity and equal distribution of power and wealth—in short, genuine development. Usually, it is assumed that the link between the effects of education/information programs and other societal sectors exists. But this basic assumption, which says that if these programs are internally effective they are also externally effective, is often neither questioned nor analyzed (Lenglet and McAnany 1977).

If it is observed that the intended participants of education/information projects are not always reached, and if it is observed that these projects are not very effective in terms of their official goals, one has to find the explanation for this and ask whether there are possibly other beneficiaries and benefits—in other words, other manifest or latent functions that cause these projects not only to continue but even to expand. By presenting the case of the Ivory Coast Out-of-School Educational Television programs, both of these issues will be considered. Subsequent pages will address the following questions: (1) Who participates in the programs? (2) What are the effects of the programs? (3) How are these effects explained? and (4) Who are the beneficiaries?

OUT-OF-SCHOOL EDUCATIONAL
TELEVISION IN THE IVORY COAST

In 1971 the first televised lessons for the first grade were broadcast in the Ivory Coast. In the 1976/77 school year, daytime educational television programs were broadcast for about 325,000 pupils in the six grades of the primary school system. These pupils were distributed over about 7,550 classrooms that were located in about 1,700 schools (Eicher and Orivel 1977). About 1,300 of these schools were in small villages; the remaining 500 were in small and middle-sized towns and large cities.

There is only one television channel in the country. Therefore, at night everybody (either in the local schoolhouse or in about 200,000 private homes) can receive the regular general television programs broadcast under the authority of the Ministry of Information. Twice a week, after the evening news, the "Tele pour Tous" ("Television for Everybody") programs (hereafter called TPT) are aired. They are aimed at the out-of-school audience of illiterate adults and youth. They carry information related to such varying issues as health care and nutrition, rural housing, cooperatives, folklore, civics, agricultural innovations, and the like. The TPT programs follow several styles of dramatic or didactic forms. The films are always shot on location in the villages, which gives them a certain flavor of vividness. Where needed, the commentary is in the French language, the official language of the Ivory Coast.

In the television schools there is usually an "animator"—one of the local primary schoolteachers—who animates the group of people watching the TPT programs together and, later, discussing the relevance of what they have seen. The TPT programs are produced by a department of the Ministry of Primary and Television Education, not by the Ministry of Information. The films are made in collaboration with other ministries and agencies concerned with rural development issues—for example, the Ministry of Health, for programs on the dangers of polluted water; the Ministry of Animal Production, for programs on animal husbandry; and the Agency for Cooperatives, for programs on cooperatives.

Who Participates in TPT?

Participation is defined as "watching the TPT program and participating in the discussion afterward." The managers of the TPT system feel that the discussion after the program broadcast is very important because it allows the animator to verify whether the spectators have understood the program and to give additional information and clarification. For the audience, the discussion is important because they can determine to what extent the program's content is relevant for their own situation. They also try to decide how they can best implement or adopt the prescriptions of the TPT program to their needs.

Much can be said about participation. First, a decline in the national audience was observed over the period 1974-77, despite the facts that more primary schools were equipped with television sets, the national population increased about 3 percent per year, and since October 1976 all primary schoolteachers were officially ordered to do out-of-school animation. The total estimated average number of TPT spectators declined from an annual national average of 16,024 in 1974/75 to 15,725 in 1975/76, and to 7,341 in 1976/77. It is assumed that these figures comprise adults only, that is, people over age 15. This assumption is not always correct. Observations show that, often, more than half of the classroom is filled with young children who come out of curiosity, to pass their time, or to be entertained. Moreover, there are indications that the animators who report the number of TPT attendants provide figures that are inflated from 10 to 20 percent.

Another observation is that a considerable number of people leave the classroom the moment the animator turns off the television set or sound (the light of the screen often being the only light in the otherwise dark classroom) to start the discussion. This fact should be taken into account when evaluating the audience figures.

When one assumes that the estimated annual national average attendance figures indicate the total number of TPT participants, one can assess what proportion of the potential audience the TPT is reaching. In 1975/76 about 80 percent of all elementary schools were in the rural areas, and one can assume that this 80 percent also applies to all the television schools, so that 20 percent of these schools are located in the urban areas. It is further assumed that a rural television school is the only television school in the village and that this village had an average number of inhabitants of 515 in 1974/75, 568 in 1975/76, and 590 in 1976/77. From these assumptions, partially based on 1975 census data, it follows that in 1974/75 there were 922 rural television schools in 922 villages with a total population of 474,830 inhabitants. For 1975/76 the figures are 1,185 villages and 673,080 inhabitants; for 1976/77, 1,322 villages and 799,980 inhabitants. The total potential rural population with access to television schools is 47 percent of the total population in television school villages, given the fact that people between the ages of 15 and 59 constitute 47 percent of the total population.

A similar calculation can be made for the urban areas. One can assume that in 1974/75 each urban television school served a total of 4,000 people and that in the course of time, when new schools were added, this figure remained stable. The number of urban television schools in each school year multiplied by 4,000 gives the total number of urban dwellers directly served by television schools. Again, taking 47 percent of this result, one finds the number of the total potential urban audience with access to television schools.

Adding the rural and urban potential TPT audiences with access to television schools together, one finds the following figures: 1974/75, 655,570; 1975/76, 872,828; and 1976/77, 986,991. As a final step, each yearly, national average attendance figure is divided by the above figures and multiplied by 100. The results of this operation show that in 1974/75 an average of 2.4 percent of the potential audience was reached by TPT programs; in 1975/76 the figure is 1.8 percent; and in 1976/77, only 0.7 percent. These figures indicate how very small the actual, as opposed to the potential, audience really was and how that audience declined over three years.

The total picture can be improved by taking into account that the above calculations are based on estimated annual averages and that there were variations. Taking the highest estimates of attendance at one program for each year, we find that the maximum proportion of the potential TPT audience reached in 1974/75 is 4.7 percent, compared with the average of 2.4 percent, whereas maximum figures for 1975/76 and 1976/77 were 3.6 and 3.1 percent, respectively. But even with the most conservative, optimistic estimates, it cannot be said that the mass medium of television reaches a mass audience, except when considering the private television viewers as part of the target audience. This will be done later in this chapter.

The target group that TPT officials have in mind is very difficult to determine. Official documents have never clearly defined what the TPT target audience should be. Roughly, it can be said that the TPT programs are aimed, first, at rural adolescents and adults who have never gone to school, who cannot read and write French, and who could profit from some basic education and information; second, at the same group in the urban areas; and, third, at the school dropouts and primary school graduates, to give them the skills and motivation to stay in the rural areas and to improve agricultural production instead of increasing the rural exodus.

The audience figures presented above include urban as well as rural spectators who watch the TPT program in the local television school. It is difficult to distinguish between the two groups of viewers, because the figures are estimates based on data from the feedback system that operates in a sample of both urban and rural schools.

Despite some continuous reports of rural classrooms filled to capacity and even more, it remains a fact that the attendance of the TPT programs has continually dropped. It is also clear that only a small percentage of the potential audience is reached by the TPT broadcasts. It is true that the TPT managers have not set a quantitative goal; there are no declarations of how many people the TPT should attract. But there is the implicit assumption that all television schools should be opened and that at least one television set should be switched on.

If, for example, in 1976/77 each television school would have had at least one television set operating, and if each animator would have attracted at least 25 adults, then at each TPT evening there would have been at least 41,300 spectators. This figure was never attained. However, 25 spectators per classroom is a rather low number. We know that for some TPT sessions the actual number of participants was higher: 35, 60, and even 100 are no exceptions. If such figures could be reached in all the television schools, the audience could be increased to 57,820 or even 165,200 spectators per broadcast.

Audience Characteristics

It appears that the main reason why so relatively few people participate in the TPT sessions is that television schools are not opened and animators are not motivated. The lack of motivation of the teacher-animator is explained by the nonremuneration of their extra services. But even in schools that are regularly opened and where teachers do some animation, it is generally observed that only few people attend.

A number of reasons have been identified as to why people do not watch the TPT programs. Some of these reasons appear to be related to the characteristics of those who do or do not attend the sessions. There are a distinct number of different groups represented. First, over and over again it has been found that about two-thirds of the TPT audience consist of men; one-third are women. Second, among the TPT spectators, the younger age groups—especially those between 20 and 40 years—are relatively overrepresented, while they are also in the absolute majority. Third, people with some form of education participate in larger numbers than their total number in the potential TPT audience would lead one to expect. This is also true for those who understand and speak basic French but have not gone to school and are illiterate. Also, research and observation concur that village authorities do not participate much in TPT sessions. There is, however, no entirely conclusive evidence for an answer to the question of whether the people with large cash incomes participate disproportionately to their number in the village population. In absolute terms, the majority of the TPT viewers fall into lower income categories, but in relative terms, there are indications that those in the higher income brackets participate more.

At the same time, it is found that there is no linear relationship between income and age of the TPT spectators. In other words, among the young as well as the old, we find poor and rich spectators, although many more poor than rich. And because there is no immediate relationship between income level and level of schooling, at least in the villages, it is not possible to make a final statement on the relationship between TPT participation and income.*

Two broad conclusions can be drawn from these data. First, the TPT programs attract more people who, through their education, knowledge of French, and other outside contacts (measured by income and sex), have a better chance to understand the television message, especially because of the French commentary (although the French is translated into the local language at each TPT session). For these people, the television and TPT programs are another means to sustain and enlarge the contact with the "modern" world of which they are already a part. That is to say, they have a contact that is probably more frequent and intense than that of women, older people, and those without education and understanding of French. Second, despite this relative overrepresentation of already "modern" groups among the TPT audience, the absolute majority of TPT spectators consist of poor, illiterate men and women. For them television represents one of the few means by which to come into contact with the outside world and to learn something about it.

The question remains, however: What are the personal motivations of those who attend the TPT sessions, or, for that matter, of those who do not attend?

Motivation

Starting with the group of villagers who do not attend the TPT sessions, there is substantial evidence that one of the great obstacles to village participation is that the sessions necessarily take place in the local school and that the TPT animator is one of the schoolteachers. Generally speaking, the school is physically, as well as sociologically, on the periphery of the village. It is a foreign element in the village culture and structure that must be tolerated and used, but only with regard to its primary purpose: the socialization of children into the norms and skills of modern society. As such the schoolhouse is a place for children, not for adults.

The teacher is accepted by the villagers as one who is trained to deal with teaching children—not more, not less. Culturally as well as ethnically, the teacher is very often a stranger and, thus, does not participate in the daily affairs of the village. Moreover, the

---

*Much of this information can be found in Etaix and Lenglet (1977).

teacher is trained as neither an adult educator nor as a development agent, which limits the teacher's technical knowledge and ability to really animate the TPT discussion group, as well as the likelihood of being accepted as an "authority" by the village population.

Thus, it is no wonder that especially the younger members of the village community, who probably have a less reserved attitude toward the school, and part of whom have even been socialized in the school, are much more likely than the older villagers to attend the TPT programs. But there are additional factors that facilitate the participation of the younger people. On the one hand, the elderly manifest the attitude contained in the following remark of an older man: "We old folks have seen a lot of things. TV is not of our time, so we'd rather leave it to the younger generation" (Grant and Seya 1976, p. 17). On the other hand, it can be documented that the younger men have a greater opportunity to come and watch television than any other category among the adults. The older people fill their leisure time with "traditional" activities. Younger women are either too busy with their heavy workload of hauling water and firewood, cooking, child rearing, and agriculture, or are not allowed by their husbands to go out at night.

Besides the opportunity to attend TPT sessions, another factor may motivate people. The people who do attend the TPT programs are in the classroom from the moment the television set is turned on (some time before the actual TPT broadcast) until it is turned off. This suggests that it is not the TPT programs but television per se that forms the biggest attraction. Thus, the entertainment function of television seems to exceed the educational function of TPT, although it must be acknowledged that these two functions are not mutually exclusive.

The attractiveness of television to isolated villagers is underscored by group and individual interviews with large numbers of these people. In general, they perceive television, in contrast to the cinema, as something accessible and free. Because some of the television content, in particular the TPT program, is related to their own circumstances, villagers affirm that television is acceptable and useful. At least in theory, they agree with the statement that television can help improve their living conditions through a series of "educational" messages (Etaix and Lenglet 1977). The reality differs, however, from the potential impact attributed to television, in general, and TPT, in particular. This is partially related to the socioeconomic status of the majority of the TPT spectators.

The majority of the TPT audience are the young, relatively poor, uneducated men who do not have any particular position in the village structure or hierarchy. This fact is important to note. If the TPT programs intend to reach the rural masses with advice and prescriptions of how they can improve their living conditions, the audience reached must be in a position to follow these counsels, that is, must have the resources and the political power to carry out the actions suggested. The majority of the TPT spectators are not in this position, and those who have money and power do not watch TPT. Thus, if TPT counsels villagers to construct a well, for example, there are many obstacles to the actual construction taking place, because those who have received the television message must first convince those who have money and power that a well is an important and necessary investment. When these latter people have been convinced, they must provide the bulk of the financial contribution and pressure the administration to provide other necessary inputs. This example concerns a communal action. But the lack of purchasing power also plays a significant role in individual actions for improving living conditions or agricultural productivity. If the TPT spectators have no money or land, or if they are still completely dependent on their father or maternal uncle for major decisions, chances are small that an action will be undertaken.

What Are the Effects of TPT?

The question is raised as to the internal effects or impact of the TPT programs: Is there any evidence that people have been sensitized to certain development problems, that they have acquired new knowledge and skills, and that they have changed their behavior or have started an action as a direct or indirect consequence of having watched the TPT programs?

On the basis of individual and group interviews, it can be confirmed that members of the TPT audience, and even part of the nonaudience, have been influenced in their thinking about problems that affect their own situations. Etaix and Lenglet (1977, p. 186) come to the conclusion that "the TPT programs attain their sensitization objective in terms of retention of TPT themes and advice when they deal with issues that people feel are crucial for them: agricultural production, clean water, better housing, etc." But the extent and depth of this sensitization effect is limited by the relatively small proportion of the primary target audience exposed to the TPT programs and by the lack of continuous support for maintaining and increasing this sensitization, as will be seen below in the paragraphs dealing with the obstacles to action.

The immediate learning effect of the TPT programs is also very restricted. That is, only a few TPT programs aim at transmitting a specific set of theoretical notions or practical skills. When this is done, the conception and actual presentation of the pedagogical mate-

rial is done rather poorly because of a lack of systematic instructional
design. This is illustrated by the study of Jouët (1976), who found
that in a half-hour film on the relationship between polluted water and
a particular disease, only 30 seconds were devoted to explaining the
disease cycle: polluted water, penetration of the parasites into the
skin, evacuation of the parasites into the water, and so forth.

Did any action occur as a result of TPT? Probably some, but
not very much. For example, one year after a certain TPT program
on public wells, about 6 percent of the 235 sample villages that reported watching this program had a new modern well, which they did
not have before the broadcasting of the program. Another 17 percent
were in the process of getting a well—collecting money, making requests to the subprefect, or waiting for technicians to drill. It was
impossible to ascertain to what extent these actions had been immediately triggered by the TPT programs. It is certain, however, that
some were and that other actions and decisions for actions were reinforced or partially influenced by the TPT series dealing with public
wells.

Also, after a number of TPT programs on water and the use of
the water filter for obtaining potable water—and after a publicity campaign on radio, television, and in the press—sales figures of water
filters for that year, in comparison with the figures of the previous
year, showed a large increase (although it is very likely that most
filters were sold in urban, rather than rural, areas). Moreover,
there are many declarations that villagers make when asked what
TPT prescriptions they have followed: construction of latrines, purchase of a water filter, construction of wells, creation of a cooperative, and the like. When verification of these accomplishments was
attempted, they appeared to be nonexistent, in many cases, or to
have already started prior to the related TPT program. Thus, it can
be said that these declarations are more declarations of intent than
actual decisions followed up by concrete actions.

Another indication of impact is reported by the National Center
for Cooperatives. After a series of TPT programs on the necessity,
advantages, and operation of a cooperative, it received a number of
requests to help create a cooperative. And, although this is not an
immediate impact, it is also known that a considerable number of
TPT spectators, either directly or through their animators, requested
additional information from the TPT department concerning the contents of certain TPT broadcasts.

The data available in this area show that TPT impact is diverse,
thinly spread, and limited. It is probably larger in terms of sensitization than in those of action. Where action is concerned, however, individual action is more likely than that of the group, and action requiring few inputs in terms of money and effort is more likely to take

place than that which requires larger inputs, although there are indications that actions with lower prestige and those that require less money do not arouse the peasants' interest as much as more prestigious activities (Etaix and Lenglet 1977).

Four main obstacles to action have been identified: technical, administrative, cultural, and structural.

Technical Obstacles

Villagers mentioned, for example, that a well could not be drilled because the soil was too hard for the drilling equipment. Because the technical problems are there to be solved, this obstacle seems minor, unless the technical solution requires large new inputs; in that case, other (structural) obstacles could be present.

Administrative Obstacles

The administrative obstacles are often of a systemic or structural nature. It is common knowledge that the administrative machinery is slow and inefficient. This means, for example, that a request for a public well is not transmitted to the higher echelons, that money deposited by villagers as their contribution for well construction disappears, and that promises by local administrators are often not executed. The administrative problem is compounded by the fact that there are other channels—via political and ethnic links in the cities—that are often much more efficient in getting access to those people at the decision-making level and in allocating funds to village projects. This means that villages or groups of people with a better informal access to the power centers of the country have a much greater chance of obtaining the support for certain actions than those who have to pass through the formal administrative system.

Cultural Obstacles

For lack of a better word, certain obstacles are termed cultural that refer especially to beliefs and customs of the villages. The obstacles are created when certain extraneously designed messages are received and interpreted by people with contrasting notions and interpretations of reality. An illustration of this obstacle is the resistance or impossibility of certain villagers to accept the scientific explanations regarding disease cycles—for example, microbes being carried from the drinking water through the human body and back into the water. Here, the rationalization may be: "Those TV explanations are good for the Whites, we have our own explanations." The television message is understood but is instantly rejected as a valid aid in understanding or changing the world.

Structural Obstacles

From what has previously been said, it should be clear that there are many internal constraints on the effective and efficient operation of an education/information project such as TPT. Objectives are not clearly defined; nor are target audiences. The reception of the programs—in this case, the animation of the listening groups—is badly organized. To this can be added the lack of finances, lack of training, and the absence of well-developed and tested software and pedagogical materials.

In addition, there are external constraints that are of a structural nature. They lie in the social structure of the country in which the project is operating, in the institutional and material infrastructure, in the political support and leadership, and in whether the project has institutional permanency (Lenglet and McAnany 1977).

A mass medium, such as television, can often arouse but cannot itself provide the resources to carry out the actions prescribed. The TPT department works with a number of client ministries and state development agencies. During the years reported, however, the field agents from these institutions have participated in neither the TPT sessions nor in the technical follow-up activities. The TPT animators were either not willing or unable to promote this follow-up.

It seems, also, that effective action can only take place if the messages are received and understood within a context of available inputs, facilities, and institutions. If, for example, the TPT programs talk about placing money in a bank account (as it did in one television series), then there must be surplus cash money and there must be banks. If the TPT program adds that money in the bank will allow receiving credit, this automatically applies only to the larger farmers who have the means to save money and who are not obliged to spend all their cash income for consumption purposes or for sending their children to school. This is just one example, but it is clear that if the TPT messages are to affect the welfare and life-style of the Ivory Coast peasant, the peasant—irrespective of socioeconomic position—should be able to apply the message by having a certain purchasing power and access to markets, credit, agricultural inputs, practical demonstrations, and extension services. As long as this is absent—and this is certainly the case in large parts of the rural Ivory Coast—very little change is likely as a consequence of TPT programs.

Evidence mentioned earlier indicates that certain social factors at the village level affect who will attend the TPT sessions and who will not. These factors also affect the direction of the discussions and the kinds of follow-up action and eventual change. The majority of the TPT spectators are relatively poor and without political power; therefore, the knowledge gained is probably not going to be applicable, because resources and opportunities are lacking.

Moreover, one of the main effects of learning and exposure to outside information is to encourage the young to leave the rural areas, especially when agricultural and other economic opportunities do not exist for them. This is an immediate contradiction with the stated intention that TPT should help stem the rural exodus.

How Are These Effects Best Explained?

At this point, it is necessary to place the TPT project back into its context of a country that has known a fast and continuous economic expansion since its independence in 1960. It is not exaggeration to state that the official Ivory Coast development model encourages the unequal distribution of power and wealth rather than limits it. The development option favors a modernization of agriculture on a wide scale for increasing the exports of agricultural products and for building an industry on the basis of the primary transformation of agricultural products. The transformation of the rural areas is a means to this end. The creation and extension of medium-sized family farms is encouraged, but so is the maintenance and improvement of large-scale agribusiness (Diawara 1976). At the same time, the traditional smallholder will disappear. This goal requires that the traditional socioeconomic structure of the rural areas undergoes a fundamental change. New institutions are required, and old social formations have to yield to modern ones. A class of agricultural entrepreneurs is created, and, inevitably, many will lose and few will gain. It is almost certain that credit and other inputs will go to the so-called progressive farmers who have already shown promising results in terms of productivity and adoption of innovations. Small family farmers will be pushed into the class of agricultural laborers and the urban proletariat or will become members of cooperatives that are usually controlled by the larger farmers and by the state (Barnet 1973). It is in this context of rural transformation and class formation that the TPT programs operate. Therefore, the operation, as well as the relative ineffectiveness, of the TPT programs in the rural areas must be explained from the following perspective: The Ivory Coast government wants this transformation process to develop gradually, with possible frictions and tensions to be avoided or at least smoothed. The state does not want nor need a political mass mobilization to reach its development goals. Probably, it needs and wants the opposite: quietness, docility, and integration. It needs tacit consent and popular participation in the development process as defined by the state. The TPT programs themselves question neither the existing power system nor the existing and newly developing social stratification. This does not exclude the real possibility (which has been ob-

served by the author) that TPT discussion sessions develop into political debates about the injustices in Ivory Coast society. But these
debates do not result in further political action.

With this in mind, the TPT programs should, instead, be analyzed in the animation rurale tradition of rural development, in which
the government explains the official development plans to the peasants
(Elliot 1974; Moulton 1977). In this sense, TPT is a political education project of the government of no little importance. In official
documents it is clearly stated that the TPT programs are an educational action "which will permit all Ivorians, urban as well as rural,
to understand the development actions, to participate actively in the
improvement of their situation and in a better distribution of the
fruits of economic progress" (Ivory Coast Republic 1975). Elsewhere
the documents state that the TPT goal is to familiarize the population "with the economic, political and administrative structure in order to free the population and to allow them to make use of the services" (Ivory Coast Republic 1976a). Also, the following objective is
formulated: "To promote awareness and analysis of existing situations, and search for adaptive solutions in the perspective of integration into the modern world without rupture with certain traditional
values" (Ivory Coast Republic 1976b).

In this perspective, the TPT programs, and many other general
television programs as well, have a typical political function. This
corresponds with the explicit sensitization objective of the majority
of the TPT broadcasts and the general tendency to transform the TPT
viewers into consumers of development services provided by the state.
However, TPT was clearly not meant to create a political mobilization
of the rural masses.

In sum, one can say: "TPT programs have only a limited internal effect. The external effect is even smaller. The TPT programs
reach only a small number of people who are not the most influential
in making development-related decisions and in taking action in the
rural areas. Thus, even in its propaganda function, TPT does not
have much effect."

The author agrees with this objection, and it seems as if the
government itself is still not convinced of the value of the TPT programs for the rural audience. There is a lack of a coherent and co-
ordinated adult education or rural information policy. Different ministries are in conflict over the areas of their authority in these matters. The TPT budget is relatively small, and, at present, there is
neither the political nor professional leadership to improve and enlarge TPT's operation. The limited effectiveness of TPT is certainly
true for the communal TPT audience—the people who watch the TPT
programs at the local school. But there are also people who watch
television in their own homes or with friends and relatives. Perhaps,
among them, other effects could be observed.

In 1975 there were an estimated 150,000 privately owned television sets in the country (Ivory Coast Republic 1976a). Because of a lack of electricity in rural areas, almost all of them were located in small and large towns. It seems correct to assume that, on the average, nine people watch one television set (Amsellem and Bouchet 1975; Lenglet 1978). Thus, there is an enormous potential audience for the TPT programs in the urban areas—up to 1.5 million people. This is considerably larger than the potential TPT audience in urban and rural schools, estimated at 872,828 in 1975. Information also indicates that 14 percent of the urban population regularly watch the TPT programs (IIOP 1975). One thus arrives at a figure of between 125,000 and 210,111 urban people who regularly watch the TPT programs in their homes. This figure contrasts sharply with the 2 percent of the rural population of 15 years and older (46,316 people) that the Institut Ivoirien d'Opinion Publique (IIOP) (1975) reports watches TPT programs regularly.

No intensive research had been done on this large unorganized TPT audience, its composition, and the possible impact of the programs in urban areas. But the IIOP (1975) found, for example, that about half of the urban TPT spectators (probably including those from both the school and the home) said that they had learned about the construction of a well and that they intended to follow prescriptions for well construction. However, only 24 percent of the urban TPT spectators could cite the subject of the last TPT program. Because there is regular contact between the townspeople and the villages from which they originate, one can assume that there is much contact and communication between urban and rural populations and that part of the TPT message is thus redistributed to the rural areas. Here, one has to assume a kind of two-step or multistep flow of communication.

Moreover, television sets in the urban areas are predominantly owned by people with at least secondary education (Ivory Coast Republic 1976c). These people watch TPT programs with more regularity than those without education, 20 percent versus 7 percent (IIOP 1975), and, because of their social position, they have high social prestige in their villages. As a consequence, they may be instrumental in getting villagers to decide on certain improvements suggested by TPT and to start actions to complete them. Thus, indirectly, the villagers could benefit from TPT. This is at least the official argument. To date, no research has been done on how urban opinion leadership influences village populations.

There is another effect in the urban areas. It was found that only small proportions of urban TPT viewers interviewed said that they did not know whether the TPT programs "taught something" (8 percent) or that they "were useful for the village" (4 percent). This can be interpreted as a general favorable attitude toward TPT's content. It means that the urban spectators are convinced that TPT serves a positive purpose for rural people. Because TPT programs —as well as television, in general—come from the government, they have a monopoly on information and are a powerful instrument of propaganda. Also, because many of the TPT programs are produced on request of and in collaboration with the state or parastatal development agencies that are responsible for the state's technical intervention in the rural areas, the TPT programs become a powerful tool for publicity and public relations for these agencies—in particular, for the urban audience. It does not seem too farfetched a conclusion that an unintended, but probably highly welcomed, side effect of the TPT programs is that they create and support a generally favorable climate of opinion in which the state can carry out its development plans. This could perhaps be the major function of the TPT programs.

Who Are the Beneficiaries of TPT?

When the original question—Who benefits from education and information?—is repeated, the answer is not entirely simple and clear. There are several elements and aspects of a complete answer in the foregoing paragraphs (although the final answer should wait further investigation):

1. It is true that, in the short run, the people for whom the TPT programs are produced and broadcast either do not have access to them in sufficiently large numbers or turn out only in limited number to watch the programs and participate in the animation sessions. The effects of the TPT programs on these audiences are minimal—mainly in terms of sensitization, rather than of action. This seems to be in line with diffusion of innovations research—that is, that mass media are most important in creating awareness and diffusing information, whereas interpersonal contacts are most important for decision making. Thus, the target audience does not immediately benefit from these programs in their daily lives, except, perhaps, that new entertainment has been introduced to isolated villages.

2. The internal effects for villages and their inhabitants, in the long run, are questionable. The obstacles to successful action are many, and the link between successful action and general development goals is unclear.

3. There is the possibility that in the future the TPT programs will, more consciously than before, become one of the means for facilitating the fundamental social changes the rural areas are experiencing. Then, it will probably not be the rural mass who will profit from these modifications but, rather, the state, the new class of agricultural entrepreneurs, and the domestic and foreign investors.

4. At present there are signs indicating that TPT caters more to the urban cadres than to the village population. It is serving the ideological and political purpose of creating and maintaining a general consensus and favorable climate for state development policies among the politically and economically dominant layers of society, rather than providing educational support to "development from below." Thus, the state and the political and economic power holders may benefit most from TPT, although indirectly.

These conclusions follow from the early contention that education/information programs must be studied in their socioeconomic and political contexts. In the Ivory Coast case, this approach was taken not only in the context of the village, where the social structure presents a variety of constraints to effective impact of TPT, but also in the context of a state that pursues state capitalist development policies. The national economy is also closely linked to, and dependent on, the forces of the international capitalist economic system, for which the Ivory Coast is an important supplier of agricultural products. Within this context, such variables as the relationship between the education/information program and other rural development activities, the relationships between competing ministries, the social institutionalization of the program, and the development of program contents must be studied. These variables are important, but only on a secondary or tertiary level.

In the final analysis, we should return to the forces and contradictions of the capitalist system as it manifests itself in the Ivory Coast. Here, we have indicated some of the forces. We have hardly touched upon the contradictions. Given the fact that there are many other ideological influences to which the peasants are exposed, and given their own concrete and daily experience with the transformation of economic and political realities, it may be assumed that the idyllic picture, as presented by the mass media, could collide with the harsh reality of daily life and provide, under certain circumstances, the impetus for revolutionary—rather than evolutionary—action. To see how the internal contradictions affect the education/information program, and to see how this program resolves these contradictions or creates new ones, should be the subject of intensive future research, for which Goussault (1976) provides some elements.

4

GUATEMALA: MARGINALITY AND INFORMATION IN RURAL DEVELOPMENT IN THE WESTERN HIGHLANDS

Jeremiah O'Sullivan

INTRODUCTION

This study examines the role of information and extension services in promoting change in the lives of subsistence peasants in the Western Central Highlands of Guatemala and is the result of the author's experience working with extension programs and rural non-formal education in Guatemala.

Guatemala, second largest of the Central American countries, with 108,889 square kilometers, has a population of 5.7 million (1973) census). The Western Central Highlands is a densely populated region with 86.6 inhabitants per square kilometer, compared with 52.3 for the country as a whole—30 percent of the country's population live in the Highlands.

Agriculture contributes some 30 percent of the internal gross product, employing six out of every ten workers. However, Guatemala has a critical problem with the distribution of land: 75 percent of the farmholdings have an average of 1.3 hectares, while some 100 large farms occupy 15 percent of all the available agricultural land, with 5,000 hectares each.

Land distribution affects both agricultural production and rural development. Production is extremely constrained on the small farms; because of the farmers' extreme poverty, few use any modern techniques. Microfincas (the smallest farms) do not produce sufficient food for family survival. With no steady opportunities for alternative employment, 75 percent of all rural families in Guatemala face poverty and gradual starvation. Almost half of all the microfincas are situated in the Highlands region, the most depressed region of the country. The agricultural production of this region is geared toward cereals with low economic productivity, using very traditional production methods. Production is low and few practical ways for increasing it have been found. The recent use of chemical fertilizers increased the production margin of these subsistence farms somewhat but has not ensured their long-term viability. Small subsistence farming appears to have little hope of transforming itself into an expanded source of production, even less so because of the rapidly increasing population that it must support.

Unequal distribution of land has many serious consequences in Guatemala. Several hundred thousand farm laborers are landless (310,000, according to the 1974 Guatemalan National Agricultural Plan). In the subsistence sector, there are almost 200,000 people working but only 7,000 employment opportunities. The average number of working days per year per person is less than 120. All of this represents a complex problem of unemployment, underemployment, hidden unemployment, and, consequently, a very low rate of productivity.

Rural living standards reflect these scarce employment opportunities. In Guatemala almost half a million families (60 percent of the rural population) have an annual income of less than U.S. $400— less than U.S. $80 per person per year, which is comparable to the levels of the poorest countries in the world today. Income determines consumption. Half the total population of Guatemala consumes only 50 percent of the calories necessary to maintain normal physical growth and to replace the energies consumed in work. Similar deficits are reported in their consumption of proteins and carbohydrates. In the Highlands, infant mortality exceeds 30 percent. Chronic undernourishment, infectious disease, gastritis, and bronchitis are the principal causes of premature death (Secretaría General 1975a).

The critical issues are subsistence farming, illiteracy, undernourishment, unemployment, underemployment, and a large sector of landless peasants—problems evident in many of the poorer countries of the Third World today. For the rural poor in Guatemala, development strategies have been proposed and carried out. This chapter will critically examine the effectiveness of some of these programs.

RURAL DEVELOPMENT STRATEGIES

The government of Guatemala is concerned with the country's food production and self-sufficiency in food. The main goal of agricultural development in Guatemala today is to increase production, and the strategy to do so is a program of agricultural extension that includes technical assistance, credit assistance, and the cooperative movement. This strategy aims to assist small and medium-sized farmers to use their resources more efficiently to achieve their social and economic advancement. An effort is being made to modernize traditional subsistence agriculture through the use of new systems of cultivation, better seeds, and fertilizers. Traditional and conservative farmers' attitudes, it is said, must evolve into modern ones; in the process, agricultural production and rural family incomes will increase.

Programs of education and information for subsistence farmers are an international concern today. However, a critical question is being posed by many development scholars: Can an agricultural extension service based on information and relatively limited credit facilities transform a static subsistence rural economy into a dynamic market economy while improving the quality of family and community life?

Coombs and Ahmed (1974), in discussing the role of nonformal education in relieving Third World poverty, cite four models of rural development: extension, training, self-help, and integrated rural development. These will be examined briefly for their relevance to the Guatemalan problem.

The extension model seeks to extend agricultural services to a constantly greater sector of the rural population. In contrast to the extension model, which emphasizes the communication of information about innovative technical practices, the training model emphasizes systematic learning of specific basic skills and related knowledge. This model involves a rather narrow, self-contained view and strategy of development based on the premise that knowledge and skills by themselves can precipitate the process of development.

The basic premise of the self-help (or cooperative) model is that the complex process of rural transformation must begin with changes in the rural people themselves—in their attitudes toward change, in their aspirations for improvement, and, above all, in their perceptions of themselves and their own inherent power, individually and collectively, to better their conditions. The integrated development model takes a broader view of the rural development process and seeks to coordinate the essential components (including education, health, housing, and agriculture) required to get agricultural or rural development moving under a single "management system." Although this model considers a role for local people in planning, decision making, and implementation, its fundamental emphasis is on the coordination of government services in rural areas.

Coombs and Ahmed suggest that the basic problem of all four of these approaches is "the narrow, simplistic and unrealistic views of rural development that underlie most rural education and other programs" (1974). The basic goals of rural development are much broader than increased agricultural production and economic growth: more equitable distribution of land; increased rural employment; improved health, housing, education, and general living conditions of all rural people; a larger voice for rural people in running their own affairs; and a narrowing of the social and economic gap between rural and urban areas. In brief, this wider vision equates rural development with the thoroughgoing transformation of rural institutions, processes, and human relationships, requiring a vigorous and forthright attack on rural poverty and social injustice.

A vast body of literature already exists that deals with the role of education and information in development and their effect on productivity and income distribution. The overall results of development efforts, so far, have not been very satisfactory, particularly as it became evident that agricultural development (which did, in fact, considerably increase productivity for some) widened the economic gap between the large landowners and the marginal subsistence farmers (Gotsch 1972; Griffin 1973).

A number of authors (Grunig 1969; Lopez 1971; Barcaclough 1972; Esmond 1974) consider the basic problem as structural—the lack of real and effective opportunity causes the small farmer to reject the technological process of change. Structural limitations include lack of land and negative conditions of tenancy; lack of, or high cost of, credit, which also limits access to the necessary inputs; low prices for harvest; insecurity and, often, market exploitation; high level of risk, which the small farmer must bear alone because there are no economic reserves if the harvest fails; and lack, or availability under degrading conditions, of public services that would satisfy the practical necessities of the small farmer (Gillette and Uphoff 1973).

All of these authors suggest that the small farmer lacks a real and effective opportunity to change. The peasant is marginalized in a system that serves the privileged few. Subsistence farming continues because it serves a purpose within the economic system; until this system is changed, there will be no real change in the lives of the peasants. The roots of the problem are in the economic sphere, and, specifically, in the system of production, not in a simple lack of education and information.

MARGINALITY THEORY: A
LATIN AMERICAN PERSPECTIVE

Over the last decade, an alternative interpretation of the complex phenomena of development and underdevelopment has taken shape in the writings of a number of scholars from Latin America, North America, and Europe. These scholars have rejected the "diffusion model" of development and replaced it with the "dependency model." The diffusion model theorists proposed that progress will come about through the spread of modernism in the form of new technology to backward and traditional areas. Through the diffusion of technology and capital, these areas will inescapably evolve from a traditional society toward a modern state. The dependency model theorists propose that, rather than being a force for development, foreign penetration and technology has created underdevelopment. Dependency theorists (Prebisch 1959; Dos Santos 1970; Quijano 1971; Cardoso 1972; Chilcote 1974; and others) hypothesize that contemporary underdevelopment was created. Ironically, the very same process (the expansion of capitalism) through which the developed countries progressed brought about the underdevelopment of many parts of Latin America.

The theory of marginality is an outgrowth of dependency theory. It has evolved through several stages over the past decade. Essentially, marginality refers to a process in which large sections of a country's population do not participate in the social, cultural, economic, and political activities of that country.

Marginality (Germani 1973; Quijano and Weffort 1973) was first used to describe the situation of people living in urban slums. The marginal sections of the cities were generally without basic services. Their residents were unemployed or underemployed and were too poor to buy the goods and services considered minimal for maintaining an acceptable standard of living. Moreover, this population was without education, did not participate in the political processes, had no access to markets, and, finally, was outside the productive process. Here was one section of society not integrated into national life. Both state and private institutions initiated actions with the expressed intention of integrating the marginal sector into the productive sector of society. As a preparation for that role, the marginalized individuals would receive the necessary education and social services so they could become functional in the productive sector.

Germani (1973) indicates that the concept of marginality had its roots in three processes: the process of the extension of the rights of man according to the principles of equality and liberty, as well as an increasing "conscientization" or awareness (from scientific studies and the production of ideologies) of violations of these principles; the process of cultural contact and the conceptualization of cultural marginality generated by anthropologists; the increasing process of modernization and its extension outside the West, and even within traditional regions of the West itself.

However, the treatment of marginality in recent years has been more specific and suggests a much deeper problem. Sociologists now suggest that the roots of marginality are in the economic sphere and, specifically, in the system of production. Marginality is seen as a chronic phenomenon, self-sustaining and caused by the incapacity of the system to provide productive employment to increasing numbers of the labor force. For Quijano and Weffort (1973), for example, marginality is

> a concept which explains the indirect, fragmented and unstable level of involvement to which growing segments of the population are submitted within the means of production that the capitalist system presently assumes as dominant, and as a consequence of this, some segments of society fulfill the role of the dominated sector within the overall social system.

Lessa (1975) argues that "the idea of economic marginality supposes the possibility of the suppression of a function without any significant readjustments within the economic system." Lessa is referring specifically to people employed in service industries, such as small shopowners and street vendors.

In Latin America, this phenomenon of economic marginality is, in the vision of sociologists who follow different ideological currents, a product of the national economic systems that are subjected to a hegemonic industrialized nucleus whose technological level is indiscriminately transferred to certain Latin American industrial processes—thus, the use of concepts such as "marginal poles," "dominating nucleus," (Quijano), and "center countries and periphery countries" (Sunkel and Paz 1970). These polarized positions are, in fact, two parts of just one system: the system of domination, of which the countries of Latin America constitute an integral part. De Janvry (1975) summarizes much of the dependency-marginality argument for rural people:

> In agriculture they are the farmers who lose control of the means of production because they cannot withstand the competitive pressure of the modern sector or the farmers who see their economic condition deteriorate as they retain traditional production techniques, but in both cases they cannot sufficiently proletariatize themselves to compensate for the income loss because they cannot be absorbed or fully sustained by the modern sector. Inevitably, they join the ranks of marginals as minifundistas and subsistence farmers.

So far this chapter has looked at the economic sector and the causes of marginality there; however, it is desirable to analyze a tendency that, according to Germani, situates the causes in the cultural order. It is necessary to reflect on the premise of this tendency because the population of Guatemala is, to a high degree, indigenous. The idea of a "cultural superimposition" is central to this perspective. Marginality is caused by the domination of one cultural group (European) over another (Indian) and it is self-perpetuating. It includes dependence on technology, concepts, and art forms and severely limits the emergence of new institutional forms.

Intimately associated with the postulate of cultural superimposition is a postulate at the psychological and sociopsychological levels. Cultural groups that find themselves in inferior situations internalize their positions of inferiority. Fanon (1963), in writing about Algerian society, observed this phenomenon among colonized black people. An inferiority complex was created in them by ethnic and racial discrimination. Such groups come to believe that they are inferior. This idea is supported by Germani (1973), when speaking about those who impute the causes of marginality to psychological reasons:

> Situations of status inferiority, and the systematic denial
> of one's rights generally cause a negative evaluation of
> one's personality, loss of identity, and other psychological
> effects which, as has been proven, can contribute beyond
> structural change to the perpetuation of marginality.

In synthesis, marginality is a situation of nonparticipation for certain groups of the population, a situation that is begun by an economic system incapable of offering permanent productive employment to those groups and that extends itself to the other spheres of social life. The marginality situation is chronic and growing. It is not a question of a structure independent of the global system; rather, it is an integral part of that same system, to the point that it would appear to be, under certain perspectives, a prerequisite for the maintenance of the present system of capitalism, dependency, and underdevelopment.

This analysis of marginality conditions this author's approach to rural development projects. These projects aim to alleviate rural poverty by increasing the productive output of the marginal farmers. No efforts are usually made to change the overall social system or to promote land reform. Within these projects, subsistence farmers continue to exist as marginal farmers with a greater share of their subsistence needs covered through their marginal agricultural production. Therefore, two hypotheses are proposed in this chapter. First, that even if more resources were available to reach more rural people, there are still some people who, for structural reasons, will continue to be nonattended by such services. These structural limitations lead to a further and more critical consideration: this nonattended group is not only marginalized by not receiving services; it is also the chronically marginalized population referred to by several authors. The second hypothesis states that the nonattended or marginalized group that lives in the Highlands is marginalized within the national system. They are marginalized in the economic, social, cultural, and educational spheres of national life.

GUATEMALAN MARGINALIZATION AND "DEVELOPMENT" RESPONSES

The Marginalization Process in the Highlands

Guatemala operates within a dependent capitalist system and, for its subsistence population, is one of the poorest of the underdeveloped countries. Characteristics typical of underdeveloped economies are evident in Guatemala: industry based on imported technology, overdevelopment of the service sector, concentration of government services in one sprawling city, and the like. In the rural areas, the complex minifundista-latifundista relationship is immediately evident, as is a large subsistence economy and export agriculture. It is useful to understand the coexistence of capitalist and precapitalist forms of production in Guatemalan agriculture. The capitalist form of production can be characterized by a tendency toward the accumulation of land and capital and the mechanization of the agricultural process. The precapitalist form, on the other hand, is characterized by food production for one's own consumption and the cultivation of small plots of land, using rudimentary technology.

In the Western Highlands, the predominant mode of production is noncapitalist and, thus, provides cheap labor to the capitalist form, which benefits from such a relationship and increases the gap between itself and the marginalized sector.

The precapitalist sector also helps to provide vegetables and basic cereals, to a large extent, for the market system and is thus connected with the economic system in another way. According to studies completed by the General Secretariat of the National Planning Council (Secretaría General 1975): "It is evident that the producers of food are receiving a proportion of the agricultural income that is continually smaller." On the other hand, in an analysis of the employment situation, it states that, "The supply of available labor is constantly growing at a rate superior to the total effective demand, which as a result has produced a constantly widening gap between supply and demand." This same analysis indicates that while the demand for labor in the urban area has grown faster than that in the rural area, it has not been capable of absorbing the supply that year after year is increased by new migrations from the rural to the urban areas. Also, the level of training of labor is constantly rising as a result of the process of urbanization and schooling. Mechanization is replacing labor, and there is insufficient development both in the industrial and in the agricultural sectors to absorb more labor. If to this situation the population growth rate is added, the problem becomes even more critical.

Returning to the phenomenon of marginality in the rural areas of the Western Highlands, the process of a growing surplus labor supply and a decreasing share in returns for food production affects two Highland groups: the migrant worker population that is gradually being displaced in the coastal plantations by mechanization (these are the people who seasonally migrate for the purpose of increasing their earnings through salaried employment) and the group that annually reaches the age for incorporating itself into the employment force, but for which the system does not create employment opportunities. For both groups the fundamental problem resides in the size of small farmholdings and the quality of the land in the Highlands. One group is forced to search for work on the coastal latifundios, and the other is underemployed on farms that could be worked with far less labor. These people work as temporary day laborers and gradually take on the new role of small storekeepers or rural traveling traders. The process of marginalization is evident here, as peasants are expelled from the land and from their noncapitalist system and move on to fulfill roles that are constantly less significant and less permanent. This process is accompanied by a migration toward more important rural centers (rural-to-rural change) and from there to urban areas (rural-to-urban), but always as a labor force that is not fully absorbed by the system.

There is also a group that, while it does not abandon the land, continues to work in agriculture without producing profits. These peasants, the owners of tiny plots of land, are identified by Bartra (1974) as pauperized peasants, another marginalized group. The pauperized peasant and the peasant who is gradually leaving the land form the core of the marginalized sector in the Highlands of Guatemala.

Some Responses to the Problem:
Development Programs

The different development programs, both public and private, that have been initiated in the Western Highlands of Guatemala have as their general objective to better the standard of living of the people of this area. Some specific programs, such as the Agricultural Development Plan (1975-79), have the objective of increasing the production of basic cereals, the staple nourishment of the Guatemalan population. Generally, the target audience for these programs is the peasants with small and medium-sized farms, for whom agricultural extension services and credit facilities are organized. A second group that is a deep cause of concern are the subsistence peasants who own very small plots of land but whose activity produces only enough food for their own consumption. This peasant is usually monolingual, lives in the communities that are most distant from the municipal center, is illiterate, cultivates the poorest land, frequently migrates to the large plantations to work as a farm laborer, and has neither the time nor the resources to experiment with new technology and with the risks of accepting credit for purchasing this technology. Given all of these conditions, this farmer will not be a good candidate for most development programs. The development programs are not designed for this peasant, because the style of life and productive ability are determined by factors that cannot be changed by these programs. Obviously, those peasants who have abandoned (or, more correctly, have been expelled from) agricultural activity or who only work as laborers are excluded from these programs.

Because development programs must prove their "effectiveness" over the short period if they are to ensure their institutional survival, these programs will ordinarily be found in those communities that are accessible by road, rather than by horseback or by footpath; will work with those farmers who have land of good quality, rather than with the owners of poor land; and will work with those farmers with whom both verbal and written communication is easier than with those who are either monolingual or illiterate. Because of the necessity of having to show results quickly, development agencies tend to work with those groups for whom success is almost certain beforehand. These groups, at the same time, represent the sector that is the closest to the institutional system and, consequently, already shares some of the values of the dominant culture. Given this situation, the two main hypotheses can be restated as they apply to the situation in Guatemala. The specific hypotheses for this study follow.

STUDY OF THE SMALL AND LARGER FARMERS OF THE WESTERN HIGHLANDS

Hypotheses

The main proposition is that extension services and credit facilities provided by the development agencies have not offered and do not offer a feasible solution to the subsistence situation of the small farmer in the Highlands. This proposition can be broken down into a series of hypotheses and subhypotheses:

1. The larger population centers have more programs within this strategy of credit and technical assistance than do smaller centers where few programs operate: the lowest level of program operation is found at the municipio level, and the action there is limited to the villages nearest the municipios; the centers that are attended in an intensive and permanent way are generally accessible by road, and those that are not attended always include those where accessibility is more difficult; the centers that are attended are connected by road to the most important regional markets; soil is generally more fertile in attended areas; and the centers that are attended are generally attended by several programs simultaneously, or have been attended by other programs previously.

2. The economic, social, and cultural characteristics of attended farmers are generally different from those of the nonattended farmers: among the nonattended farmers, there is a higher level of illiteracy and a lower level of bilingualism; among the nonattended farmers, the annual family income is lower and more equally distributed; the highest levels of migration are found among the nonattended farmers; the average size of the landholdings of the nonattended farmers is less than the average size for the attended farmers; the attended farmers include a greater percentage of Ladinos than do the nonattended farmers; nonattended farmers generally affiliate themselves with more traditional organizations (for example, cofradias and religious associations), while more attended farmers belong to development organizations (such as cooperatives and Catholic Action).

Hypotheses 1 and 2, together with their respective subhypotheses, make up one part of the general hypothesis that both the individuals and the centers attended by the development programs are more advantaged than the people and the communities not attended by these programs. The next two hypotheses, however, go one step further and suggest that the action of the development programs and the use that small subsistence farmers can make of the services of credit and information given by these programs are, in fact, structurally limited and that the changes these programs achieve through the introduction of new technological practices do not produce significant differences in the quality of life of the people being served.

3. When the development programs, in fact, reach the people situated in the group of subsistence farmers, these programs will not produce significant changes in their life-styles: family income of the small subsistence farmers who are attended by the development programs is not significantly greater than family income of the nonattended small farmers; the diet of the small attended farmers is equal both in quantity and type of food to the diet of the small nonat-

tended farmers; the total crop production of the small attended farmers is equal to, or not significantly greater than, that of small nonattended farmers; the small attended farmers increase income through the same channels as do the nonattended farmers—migration, seasonal work as laborers for the wealthier farmers in the community, and the like.

4. The reasons why the small attended farmers do not significantly differ in the quality of their life-style when compared with the small nonattended farmers are basically structural limitations.

The average size of the landholdings and the quality of the land of the larger farmers permit more variations in their crop selection, in absolute terms, than does the average size of the small-farmer holdings, whether these small farmers receive extension and credit services or not.

Methodology of the Study

This study was conducted in the area selected as a first priority for the government program of nonformal education in the Highlands region of Guatemala. Research was restricted to a total of 14 <u>municipios</u>* within the three departments of Quezaltenango, Solola, and San Marcos. A total of 600 people was determined as a reasonable sample, representing somewhat less than 10 percent of the total number of rural families in this area. This sample of 600 household heads was then subdivided into two main groups: 250 attended farmers and 350 nonattended farmers (these latter represent a far greater proportion of the population). Attended farmers were defined as those farmers who, during the agricultural cycle 1975/76, used the agricultural credit service of any of the four following institutions: Directorate General of Agricultural Services, Ministry of Agriculture (Dirección General de Servicios Agrícolas [DIGESA]), National Bank for Agricultural Development (Banco Nacional de Desarrollo Agro-

---

*As the term <u>municipio</u> is employed in Guatemala, it would be somewhat erroneous to translate it as "municipality." To be sure, it does mean that, but as it is used here, the closer translation into English would be "county" because it is a dispersed geographic area, sometimes of considerable size, having its own governing capital or cabecera. The term <u>aldea</u> likewise can be translated as "village"; but in Guatemalan rural usage it is more akin to "township," because it, too, can cover an extensive area of dispersed homesteads and have no village characteristics whatever.

pecuario, S.A. [BANDESA]), National Wheatgrowers Association
(Gremial Nacional de Trigueros [GREMIAL]), and Agricultural Cooperative (Cooperatives de Servicios Agrícolas [COOPS]).

Additionally, the attended farmers were selected from municipios defined as attended, and, within these, in attended communities. Criteria were established to determine the municipios and communities attended. The nonattended farmers lived in municipios and
communities defined as nonattended, because relatively few of their
citizens received any credit or extension services from any of the
above-mentioned agencies. Selection of the nonattended farmers
within the three departments was random.

For the fieldwork, ten young Indian men were trained as interviewers; they were responsible for the collection of all the data. Two
Guatemalan agronomists gave constant advice and help at each stage
of the research. They helped design the questionnaires, train the
team of interviewers, and supervised the data gathering. The data
were gathered in the field during a three-week period in January 1977.

The Small Farmer's Perceptions of the Problem

Before considering the quantitative questionnaire data collected
in the field, this study presents some of the personal views of the
subsistence farmers. The reality of their daily struggle is one of
exploitation and oppression. The very presence in their community
of people who are asking questions, taking notes, and looking for information is perceived as a real danger for the community. Unhap-
pily, there is a long and sad history of exploitation and unjust expro-
priation of Indian land.

Every effort was made both before and during the actual fieldwork to maintain close communication with community leaders and Indian authorities. An open-ended semistructured interview was proposed for a small subgroup of the nonattended farmers. Two members of the interview team were selected for this task. The interviewers walked along some pathway in the rural area; when they saw
a peasant working his land, they chatted for a while. No effort was
made to structure the interview or record the peasants' comments
at the time or to select specific peasants. The interviewer did have
a few basic ideas that he wished to discuss (education, agricultural
services, and the like), but these were only introduced if the peasant
actually made reference to them. Once the conversation was completed, the interviewer walked on and, as soon as it was convenient,
made notes of the main points of the conversation, including verbatim
comments made by the peasant.

A total of 22 interviews was completed during three days of
intensive work. Sometimes, the conversation lasted several hours.

Every effort was made to reach the most distant hamlets of several isolated villages. The themes most frequently discussed were education, poverty, outside help, confidence in others, harvest, and possible paths toward a better life-style. There is a generally fatalistic perspective in many of these comments, but it must be remembered that most of those interviewed live in conditions of extreme poverty, constant hunger, and disease. Their comments often reflect a clear awareness of their problems and the reality of poverty as the determining factor in their lives. Their comments speak for themselves.

Education

"The people do not want anything. They do not want to study . . . they say . . . what is the use of studying? It is better to work and earn some money, study only teaches laziness; worse still for the children, it is very difficult; and, moreover, it is not study that will give us our food, but, rather, our hands and our lands. The people do not believe in education, they have no time to study. The situation is difficult, and for this reason they abandon their studies or classes. Perhaps the classes are of some use, but we cannot afford to lose time.

"The education of the poor is something that is not thought of. We are more concerned with finding a few cents to sustain our family. Moreover, we are even more confused because of several religions that want to teach us and we are not able to find the right road. Some talk about Heaven and others about the earth; really everything is so confused. We no longer believe in all of this, and, moreover, because we are very poor, everybody uses us."

Poverty

"The situation is getting worse, because of the price of everything. Because of our poverty we cannot buy anything. We do not get any better, because the peasant's salary is never increased—it is still the same.

"On the other hand, the students have got it better. When they want anything they ask for it, but we are not considered, and the students do not see that we suffer more because of what they are getting. The situation is no better. Nobody gives us any advice of how to better our harvest. Moreover, ungrateful poverty forces us to leave our homes and our children and search for a living on the coast. We have to abandon our lands and our plantings; and when we return, our plantings are lost, because we have no one to take care of them or to defend us. Why? Because there is no one who takes an interest in us. It is true that you can hear many things on the radio. For instance, they say there is a law that protects the peasant, but we have never seen it, nor do we know about it. For instance, they say it is forbidden that the people go to the coast in trucks like animals and that they should take us in pickups or buses. But that is a lie, because it has never been fulfilled. Why is nothing done about it? Because the government says nothing."

Help from Outside

"When anyone comes to visit, the people do not like it because of all the times they have been deceived by institutions and others who are always asking many questions. For this reason, one day when the people from the Ministry of Health came, they were rejected, for they have often come here with promises and then do nothing.

"The people fear anybody who comes from another place for two reasons: because of ignorance and because they fear they may be robbers, because many things have happened in these communities, caused by people who come here in jeeps—particularly by night. The people get very worried, because they have suffered many serious consequences."

Confidence in Others

"We don't talk about our problems to other people; it is useless to tell them to another person who may be in an even worse situation. They can't give us any help and, indeed, it is better to endure suffering alone and not trouble your neighbors, and ask God to help you find the cents so that you can continue to live.

"You don't talk about your poverty to anybody. It would be shameful to tell it and how we live in our family. Moreover, it is better not to say anything, because if you are a little better off the others are spiteful of you, and if you are poorer they criticize you, so it is best not to have confidence in anybody. We poor peasants can't find a way to better our lives; we are ignorant, we don't know how to use our money. Sometimes they loan us money but, because we are ignorant, we don't know what to do with it, so the first thing we do with it is drink it, or we buy things that are of no real use to us, and when we have spent all the money we have to go down to the coast and earn enough to pay back the loan, or start to sell our few things to pay it."

Harvest and Fertilizer

"If we want to better our harvest, it is necessary to experiment with new seeds to better our planting system. Fertilizer is used by most people, but they have no real exact information of how to use it.

The only thing we know is what we get from our harvest. That is all we know, and this is why we are so backward.

"This is why we don't want to have commitments with BANDESA, because we are not capable of working the money, and it is better to be as we are today and not leave our children in debt.

"We don't use fertilizer because we don't have money to buy it; and natural fertilizer is not used either, because we don't have animals. Stubble is the only thing we have—it's all we have—after it we can only ask God to bless our harvest. He is the only one that helps us in this world."

Possible Solutions

"The only road to a better life is understanding one another as brothers and fighting together for the good of all, so that the 'gringos' and the government will not continue to exploit our ignorance and backwardness. The future is in our hands, but we cannot achieve the unity with others, or we don't know how to organize ourselves to have the force to claim our rights from the government.

"The problem of our community will only be solved by ourselves. We have no hope in anybody, and we cannot count on anybody. We are better to fight on our own as we have done so far.

"There is nothing that can be done. For this reason, our situation is painful and we feel really abandoned because nobody wants to help us, and if we demand our rights from the government we get nowhere. The Ladinos, however, are organized. The government helps them whenever they ask for anything. It doesn't matter how many requests we make, they will never solve any of our problems. They will only dump our petition in a wastepaper basket or in the drawer of some desk, and there it ends. It is useless giving our data to anybody from outside. They only come looking for information to see how we are doing, but they never offer a solution for our problems."

Comment

The above quotations represent only a small part of the many pages of testimony offered by these subsistence-level peasants. They tell of unremitting poverty, marginalization from the productive structure of the country, of a whole sector without rights and without any real claim on the benefits that are part of a citizen's rights. This testimony also suggests a person who recognizes exploiters and the people and programs that have come to the Highlands with promises that always end in deceit. This peasant sees a need for education, but education needs to be functional—education that will produce something useful and train the peasant to fight against misery, education that will produce better harvests.

The scarcity of land is a critical problem, but perhaps even more critical is the scarcity of resources to work the land. The only resource that the Indian has on the subsistence farm is labor—in fact, a great deal too much labor for the land possessed. Technical resources such as fertilizers, chemicals, and mechanization are scarce or nonexistent. Practically half of the nonattended farmers do not use fertilizer, but almost all of them would use it if they had the resources to purchase it. The poor, subsistence farmers generally have the poorest land—land that must have fertilizer if it is to produce anything; when they cannot afford to use fertilizer, the production is extremely low. Poor production means less to eat and the necessity of finding alternative employment. If employment cannot be found, the only alternatives are hunger or migration to the coastal plantations or urban areas.

General Characteristics of Sample Farmers

In comparing the data on both groups of attended and nonattended farmers, the following conclusions were drawn.

Farmers who are attended by extension agencies are different from nonattended farmers because of where they live. A farmer has a better possibility of being attended if he lives in an urban area. If the municipio where the farmer lives is attended by one of the development agencies, it is very probable that other agencies will be working there also and that the farmer can get credit from more than one agency if requested. Attended areas are connected by road to market centers. Table 4.1 presents a summary of these characteristics. The findings confirm several of the subhypotheses of Hypothesis 1.

Language is a critical communications barrier in a farmer's relationship with the extension agents. Three of the four extension agencies have no agents who speak the local Indian dialects; only a few of the cooperative institutions have bilingual extensionists. Perhaps not surprisingly, three of the four agencies did not give extension services to farmers who only speak Indian dialects: 60 percent of nonattended farmers are illiterate and 30 percent speak only Spanish. Table 4.2 presents a summary of these characteristics. These findings confirm the subhypotheses of Hypothesis 2.

Significant differences also separate the two groups with regard to education. Many more nonattended farmers are illiterate than attended ones: 63 percent of the nonattended farmers did not go to school at all; in contrast, only 36 percent of the attended farmers did not attend school.

The National Planning Council considers an annual income of U.S.$500 as the minimum necessary for survival of a family, yet 70

TABLE 4.1

Selected Macrocharacteristics of Attended and Nonattended
Populations

	Attended	Nonattended
Number of municipios where at least one extension agent resides permanently[a]	4	1
Number of villages where at least one extension agent resides permanently[b]	2	0
Number of municipios accessible by road[c]	6	4
Number of villages accessible by road	10	5
Number of municipios with road connections to markets	10	4
Number of municipios attended simultaneously by all four agencies	5	0

[a]A total of six attended and six nonattended municipios.
[b]A total of ten attended and ten nonattended villages.
[c]It is somewhat difficult to define what is an accessible road.
The department capitals are accessible by paved roads. All the municipios are accessible by unpaved roads, but in at least two of the nonattended municipios (Santa Caterina Tx. and Comitancillo), road communication is often not possible during the wet season.

Source: Compiled by the author.

TABLE 4.2

Social, Economic, and Cultural Characteristics of Attended and
Nonattended Farmers
(in percent)

	Attended	Nonattended
Education		
Illiterate	35	60
Bilingual	61	53
Spanish only	31	8
Annual family income (U.S. dollars)	1,279	428
Level of migration	0.7	6
Average farm size (cuerdas)	59	20
Organizations		
Traditional	3	6
Modern	65	45

Note: 1 cuerda = 0.11 acres, thus 59 cuerdas = 6.5 acres and 20 cuerdas = 2 acres.

Source: Compiled by the author.

TABLE 4.3

Average Family Income
(in U.S. dollars)

| | Attended | | Nonattended | |
Source	Average Income	Percent of Total Income	Average Income	Percent of Total Income
Agriculture*	608	48	161	38
Laborer	58	5	32	7
Salaried	291	23	44	10
Artisan	57	4	52	12
Trade, commerce	86	7	24	6
Migration	6	—	24	6
Animals	173	13	91	21
Total family income	1,279	100	428	100
Total nonfarm income	671	52	267	62

*Agricultural income does not include any cost for family labor.

Note: This table is based on all sources of income for each family member.

Source: Compiled by the author.

percent of the attended group did not reach this level on farm income alone. Almost none of the nonattended group reaches a farm income of U.S. $500. Although off-farm income is a significant proportion of people's income, in this sample, as is evident in Table 4.3, 20 percent of the attended group and 80 percent of the nonattended farmers still have less than U.S. $500 from all sources.

Farm Productivity: Impact of Land Size and Services

The evidence of the previous section suggests that the development agencies are reaching only a small portion of the farming population and that the farmers they actually reach are the relatively advantaged ones. It is reasonable to conclude that the development agencies are not reaching the poorer farmers. Similar findings have been reported for many other countries.

The next question proposed was: Given the size of landholding of most of the Highlands farmers, would it do them any good if they did have access to government extension services? Three relationships were studied to answer this question:

1. The interaction between the size of a farmholding and whether a farmer was attended by a development agency and its effect on farm output were studied.
2. The effects of the level of technology employed, controlling for money invested, were examined to determine whether the information that development agencies imparted makes any difference in farm productivity.
3. A multistage model for farm productivity was developed.

The three central variables used were farm costs, farm output, and level of technology.

Farm costs were subdivided into three categories: inputs, other costs, and labor. Farm inputs included seeds, fertilizer, insecticides, and herbicides. Each farmer was asked the exact quantity of each one of these inputs used per cuerda of land. Input costs were specific to each crop and to each farmer. Other costs included the interest paid by the farmer on his institutional loan. Equipment and tools were also costed. Equipment basically included harvesting machines; tools included machete, hoe, pick, and the like. Transportation costs, if incurred, were estimated. Land, if rented, was also included. Hired labor was costed, based on the number of laborers per day at the rate paid by the farmer.

For the farm output, each farmer indicated the exact production per cuerda for each of the products cultivated. The value of the harvest for each product was the market selling price in Guatemala at the time. A summary of the breakdown of farm costs per cuerda is reported in Table 4.4.

The level of technology included inputs such as hybrid seed, fertilizers, and chemical products. This is the basis of many of the significant differences in agricultural production in the world today. An agricultural technology scale was created in this study and this scale was used subsequently in sections of the various causal analyses. A total of 35 agricultural practices was measured, and on each practice each farmer was given a score of zero to five; a zero score indicated that the farmer did not apply any element of the recommended practices; a score of five represented the use of the most acceptable practice.

Three steps were undertaken in the construction of the technology scale. A first step was a test of reliability of the composite scale, and for this statistical list Cronbach's Alpha Reliability Test was used. A second step was the use of a correlation matrix to show the interrelations among the variables. A third step was the use of

TABLE 4.4

Breakdown of Farm Costs per Cuerda for Attended and
Nonattended Farmers

Cost Category	Attended		Nonattended	
	Dollars	Percent	Dollars	Percent
Agricultural input (seeds, fertilizer, chemicals)	5.1	67	2.9	63
Other cost (transportation, rented land, animals, machinery)	1.4	19	1.1	24
Laborers*	1.1	14	0.5	13
Total cost	7.6	100	4.5	100

*Number of person-days per cuerda: attended, 6.5; nonattended, 6.5.

Source: Compiled by the author.

factor analysis. For this investigation, factor analysis was used to confirm the hypothesis that a specific set of items made up a unidimensional scale.

Several strategies were attempted in the development of this agricultural technology scale. Initially, all 35 items or practices were included; however, the factor analysis suggested that a subset of items related specifically to investment in inputs, fertilizers, and chemical products underlay the scale. A second strategy was to divide the items between investment and noninvestment practices and also to divide them into ecological zones. However, the effort to create a noninvestment scale was not successful. Thus, if one controls for available resources, there is very little evidence that technological innovativeness exists among the Guatemalan farmers. A third and final strategy was developed. This consisted of a scale using only a series of practices that required economic investment. Two scales were created, one for wheat and one for maize-farming practices.

Farm Size and Productivity

The techniques for measuring farm costs and farm output have already been discussed. Farm costs were shown in Table 4.4; output was estimated in dollar value at 17.9 per cuerda for attended,

FIGURE 4.1

Total Value of Harvest

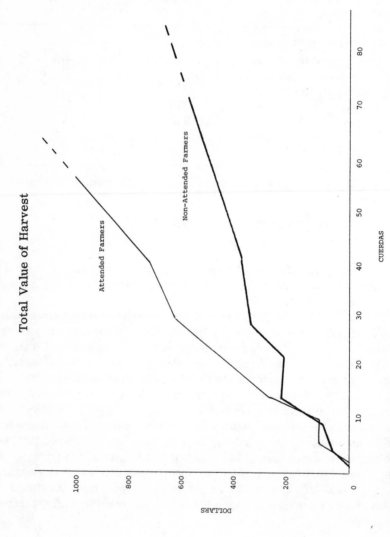

Source: Compiled by the author.

FIGURE 4.2

Farm Income

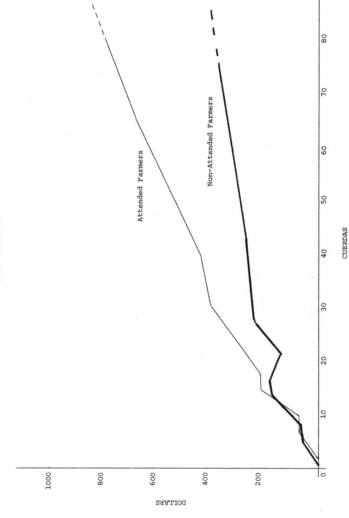

Source: Compiled by the author.

and 12.5 per cuerda for nonattended, farmers. It is now possible to
see how these two factors related to each other. Figure 4.1 represents the total value of each farmer's harvest in relation to the total
number of cuerdas for both attended and nonattended farmers. What
can be immediately noted is that for low levels of landownership, agricultural product of attended and nonattended farmers is practically
equal; up to about 18 cuerdas, there is no important difference between the groups. However, from 20 cuerdas upward, the difference
widens continually.

Figure 4.2 represents farm income and, once more, a very
similar, if not quite so extreme, pattern is evident. Farm income
here represents the difference between total value of the harvest and
farm costs. Absolute farm income for small farmers, both attended
and nonattended, is very similar; among the larger farmers, once
more, the differences are impressive.

An Explanatory Model

Farm income for both attended and nonattended small farmers
is essentially the same, whereas, for medium- and large-sized
farms, attended farmers do considerably better. The interesting
question that results from this interaction is: What is the causal
mechanism? or What is it that determines a farmer's output? Total
agricultural output is, to a great degree, a function of the amount of
land a farmer owns. As a general rule, if a farmer has little land,
there is little output. Indeed, in this study, about 50 percent of the
variance in total output is associated with land size. However, it is
also necessary to look at the influence of other factors—such as investment, level of technology employed, and such background factors
as education and outside income—as predictor variables in determining a productive farm. What accounts for the remaining variance?
The statistical technique used most often by economists to make estimates of production functions is regression analysis. The two basic
elements included are capital and labor. Capital investment is measured through farm costs for inputs, land value, and technology used.
Labor is measured by the amount of human effort invested in the farm
during the agricultural cycle. A third input, the capacity to make
use of both labor and capital with maximum efficiency, is represented
by the technology scale when the level of farm investment is controlled.

Table 4.5 reports the means and standard deviations for each
of the variables in this production-per-cuerda regression; Figure
4.3 indicates how the beta coefficients relate to production per cuerda,
the dependent variable.

Fundamentally, what this equation is reporting is that farm
costs are the significant factor in determining the per-cuerda production for all farmers. Those farmers who invest more produce more.

TABLE 4.5

Value of Production-per-Cuerda Regression

Variable (N = 567)	Mean	Standard Deviation
Production per cuerda (U.S. dollars)	17.1	22.1
Maize technology (scale from 0 to 50)	13.6	8.8
Farm cost (dollars)	6.1	10.7
Quezaltenango (department)	0.2	0.4
Land quality (0 = level, 1 = broken, 2 = hilly)	0.4	0.4
Family labor (number of days of labor contributed by the family)	6.0	5.7
Number of persons per family (per cuerda)	0.4	0.6

Source: Compiled by the author.

The unstandardized coefficients suggest that for every dollar that a farmer invests in farm inputs, given average values on other variables, there will be a return of U.S.$1.50. A second important conclusion is that the level of technology does not contribute to productivity. It is not statistically significant and has a negative beta weight. Indeed, it means that innovativeness is not a significant predictor, since practices not requiring economic investment were introduced into the regression equation and did not predict productivity. (The additional r^2 associated with the whole set of items was only 0.006; most of the individual beta weights were negative and none were significant.) It is now clear that farming practices not requiring investment do not affect productivity, indicating that such efforts are not rewarded. Thus, the reasons why farmers do not use them consistently seems clear—the farmers themselves know that they do not help productivity.

This regression equation was also broken down between small and large farms. Small farmers were defined as those with two acres or less and large farmers as those with more than two acres. For the small farmers, farm costs continue to dominate—the beta coefficient is, in fact, 0.79 (0.76 for the total group, and 0.58 for the larger farmers). Again, only farm costs and family labor are significant. For the larger farmers, the beta coefficient (unstandardized) declines to 1.3, suggesting a lower productivity level for these farmers. Family labor also declines, reflecting the fact that many of the larger farms depend more on hired labor for some part of their agricultural activity.

FIGURE 4.3

Beta Coefficients of Production-per-Cuerda Regression

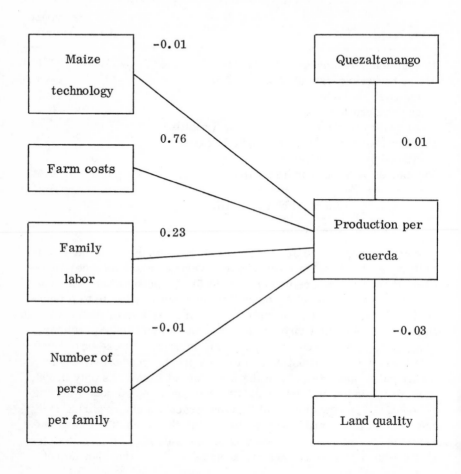

Unstandardized Coefficients:

Maize technology = -0.00	Land quality = -1.40
Farm costs = 1.60	Multiple r = 0.92
Family labor = 0.90	r^2 = 0.85
Number of persons per family = -0.30	Adjusted r^2 = 0.85
Quezaltenango = 0.60	Standardized error = 8.64

Source: Compiled by the author.

Determinants of Investment

For given land size, economic investment accounts for most of the variance in the farmer-productivity equation. A further step in the analysis was undertaken to help determine which group of farmers invests. The sample was again broken down into two groups—farmers with less than two acres of land and those with more than two acres. Although the complete statistical analysis will not be presented here, the results are of considerable interest. Among the small farmers, none of the independent variables were good predictors of investment, suggesting that what farmers invest in their farms is not affected by land size, education, or supplementary income. Credit is positively related to farm costs; however, the coefficient is quite low. The surprising conclusion is that, for small farmers, it is not at all clear what determines level of investment. Education is not a good predictor, nor is off-farm income. It does not make a difference if the farmholding is large or small (within the two-acre category). Access to credit makes little difference. Among the large farmers (with more than two acres), access to credit is a significant predictor, as are education and residence in the department of Quezaltenango. These are important relationships and they support some previous findings. Credit is related to investment, and education is a significant predictor. Land size is also significant, but negatively related. That is, as farms get bigger, production per cuerda falls. These findings support earlier findings that farm investment and productivity are highest among farmers with smaller plots (for this subsample, those with two to five acres).

Role of Education and Information

Much literature exists on the issue of the role of education and information in people's productivity and income levels. Chapter 6 reviews some of these studies. The vast volume of findings available seems to suggest that, in general, education increases farmers' productivity—but only under certain conditions. A question of this study is precisely this: Under what conditions can education help increase productivity?

Education has been examined both as formal and out-of-school, or nonformal, education. Of the total sample of 600 farmers, 50 percent had no formal schooling whatsoever, and 80 percent either had no schooling or had abandoned school before completing third grade (90 percent among the nonattended group), generally considered the level at which people can still be considered illiterate. There is, on the other hand, a small group of farmers (15 cases) who are all professional people and who have secondary or university education.

FIGURE 4.4

Standardized Coefficients in the Maize Technology Scale
(N = 567)

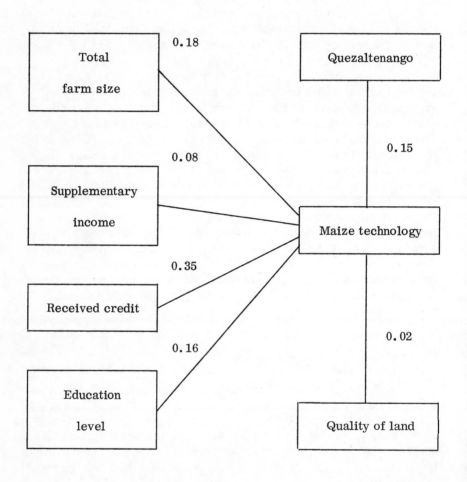

Multiple r = 0.62

r^2 = 0.39

Adjusted r^2 = 0.38

Standardized error = 6.91

Source: Compiled by the author.

None of this group, however, seem to work their land; this responsibility is left to an administrator.

Formal education, this study found, is not a good predictor of productivity, although it does predict level of investment among larger farmers. Few of the smaller farmers have formal education, and the failure of education to predict either productivity or investment among this group is not surprising. In trying to find another role for education and information in this study, the likelihood of education having a role in predicting the use of technology was explored. In a certain sense, level of information was being measured indirectly through the maize technology scale, particularly when actual investment was controlled. Lockheed, Jamison, and Lau (forthcoming) and others have pointed out that educated farmers are more apt to critically evaluate new and improved inputs and better distinguish the random from the systemic elements in these innovations. The equation in Figure 4.4 tries to determine what role education and other previously named predictors have in determining a farmer's level-of-technology use. All predictors, except quality of land, are significant on the F-distribution and positively related to maize technology. The underlying trend, evident in the beta coefficients, suggests the importance of economic resources in their relationship to technology. The best predictor, as expected, is whether a farmer received credit for purchasing inputs. The second largest beta coefficient is for total farm size, which confirms the conclusion reached by other researchers that technology is most likely to be adopted by larger farmers for whom it is most appropriate. Education is the third predictor and operates among farmers for whom one year of formal schooling is the mean. The conclusion must be cautious: education does contribute something to use of innovative practices, but how and to what extent this may influence productivity is not at all clear.

Other Factors in Subsistence Agriculture

Family income has been discussed already. This study shows that farm income is lower than nonfarm income for every group of attended farmers with less than 35 cuerdas. It also shows that subsistence farmers with little land who live in rural areas have as their main sources of supplementary income employment as laborers with the wealthier farmers, craftsmen, or migrants to the coastal plantations. Owners of small farms who live in urban areas generally hold full-time employment—some with the national government as bureaucrats or teachers, while others work as shop owners, tradesmen, or in semiprofessional employment. It is evident that the vast majority of the nonattended farmers live in conditions of extreme poverty. Over 80 percent of these small farmers do not even reach this minimum subsistence level. Even if the extension agencies were able to do what they have not been able to do thus far—that is, provide credit and useful information to the small farmers—most of the Highland farmers could not live off this land. One recalls that among owners of small farms, mean income is in the range of from U.S. $12 to U.S. $15 per cuerda. Even where productivity increased 50 percent so that mean income was in the U.S. $15-18 range, no farm smaller than 25 to 35 cuerdas could produce a U.S. $500 income— the minimum level. About 80 percent of the nonattended farmers own less than 32 cuerdas. And, in addition, one must question the possibility of a 50 percent increase in farm income.

A final factor—diet—was examined for the farmer sample. Consumption of eight foods was compared between attended and nonattended farmers. Of these eight foods (corn, beans, eggs, milk, and the like), the nonattended farmers consume less, on the average, in every case. A factor that is important in people's diet is place of residence. People who live in the more isolated regions with little off-farm employment opportunity (the poorest of the poor) also have the poorest diet. Ordinarily, foods such as bread, cheese, meat, and milk are not available on a regular basis in most of rural Guatemala. Many rural people never drink milk nor eat cheese and probably eat meat less than once per week. Farmers with off-farm income obviously have better possibilities for purchasing food.

CONCLUSIONS AND POLICY IMPLICATIONS

General Conclusions

The general purpose of this study was to examine the role of information and extension services in promoting change in the lives of subsistence peasants in the Western Highlands of Guatemala. Through an analysis of these peasants and the agricultural extension programs, it was hoped to understand better the social and economic reality within which the subsistence farmer carries on daily life and the system of traditional or marginal agriculture used. Based on the findings, some concrete suggestions will be made here that may help the situation.

The general hypothesis that was proposed for this study was "that the extension services and credit facilities, offered by the development agencies, have not offered a viable solution to the situation of subsistence of the small-farm owners in the Highlands." The extensive data base generated in this study permitted in-depth analysis of several critical variables. Obviously, considerably more analysis could be done and many other hypotheses tested; however, for the objectives of this study, significant conclusions can be proposed and their impact on the lives of the subsistence farmers in the Highlands can be estimated.

Attended and nonattended farmers are significantly different from one another because of where they live. A farmer has a better possibility of being attended if living in an urban area, in either a municipal town or a departmental capital. If the municipio is attended by one of the agencies included in this study (for example, an agricultural extension agency), it is very probable that all four agencies will be working there, and that the farmer can get credit from more than one agency if he requests it. The municipio is connected by road to the departmental capital and has access to local markets. It is probable that if the farmer is attended and does not live in an urban area, the community where he lives is accessible by road.

Nonattended farmers can be recognized relatively easily. They have an average of about two acres of land, that is, about a third of what the average attended farmer has. Six out of every ten nonattended farmers are illiterate and fewer than 10 percent speak only Spanish. Their total family income is about a third of what the attended farmers earn. Moreover, nonattended farmers live in more isolated rural areas with less access to basic services such as education, potable water in the home, and any nonformal education services. The nonattended farmer is considerably poorer than the attended farmer, not only because of lower income and less land but also because of fewer opportunities for other types of productive employment. There are fewer opportunities for employment in rural communities than in more urban communities, and where employment is available (such as farm labor) salaries are considerably lower.

The National Planning Council of the government of Guatemala considers an annual income of U.S. $500 as the minimum necessary for survival, yet 70 percent of the attended group do not reach this minimum survival level on farm income alone. No category of the nonattended group reaches a farm income of U.S. $500. Although off-farm income is a significant proportion of people's income in this sample, 20 percent of the attended group and 80 percent of the nonattended farmers earn less than the survival level. Overall, this suggests a critical level of poverty for the majority of the rural residents. The main cause of this poverty, which was consistently reflected throughout this study, is land distribution: 70 percent of the population have less than 30 percent of the total land. In absolute terms, more than one-half of the total nonattended group and one-quarter of the attended group have less than one acre of land per family.

The importance of land size was further emphasized as a result of the first multiple-regression analysis that attempted to predict the total value of the harvest. Here, land size was the best predictor of total harvest, accounting for 50 percent of the variance in output. This result suggests that what a farmer produces is basically determined by the size of the farm.

If land size determines a farmer's total harvest, what determines the level of productivity? Productivity is determined by a farmer's economic investment in the plot of land. Each U.S.$1.00 that a farmer invests gives an average return of U.S.$1.50. Outside of investment, nothing else really predicts productivity.

A third and final equation tried to answer the question, What predicts what a farmer invests? The data presented in this study cannot satisfactorily answer this question. On the very small farms (less than two acres), the level of investment and return are very similar for both attended and nonattended farmers. While the attended farmers get credit from one of the extension agencies (mainly the cooperatives for this size of farm), the nonattended farmers do not, yet they also invest a similar amount. Off-farm income and level of education are not good predictors of investment, so the question remains: Who invests and where do they get the resources? Several possible explanations were proposed, yet a complex question remains: Why do some farmers invest while others do not? Those who do invest have a reasonably satisfactory rate of return for their efforts. Among owners of larger farms, residence in the department of Quezaltenango, level of education, and access to credit all help predict who invests in their farms. These three predictors help explain some 20 percent of the variance for farmers with over two acres of land.

The role of extension agencies seems very limited throughout the Highlands. Even among the group of farmers selected as attended by these agencies, 50 percent claim to have had no contact with extension agents during the year when they were officially on the list of being attended; 20 percent of the farmers answered categorically that they had not been helped by the extension agents. The farmers were not asked why they felt that they had not been helped; however, several farmers did complain of the bad quality of the seed that they had purchased from the agency the year before. The level of attention, overall, seems very low and, on the smallest farms, where subsistence agriculture is extremely marginal, there are no basic differences between attended and nonattended farmers. Attendance does make a significant difference among the farmers with more land, however, because these farmers have more off-farm income, more education, and are better situated for access to markets, and the like. The overall effect of being attended is conditioned by these other factors.

The extension agencies are expected to fulfill a dual role: provide information and provide institutional credit. Although credit is limited by the actual resources assigned by the national government, information should be much more readily available. This study suggests that this is not so, not only because there are few extension agents—because these agents do not speak the Indian dialects, and because few attend at the village level, and the like—but also because the possible role that information can play is very limited. Indeed, it could be argued that extension services are limited to credit. They do not, or they cannot, provide information. It may be, however, that the extension agents do facilitate the flow of information to farmers but farmers are unable to use it because it does not seem useful or relevant to them or they do not understand it. The output of a farm is determined fundamentally by its size, and the productivity of a farm is determined by the level of investment—level of investment means economic resources.

Policy Implications

The first objective of the Guatemalan National Agricultural Plan is to increase agricultural production. The data presented in this study suggest that if the government's goal is to obtain the maximum possible food production for each unit of scarce and limited resources (arable land and capital), these resources should be directed to the smaller farmers, because they use the land and capital inputs more efficiently in food production than do the larger farmers.

However, there is a further and much more critical dimension of this problem. Though small farms are indeed productive farms, their owners are still critically poor and many manage to farm even when their income is below the minimal survival level proposed by the Guatemalan government. Most small farmers fundamentally depend on off-farm income for their survival. The farm is only one means of support and, for many, not the most important. The farm provides the basis for sustenance, but the rest of their livelihoods must come from other sources. Owners of small farms have relatively little contact with any of the extension agencies, and probably relatively little interest in them except for purchasing fertilizer. And, basically, the farmers are right. The extension agencies can significantly change neither their farm productivity nor their income levels. This study shows that there are no significant differences between attended and nonattended small farms, as far as farm income is concerned. Extension agency activity will not improve the income of the very small farmers, given the present structural limits in the Highlands.

The purpose of this study was to examine the role of information and extension services in improving the lives of the subsistence farmers of the Highlands. The problem of providing relevant information to small farmers is the subject of several recent research projects. The measurement of this variable has generally followed an analysis of the number of extension contacts that a farmer has during a specific time period. No relationship is established between extension contacts and productivity, but if the analysis of this Guatemalan data were limited to extension contacts, the results would be very poor. Rather than follow this line of action, it was decided to examine extension contacts or attendance within a production-function analysis. The results of this approach have already been discussed, the most important one being that there are no significant differences between attended and nonattended small farms in their productivity. Among medium-sized farms, there are significant differences between those farmers who are attended and those who are not. However, the "causes" of these differences are the result of the economic investment that each farmer makes on the farm and the size of the holding. Another very significant finding is that off-farm income is extremely important for small and medium-sized farmers and, to the extent that farmers have relatively high off-farm incomes, they will be able to invest more on their farms. Overall, information does not contribute significantly to output or productivity. The low level of knowledge evident in both the maize- and wheat-technology scales suggests that people are using fertilizers (really the only element of modern agricultural technology in widespread use in the Highlands today) with very little knowledge of their properties and their appropriate application. The traditional innovation model that suggests that knowledge of something leads to its adoption may be inapplicable; a more appropriate model would suggest that the application of some practice, such as the use of fertilizer, leads eventually to some knowledge of it.

There is a great need for situationally relevant agricultural information in the Highlands of Guatemala; and, although this information will not change the income level and the life-style of the marginal peasants very significantly, it will at least help them do better than they are doing today and might increase their productivity a little. Even situationally relevant information, however, will not change the extreme skewness of income distribution.

Two recent studies in Guatemala concerning agriculture may be relevant to this pessimistic conclusion. Although both seem to arrive at more positive conclusions, a closer look will reveal that they are not contradictory to the findings of this chapter. Daines and Howell (1975) found that credit appeared to have a significant impact on all farm sizes studied, especially the smallest ones (zero to one hectare). The changes, however, among the smallest farmers were not due to increased production because of added technology but to changes in crop composition (from raising basic grains to vegetables and flowers). This solution, although useful for the small number of farmers studied, is not a feasible one for most subsistence farmers in the Highlands, because only a few places are suitable for these crops and no market infrastructure is readily available for any major increase in this crop production even in areas where it is suitable.

The Basic Village Education experiment (Academy for Educational Development 1978) provides some evidence that through radio, monitors in listening groups, and agronomists, small farmers in experimental sections of the Eastern Lowlands and the Western Highlands significantly increased knowledge and new agricultural practices. Some evidence also exists to show increased production—especially where agronomists could reach the farmers. A careful look at the evidence seems to indicate one conclusion similar to this study: innovations that are most relevant to increased production are resource related, not information related. Also, if the agronomist seems to be a key to helping farmers increase their production (as opposed to simply providing more information to increase knowledge, as radio by itself seems adequate to do), then the costs of agronomists in sufficient numbers to cover the mass of subsistence farmers seem too high for the Guatemalan government to undertake.

In all of these studies, the policy conclusions are based on empirical data that may be valid but rest on certain assumptions that are not explored with subsistence farmers in mind. Given the number of subsistence farms in the Highlands, the real solution to the problem must be for them, as well as for the already better-off, small, cash-crop farmer who can take advantage of the innovations that are offered.

The lack of organizations to promote and defend the rights of poor subsistence farmers creates a situation of isolation and institutional abandonment in the Highlands. Most organizations that exist are for Spanish-speaking, or Ladino, people; the Indian population does not really have anything except Catholic Action, despite the fact that one of the objectives of the National Agricultural Plan is to "encourage rural organization at all levels, especially local, so as to facilitate the development of associative forms of production" (Secretaría General 1975a). The only organization mentioned by the Indian people in our survey was Catholic Action, and, although this organization does have some social goals and promotes some new farm technology (such as fertilizers), it is not likely to provide needed organizational structure to improve agricultural output.

The cooperative movement works among owners of small farms; however, the majority of the farmers in the Highlands have smaller landholdings than the average cooperative member. Some cooperatives are directed by Ladino people, and the Indian people play only a passive role, basically using the cooperative to purchase fertilizer.

In fact, the cooperatives, because they do not get any government subsidy, charge higher interest rates and a higher basic price for agricultural inputs than do government agencies.

Effective Indian participation through effective local organizations is indeed a crucial need. This may be a first step for the functionally marginalized Indian farmer to emerge from poverty and a position of inferiority in the social, political, and economic structure of the Guatemalan society. However, there is very little evidence to suggest that there is any real possibility of change for the Indian in the structure of Guatemalan society today, not only because of race but also because within the sociopolitical and economic structure of that society the level of participation of the landless peasants and the subsistence peasant is determined by the structure of that society, and neither extension programs nor information programs can do much to change that reality.

5

BRAZIL AND GUATEMALA: COMMUNICATIONS, RURAL MODERNITY, AND STRUCTURAL CONSTRAINTS

Eduardo Contreras

INTRODUCTION

For a long time, communication has been seen as a crucial component in modernization of developing countries. The specific research tradition that has fully exploited that tenet is diffusion research. However, there is an earlier and broader tradition that has linked modernization and communication under the rubric "mass media and national development" (Schramm 1964), which stems from the pioneering work of Lerner (1958).

The object-problem of this chapter is the impact of communication on modernity. The setting chosen is rural, the level of analysis is that of individual modernization. The central thesis is that communication has not played an important role in rural development in developing countries because of a series of structural constraints under which it has operated and presumably will continue to operate. Put another way, communication processes cannot be seen in isolation from the particular societal arrangements under which they have developed and the restrictions through which they exert their influence.

Those societal arrangements are treated here as structural constraints. At an individual level, they are expressed as opportunity

This work is based in part on the author's "Communication, Rural Modernity and Structural Constraints" (Ph.D. diss., Stanford University 1979). Part of that work was supported by a 211(d) grant from the U.S. Agency for International Development to Stanford University, Institute for Communication Research. Special thanks are due to Everett M. Rogers and Jeremiah O'Sullivan-Ryan for allowing the use of their raw data-sets for Brazil and Guatemala, respectively.

ranges. The problems with which this study deals have to do with the interrelationships among structural constraints, communication's performance and potential under such conditions, and the interaction of these factors as antecedents of individual modernity outcomes.

The first part of the study deals with a theoretical discussion of modernization and communications, communication expectations in rural sectors, and diffusion strategies. Next, the specific problem of rural communication under structural constraints is discussed, setting the stage for an analysis of data gathered in Guatemala and Brazil. A summary description of these and the variables involved follows. There are then two separate but parallel analyses undertaken, and some general conclusions and policy implications round off the discussion.

THEORETICAL DISCUSSION

The Modernization Paradigm

Modernization theory may still claim a role as one of the dominant paradigms of contemporary social science. Its concern is making sense of the complex change processes that societies have been undergoing for the last two centuries. Its basic typology is that of traditional and modern societies, ideal types that serve only as landmarks for its substantial concern: the process of transition itself.

There is no attempt in this chapter to make a detailed critique of modernization theory, because it would distract from more relevant concerns. One must note, however, that modernization has been accused of being a euphemism for Westernization, so that the unique path and ultimate goal for modern nations can be inferred from the most advanced capitalist states of today. As a policy, it has also stirred up hopes rooted in particular processes to be initiated (and financed) to trigger modernity. It might even be argued that the regularities unveiled in modernization processes reflect less an inherent abstract universality than historical vicissitudes because of the successful diffusion of the particular paths some dominant industrial societies underwent and forced upon underdeveloped or traditional societies.

Now, perhaps because of the crisis of both modernization theory and policies, one can speak more of a loose and problematic paradigm,* and it is in this sense that it provides a theoretical background

---

*The paradigm is problematic in the sense that it seems there is no one way, let alone one key societal element, that can be singled

for this work, which is, in a way, a critique "from within." New theoretical insights and a reevaluation of the vast empirical literature that has flourished around modernization are necessary. The theoretical aim of this work is to contribute somehow to that process, specifically for communication aspects.

Communication and Modernization

The 1960s were undoubtedly the golden age for communication's role in modernization, that is, for advocating the crucial role that communication, particularly mass media, would play or, indeed, appeared to be playing in national development. Two landmark studies, Lerner's The Passing of Traditional Society (1958) and Schramm's Mass Media and National Development (1964), set an overall optimistic tone. Communication was presented not only as having "brought about the downfall of traditional societies" but also as a privileged perspective for analysis (Pye 1963). Later, Schramm (1976a) conceded that "a grand design for economic and social development seemed almost within our grasp ten years ago, but has consistently eluded us and now looks to be actually more remote."

Diffusion research was the best-suited tradition to accommodate a wide array of rural communication endeavors and experimentations. The rural setting was the natural habitat for traditional individuals. Peasants continue to be the world's largest population, and they were being left out of the mainstream of modernization. Rogers (1969) made the case for a worldwide subculture of peasantry; and, although a careful rereading of descriptions of traditional individuals does uncover implicit structural constraints (precisely those rigid features that make up the traditional societal typology), the emerging pattern was not one that stressed these societal structures but one that stressed individual characteristics as hindrances to change.

It happened that research in the United States had already uncovered some important operational processes in rural diffusion. Strong generalizations on the rate of adoption, characteristics of the various categories of adopters (particularly the innovators), and the role of mass and interpersonal communication were believed to obtain cross-culturally. A detailed treatment of these ideas can be found in Rogers (1962), or in Rogers and Shoemaker (1971).

---

out as constituting the crux of modernizing efforts. It is loose in that, after the demise of the view that economic growth (with clear-cut clues as to "how") would by itself foster accompanying societal and individual changes, it is embodied in different levels of analysis of the social system and favored by different disciplines.

In terms of the present discussion, it should be noted that diffusion theory acted (and acts) as a particular communication paradigm focused on the individual farmer. Modernization theory seems to have been operationalized at the rural level as the process of adoption of innovation. While Frey's (1973) assertion that "there would seem to be a veritable gulf between the diffusion of 2-4D fertilizer . . . and the modernization of a society" holds, it is unfair to sum up, thus, the contribution of diffusion to modernization and communication. What is indeed fair is to suggest that communication policies and practices became as much prisoners of the assumptions of diffusionism as they were infatuated with the grandiose role early modernization theory promised.

Some Features of the Rural Problem

The mere magnitude of rural populations is part of the problem. Developing nations have a very large and slowly decreasing rural population, but the real issue has to do with its poverty. The World Bank estimates that 750 million people live in poverty in the developing countries (of which 85 percent are in absolute poverty, defined as U.S. $50 or less annual per capita income equivalent). More than 80 percent of the poor are thought to be living in rural areas. The bank's new sectoral policy for 1975-79 expects to reach 100 million rural people, of which 60 percent are poor. During the same period, the rural poor will have increased by 70 million (World Bank 1975).

One important factor in rural poverty is the land tenure system. At least for Latin America, an anomalous pattern of land concentration in few private hands is the most typical feature of the rural sector. Less than 10 percent of the agricultural holdings account for over three-quarters of the available land. In some countries, as little as 0.1 percent of holdings are over 2,500 hectares and yet account for 20 percent of the area of Colombia, 26 percent in Ecuador, and 60 percent in Peru. On the other hand, a substantial amount of small owners have to make do with subsistence-level plots. Thus, in Brazil half of all rural holdings are less than ten hectares and use only 3 percent of the area (1970 data); in Guatemala, almost nine out of ten plots are under five hectares and barely account for 1.3 percent of the area (1964 data; all above figures based on UCLA 1976).

The preceding discussion has identified two relatively fixed constraints: the magnitude of a predominantly poor rural sector and the patterns of land tenure. There is no indication that any of these factors will vary dramatically in the foreseeable future throughout Latin America.

Assuming that the future for most of the rural poor is to live and die in the countryside, so no urban outlet solution is available, two possible agricultural strategies can be suggested. One is a better use of the most underused resources in Latin American agriculture: land and labor. Restrictions for that being a substantially feasible path have been presented. The other one is technology to increase productivity per unit within the existing limitations. The latter view is precisely the realm of the diffusion of innovations.

Because the legitimate bias of this work is communication, the next section presents a panorama of the rural communication situation for Latin America. This completes the constraints under which diffusion and extensionism, presented in the last part of this section, is better understood.

Media Expectations in Rural Settings

Why should communication (one must ask) be expected to play a role in development without any regard for the notion of structural constraints? One should recognize that it has not been established that communication plays an essential role in modernization. That communication is part of the complex interaction of processes involved in modernity is well documented, but such a statement is trivial. What matters is whether communication can really be expected to function as a prime mover or antecedent in such a process, and under what conditions.

What could mass communication offer? First of all, it obviously has the ability to reach many people rapidly and with the same messages. If no such capacity existed in a country, it had to be created by expanding the communication facilities (thus, for example, UNESCO's minimum requirements for radio or newspapers per thousand). Audiences were what, in fact, was needed. People had to receive information about the system (in many cases, as in Africa, on the emergence and constitution of the nation-state itself) and their demanded and expected roles. They had to be socialized into new ways of living, trained in new skills, and transformed from their deep-rooted traditional mores. New values had to be instilled, countermodernizing forces dispelled, new loyalties developed, aspirations reformulated or encouraged. In short, the social system had to communicate required information and values so people could meet the role demands that an emerging modern society had to ask from its participants.

A critical assumption in this optimistic viewpoint is that the content of mass media is, by definition, modern oriented. Regardless of any specific messages, in the context of a traditional society, media are a modern input. But most studies have not proceeded beyond an evaluation of modern content, in general. At this level, media would seem to create a "climate for modernization" (McNelly 1966). More than any specifically identifiable and instrumental messages, what appears to matter is the climate conducive to modern ways of life. McNelly, however, tries to be more specific within that realm. He contends that, for Latin America, the media are full of messages relevant to modernization. "Much of the content of media, including advertising, is informative, educative, or propagandistic in nature, designed to inform or persuade people about various kinds of modernity" (McNelly 1966). Rogers (1969) also accepts this view in his Colombian study. It also seems to be the position of Inkeles and Smith (1974).

Barghouti (1974) questions the assumption that there is an overall modernizing climate provided by the media, or that it is worthwhile to invest in media if that were the only outcome. He finds that in Jordan's rural development, media have played an important developmental role as sources of political information, but they are not instrumental in the provision of agricultural information. The consequences of the assumption can now be clarified. By assuming that content is promodernization, he argues, one receives the impression that modernity is inevitable once the media are available and used. The climate notion thus "conceals shortages" in the provision of needed information.

Besides the fact that many authors challenge the notion that any media content is modernizing in the context of a rural society, there is agreement in that there is a very limited amount of information that farmers can use.* If such information exists, it is bound to be directed almost exclusively to big farmers, that is, those who have established links with the modern sector and who can adopt (purchase) what is suggested.

It can be suggested that, because little relevant content is available for agricultural modernization, media cannot be expected to fulfill needs in that aspect. Where there is such content, it will probably be tied to structural constraints of the audience, implying differential usefulness of media.

---

*An exception to the contention that little relevant modernizing content is present in mass media can be found in rural communication projects using mass media, of which the most notable example for Latin America is the radio schools (see, for example, Spain, Jamison, and McAnany 1977). Such instances are not considered here, since they fall outside the scope of the data-sets to be analyzed. Although such projects are not considered, since they alone would constitute another chapter, some implications for them are set forth in the final part of this chapter.

However, the position will be sustained here that the general modernizing function of media can be expected to have an impact on rural audiences. People are socialized in cognitive, affective, and behavioral domains by exposure to mass media. Media can affect desires, expectations, and the awareness of choices, but they cannot, per se, provide the removal of structural constraints standing in the way of modernization. If the environment is supportive, communication's potential would be enhanced.

Diffusion of Innovations as a Communication Strategy

Galjart (1971) contends that the modern/traditional dichotomy has failed to explain agricultural development in poorer countries, and he proposes three factors that would be more suitable to that understanding: ignorance, unwillingness, and inability. Ignorance would refer to lack of knowledge: the farmer does not know of the innovation or, if there is some awareness, lacks the know-how. Unwillingness does not imply ignorance or an incapacity to innovate but the presence of values and attitudes that prevent innovation. If the first factor calls for information, the second one points more directly to what has usually been dealt with as the cultural barriers to modernity.

To a great extent, the mixture of these two factors has permeated the notions of the traditional farmer and set forth particular strategies of intervention. It can easily be seen that the problem thus restricted can be reduced to the individual level: a farmer who lacks information and whose attitudes are not congenial to change.

Somehow, perhaps because of the fact that diffusion theory borrowed heavily from evidence and interpretations primarily developed in and for a very particular rural setting—that of the United States—little attention was paid to the structural features of traditional rural environments that hampered a communication approach for overcoming the barriers to modernity. Galjart's third factor, inability, refers precisely to such barriers. At the individual level, it means the farmer is unable to change, even if he knows what could be done and desires to do so, because of situational limitations. This inability factor has been largely ignored in diffusion research.

The question asked was, Who are those who innovate first? rather than, What are the social consequences of a diffusion process operating as the model predicts? In policy terms, the first question was the more important. There was a need to identify an entry point into the traditional sector. Thus, the characteristics of early adopters are thoroughly studied to provide guidelines for eminently practical and urgent concerns. So, too, are the communication channels that seem best suited for them.

Just as Lerner (1958) found his modern individual to be urban, literate, a media user and empathy-imbued, so diffusion theory also had its modern persons in the form of early adopters. The early adopter is empirically characterized (as compared with rural peers) as having more education, greater contacts with change agents, and higher exposure to mass media and interpersonal channels. The early adopter participates more, is more of a cosmopolite, seeks information, and has greater knowledge. The attitudes all seem to point in the right direction: the early adopter is positive about change, risk, education, science, and the like; is an achiever and has higher aspirations; is also a person of higher social status; and has more land (see app. A in Rogers and Shoemaker 1971). As in some conceptions of the modern individual, there is here a mixture of personal and background characteristics. The issue is that, in this case, there is no immediately perceivable correspondence between the personal characteristics of modern man and the rural environment in which he is situated.

At this point, the concerns of theory and practice intermesh, because the development of diffusion theory derived from what diffusion practices were doing. "Diffusion generalizations adequately draw conclusions about current practice, but this may be very different from offering recommendations for optimal practice" (Röling, Ascroft, and Chege 1976).

As long as the goal was to reach at least the most receptive farmers (in a context characterized as traditional)—assuming that the "trickle-down effects" went unchecked and the generalization of diffusion practices became normative for extension agencies precisely because of their generalized diffusion—the question of potential inequities was not to be an issue. And obviously, from an extensionist's point of view, the strategy of concentrating on the modern or progressive farmers has had its advantages, which Röling, Ascroft, and Chege (1976) describe.*

The adoptions that in principle were available for all farmers in practice were only implemented by the most resourceful of those farmers. Even if the S-curve of diffusion reached its total population

---

*Briefly, such farmers have larger farms (greater effect of the extensionist's advice on total productivity), are, or can be expected to be, the core of commercial farming, are eager for information, and follow technical advice easily. They can demand assistance, and complain if not attended; they have the resources needed for implementing new ideas; and they are homophilous with the extension agent.

plateau over time, the fact is that early innovators stand to benefit more (at that stage of the curve, the innovation is still new among the population).

STATEMENT OF THE PROBLEM

The attempt here is to reconstruct the role of communication for rural modernity under structural constraints. The author will try to make a case for communication. By giving a preponderant role to societal restrictions over communication, it is hoped that more precise and less "oversold" roles emerge for communications, a matter of particular importance to policy and projects.

Theoretically, and at an adequate level of abstraction, communication can be considered the key societal process. What is argued here is that there can be no unexamined theoretical reductionism from a generally valid statement to a consideration of particular communication processes operating under specific societal restrictions and being expected to play an important prodevelopmental role. Without regard for precisely those "particularistic" factors of history and structure, the developmental role of communication is unduly overemphasized and, in the process, oversimplified.

The present work concurs partially with Grunig (1971) in that "structural change is the essence of development and communication a complement—after structural change has taken place—and not that development is a communication process complemented by structural change." In the absence of structural change (which may be defined as both the process of removal of key identifiable structural constraints and the provision of new societal arrangements oriented toward a more equitable distribution of Good), attention will be paid to the existing structural constraints of rural society that presumably affect communication's impact.

A clarification must be made, however. It could possibly be inferred that there is no worthwhile communication activity before structural change takes place. This null position is not taken here. What is implied is the following: first, that without structural change communication effects will be limited both in terms of relevant information conveyed and audiences reached and affected and, second, that the notion of communication as the key element for change should be abandoned as misleading.

A clarification of terms is due, at this moment, in regard to structural constraints. Structural constraints are societal obstacles that restrict the opportunities of an important number of individuals to participate fully and equitably in the development process and in the sharing of the benefits of a given social system.

Inherent in the notion of structural constraints is a situation of inequality in allocation of society's good, and a process of conflict and power struggle, because for some groups it is advantageous to conserve a particular social arrangement that allows for their own development as a group or, in a stricter sociological sense, as a class.

The notion of structural constraints has to be normative. What are constraints for the vast majority of rural populations are precisely the societal arrangements that allow rural oligarchies to occupy a predominant role in society. It is conceivable that a notoriously unequal allocation or appropriation of resources can have positive effects on national growth, even if at an unbearable social cost. The values of equity and concern for the lives of the rural poor must then be accepted as underlying the concept of constraints. These are defined as structural in the sense that the individual alone cannot affect them but suffers the consequences.

Given a variety of methodological and data restrictions, the level of analysis of this work is the individual. The shift of levels implies that the notion of structural constraints must be translated into that level of individual characteristics, that is, it may be stated that the individual has assigned attributes that reflect to a greater or lesser degree the impact of social determinants. These define the opportunity structure, that is, the ability, not the abstract desire, to engage in modern behavior.*

It is suggested here that being subjected to structural constraints creates different outcomes in modern attitudes and behavior, because some farmers have their opportunity range severely limited while others, relatively freed or even profiting from the structural constraints, are offered the objective opportunity to be innovative.

It is a very important empirical point to assess the rigidity or relative flexibility of a system characterized by structural constraints, to be expressed as individuals' opportunity ranges. It is postulated here that for most persons these restricted ranges effectively limit their chances of becoming modern, specifically in behavioral terms. But some people do manage to take advantage of slight alterations in structural constraints. Objectively, their opportunity range has expanded. If they desire, the chances for modernity are available, even if in a limited way.

What are some identifiable structural constraints? The one synthesizing phrase is "lack of resources" for the individual—socially, a distribution of resources such that the majority of the population

---

*The notion of opportunity structure is very loosely adapted from Kahl (1968).

have none or very limited amounts. The crucial constraint is held to be land tenure patterns. It is proposed to call this land factor a first-order structural constraint in contrast with other constraints, which will be called second-order ones. Such a distinction is theoretically relevant and policy useful: first-order constraints concern relatively fixed resources (that is, land size), the alteration of which implies major transformational social policies affecting the status quo and the power structure of society, because they imply redistribution of resources among social groups. For all practical purposes, this alteration lies beyond the realm of normal rural development policies. Second-order structural constraints are other societal resources that are generally lacking in the rural sector but that can be, and usually are, the object of ameliorative social policies. They do not imply an alteration of first-order constraints. They are intended precisely to overcome some of the consequences of such constraints without forcibly having to address the underlying basic social arrangements.

Lack of these resources can be said to typify second-order structural constraints. Such resources include education, social organizations, credit and extension services, marketing facilities, communication, and mobility.* The presence—even if limited—of some of these second-order resources presumably affects the opportunity range of individuals.

Thus, second-order structural constraints will be considered as reinforcing or partially altering the basic restriction for the diffusion of modernity. In terms of individuals' opportunity ranges, it will be asked whether having more schooling, receiving credit, belonging to a co-op or obtaining extension help broadens the opportunity range primarily defined by the land-resources factor and, if it does, whether it has any detectable impact for the individual. It is postulated that little impact will be detected, that, in the main, resources will be concentrated on those whose basic opportunity structure already enables them to become modern.

As a corollary, the implication is that the existing gaps created primarily by the land-resource factor will be reinforced and even tend to increase.

For purposes of a more detailed analysis, communication is treated separately from other second-order constraints. Given data limitations, communication is understood to be primarily mass me-

---

*Mobility is presented as part of the opportunity range, because, at a sociological level, one of the features of structural constraints is the relative fixation of people to a limited geographical environment. For the individual, "moving out," even if occasionally, is a broadening of one's opportunity range.

dia exposure and interpersonal modern communication or change agent contact. It is postulated that the association between mass media and modernity outcomes is linked to opportunity structures.

DATA-SETS AND VARIABLES

Only the minimum needed information on data-sets, variable constitution, and quality of measurement is provided here. A detailed treatment can be found in Contreras (1979).

The Brazilian Diffusion of Innovations Project

The Brazilian diffusion of innovations project was conducted by the Department of Communication at Michigan State University, under the direction of Everett M. Rogers, and was sponsored by the U.S. Agency for International Development (AID). It was located at the Federal University of Minas Gerais and involved the Brazilian rural agency for credit and extension (ACAR). Further information is found in Rogers, Ascroft, and Röling (1970). Phase 2 of the project, used here, was based on 1,307 interviews with farmers in 20 villages of the Minas Gerais region during late 1966. Sampling design was purposive at the village level: 80 villages represented the "least" and "most" successful in adoption, as defined by ACAR agents. The 20 units were chosen for a later experimental stage. The pool of respondents used here are 1,015, given the fact that one village had been "lost" from the available data-set and that land renters were excluded from the analysis. The villages are atypical in that they have a greater-than-average change agent effort, whether successful or not. The individuals sampled, however, are not restricted to ACAR clients.

The Basic Rural Education Project in Guatemala

The government of Guatemala proposed a new program of nonformal education in its 1975-79 sectoral plan, to be implemented in the Western Highlands region. Three donor agencies—UNESCO, the United Nations International Children's Emergency Fund, and AID—were involved in the project. Stanford University, Institute for Communication Research, had a subcontract for the areas of research, evaluation, and delivery systems. Emile G. McAnany and Robert C. Hornik conducted the subcontract. Jeremiah O'Sullivan and Eduardo Contreras were stationed in Guatemala. A base-line survey was conducted in late 1975. A second survey was undertaken by O'Sullivan in early 1977, which is the one used here. Actually, two random samples were selected. The first one (N = 250) represents attended farmers (that is, those receiving assistance, primarily credit, from agricultural agencies). A second sample (N = 350) represents non-attended farmers and most clearly approximates the bulk of the Highlands population. Complete details of this random multistage sample are found in O'Sullivan (1978b), as well as in Contreras (1979).

Variables

A word about reliability and validity issues is needed. Overall, this author is satisfied with both aspects regarding the nature of the sampling and chosen variables for the present purposes. The Brazilian data-set was checked against other publications derived from the diffusion of innovations project. For Guatemala the 1975 base-line research and other surveys for the region were used. The above is in addition to internal consistency checks for both sets. A lengthy discussion is not in order here.

It is obvious that no operational equivalence of measures could be aimed at; rather, variables were chosen to allow conceptual comparisons, while taking advantage of unique strengths of each data-set, compensating for what the other one lacked.

First-Order Structural Constraints

For Brazil the simplest notion equated the individual's first-order opportunity range with the total amount of land possessed. Advantage was taken, however, of a variety of measures, and the constituted variable is called "assets." Assets represents the regression equation for farm income, the main predictors being total amount of pasture and planted land and number of cows, the two of which account for 97 percent of the 37.4 percent explained variance. The logic lies in the question, What farm income would have been expected given the amount of land and type of land use an individual had? By applying regression coefficients, each farmer obtains a score on assets, which is the predicted farm income from (essentially) land and cows. Simultaneously, an outcome variable called "farm income residuals" is obtained as the difference between actual and predicted farm income for each subject.

In the Guatemalan case, the variable assets is created by predicting the total value of agricultural production from (essentially) amount of land and wheat cultivation use of land. These two variables account for 99.8 percent of the 81 percent explained variance. Total value is not the net income, but the potential cash value of each respondent's production, assuming it had been transacted. Thus, sub-

sistence and market farming alike are assigned a value to their production, regardless of actual sale.

Second-Order Structural Constraints

Credit. In Brazil the best item proved to be the actual loan the respondent had obtained, if one had been received. In Guatemala,
lacking such information, respondents were assigned values according to years of credit use, if credit was used at all.

Participation. For Brazil participation was an index of membership
in a number of community organizations. Alternatively, cooperative
membership alone is used, but results are wholly consistent. In
Guatemala no adequate measure was found, mainly because of the
real fact of very limited participation in the region. Being "attended"
or not is a surrogate measure, but, given some self-selection problems, it is not truly adequate either.

Mobility. This author prefers to speak of mobility, rather than of
cosmopolitanism. The item is simply measured by the number of
visits to the city in the past year for Brazil, and by a Guttman scale
composed of trips to the department and national capitals in Guatemala.

Education. Rather than measuring schooling, there was an interest
in the present educational ability of the respondents (this, in turn,
created problems with the media variables). In Brazil an index of
educational ability was composed consisting of years of schooling, a
literacy test, an understanding test, and the frequency of letter writing (alpha reliability coefficient for the scale is 0.819). In Guatemala
the index included last grade completed, ability to read, and ability
to write (self-reported); the alpha was 0.855.

Communication. In Brazil an overall mass media-exposure index
was devised as a weighted combination (by factor analysis) of exposure
to radio, newspapers, movies, and television. Despite statistical
manipulations, the alpha was only 0.637. Other measures are also
used on occasion; for example, interpersonal communication is
measured by change agent contact, that is, number of contacts in the
last year.

For Guatemala, media exposure takes the form of a Guttman
scale composed of radio exposure, radio ownership, radio use for
news/education, and newspaper exposure, in that sequence. The
scale performs as well as a radio scale only (with a 0.812 alpha).
Interpersonal communication is a Guttman scale of three items:
whether the change agent visited the community, whether the agent
helped the people, and whether the respondent had contact (talked)
with the agent.

Outcomes

Innovativeness. In Brazil innovativeness is the sum of adopted practices as expressed in length (years) of adoption, divided by the number of available practices for the village. Practices were identified
by ACAR agents, and they are not identical for each community. Another measure, adoption, is an index composed similarly but without
time-weighting of practices.

In Guatemala there are no similar measures. Of those used,
one should report an opinion-on-chemicals scale (composed of attitudes toward fertilizers, insecticides, herbicides, and disease-con-
trol chemicals) and a similar use-of-chemicals scale (alphas are
0.708 and 0.670).

Farm Income Residuals (Brazil). Farm income residuals is the counterpart of assets, that is, the unexplained variance for farm income,
once regressed on land-related predictors (thus, actual farm income
minus assets).

Values and Costs per Unit (Guatemala). Little residuals for value of
production were left. Thus, total value is divided by land, giving a
productivity figure (value per unit). Costs per unit are obtained similarly. Of the costs, the inputs-per-unit variable is used here, representing the unit cost of the use of chemicals.

THE GUATEMALAN CASE ANALYSIS

The Western Highlands region in Guatemala is populated by a
third of the country's inhabitants. Over three-quarters of the area's
rural population are Indian. Minifundia and subsistence farming pre-
dominate. Land is topographically uneven, eroded, nonirrigated,
and poor in fertility. Maize is the predominant crop. Wheat, beans,
and vegetables are also cultivated.

Land tenure is inequitable, both for region and country. Of the
nation's farms, 3 percent hold 62 percent of the land under cultivation.
In the Highlands, 5 percent hold almost half of the available land.

A little less than half of the farmers have had no schooling.
Few attain more than three years of primary. Farmers express a
desire for more education (practical, agriculture-related courses),
yet few appear to have attended courses, which are only marginally
available through some rural projects.

Two-thirds of the sample—and virtually all of the population—
have no credit use. There is limited mobility. Many have never been
outside their village. There is, however, another type of mobility—
every year thousands of farmers are carried by trucks to the large
export-oriented coastal estates. This seasonal migration is, for
many, their only source of cash income.

Radio is the only "mass" medium. There is at least one-third of the population that can be called a stable audience. Another third and up to one-half have no access to radio at all. Occasional contacts with change agents are restricted to a fraction of the population, which this author estimates at less than 5 percent. Given the nature of the 1977 sample used here, the role of the extensionist appears inflated. Even for attended farmers, alone, such contact is not so widespread or frequent.

This author's reading of the Guatemalan evidence indicates that there is no reasonable basis for assuming that the factors inhibiting modern behavior are fundamentally cultural resistance or mere ignorance; rather, it may be crudely put as a question of resources. Farmers seem quite rational and open regarding acceptance of modern inputs. Whether such modernity potential is realized has much to do with resource availability. There are a number of practices that do not demand cash outlays, such as contour plowing, seed selection from their own crop, spacing, use of organic fertilizers, and compost piles. These are not correlated with income, land, or ethnic origin. The situation is different for purchased innovations, such as chemicals. While all types of farmers have crop problems, and few have negative opinions on any one chemical, the striking difference between poor and rich farmers is in the actual use of chemicals.

Table 5.1 provides a correlation matrix that shows the extent to which the variables constituting the opportunity range can be thought of as a set. Table 5.2 presents the correlation matrix for opportunity-range and modern outcome variables. The attribution of plausible directionality of the relationships in both tables is left to the reader. There is at least evidence for speaking of opportunity ranges as a set,

TABLE 5.1

Correlation Matrix of Opportunity-Range Set, Guatemala
(N = 593)

	(1)	(2)	(3)	(4)	(5)
Assets (land)	(1)				
Credit	38*	(2)			
Mobility	29	37	(3)		
Education	32	30	39	(4)	
Media exposure	24	26	32	35	(5)
Interpersonal communication	29	41	35	36	22

*$r \times 100$; all r's significant at 0.001 level.

Source: Compiled by the author.

TABLE 5.2

Correlation Matrix of Opportunity-Range Variables and Modern Outcomes, Guatemala
(N = 593)

	Assets	Credit	Education	Mobility	Media	Interpersonal (change agent)
Innovation ignorance[a]	-21[b]	-30	-23	-31	-27	-30
Opinions: credit	34	47	27	31	20	31
Opinions: chemicals	20	24	18	25	22	25
Change of practices[c]	17	36	30	29	19	51
Use of chemicals	47	49	44	44	39	45

[a]Index based on "don't know" responses to innovation items.
[b]r × 100; all r's significant at 0.001 level.
[c]Dichotomous variable (Have you changed your practices lately?).

Source: Compiled by the author.

which is to say that second-order ranges do not appear to countervail the impact of basic constraints in land. It also appears that opportunity ranges do affect outcomes, but this is also true for communication. Thus, simple associations may give credence to the theoretical expectations held here, but they may also distort as much as they reveal.*

Multiple regression analysis is used here to extricate the relative contributions that a variable brings to the explanation of an outcome.† Although regressions were performed for four outcomes, only that for use of chemicals is reported here, because results are basically redundant.

Predictor variables were entered as four sets, as presented in the next summary table. Three regressions are shown in Table 5.3. One deals with the entire sample. The other two aim at determining whether there are different patterns of prediction for subgroups. For that purpose, one group is composed of farmers attended by an extension agency, an adequate approximation to larger and resourceful farmers; the second group is the nonattended farmers, which approximate best the bulk of the Highlands population.‡

For farmers in the high range of the opportunity structure, resources and education-communication are the essential predictors of chemical use, which is high. For the opposite group, whose use of chemicals is very low, less resources are involved (and, if at all, through credit), and the education-communication contribution is lower. Mobility's contribution to variance suggests that those users have established market links and shifted somewhat from subsistence agriculture, a fact given more credibility when the bilingual/Spanish factor is considered.

---

*The relationship of modernity outcomes to the postulated predictors was also examined by breakdown analysis. This author is satisfied that relationships are essentially linear. Thus, the correlation matrices are sufficient at this time.

†Since the interpretation of the particular contribution of one variable—in terms of explained variance or r^2 changes—depends very much on the exact placement of such variable in the set of predictors, variables were entered following theoretical criteria, and alternative solutions were also explored. The problem is more important in the Brazilian analysis than it is here. In general, when two predictors are highly correlated, the second-entering variable loses strength.

‡One should, of course, ask if use of chemicals would be useful for small farmers if they could afford them. Apparently the answer is yes, from what was discussed earlier, regarding use of practices that do not demand cash outlays.

TABLE 5.3

Multiple Regression: Use of Chemicals, Guatemala
(percent of explained variance in rounded values)

	All Farmers (N = 593)		Attended Farmers (N = 107)[a]		Nonattended Farmers (N = 350)	
	Total	Explained	Total	Explained	Total	Explained
Assets and credit	33	60	15	33	9	24
Mobility	7	13	4	9	10	27
Communication[b]	8	14	18	40	9	24
Other[c]	7	13	8	18	9	24
Total explained variance	55	100	45	100	37	100
Mean value for use of chemicals	1.2		2.37		0.71	

[a]Does not include cooperative members, who are mostly small farmers.
[b]Educational abilities, media, and interpersonal.
[c]Dummy variables for region and language. Farmers living in or nearby Quezaltenango, the urban center of the Highlands, and being Spanish-speaking or bilingual have some advantages.

Source: Compiled by the author.

The analysis could have stopped here. In fact, many studies in the diffusion of innovations do not go beyond the adoption of the recommended practice, but the question of whether improved practices make a difference in the lives of the adopters is left wide open. It is not usually established if changed practices have a significant effect on productivity.

The question is not only of improved practices leading or not leading to higher agricultural productivity. There is also the issue of the differential societal impact of said changes in practices and, presumably, productivity. O'Sullivan, in Chapter 4, contends that small farmers, even if attended (and thus given some opportunities to modernize), do not change their disadvantaged condition of marginal farmers.

Path analysis is used here for a closer examination of these issues. By using the beta coefficients from multiple regressions, rudimentary causal paths are established for different subgroups. The reader is reminded that the model presented here is but one of the "plausible" ones.*

The variables that were selected for the path models are, from distal antecedent to predicted outcome: assets, education, media, mobility, interpersonal, credit, cost inputs per unit, and value per unit (or productivity). Several decisions on selection of variables had to be made to avoid overstressing the model. The only one worth discussing is use of chemicals. This variable is superseded by cost inputs per unit. This latter variable represents much more accurately the use of chemicals in terms of amounts and costs involved. Use of chemicals did provide an adequate discrimination for earlier purposes, but is no longer useful.

For the sample as a whole, Figure 5.1 presents the path model, along with some statistics. It also illustrates the complexities in-

---

*In path models, there is tension between realism (incorporation of as many variables as possible) and parsimony (incorporation of a few variables in simple relations). There is no inherent solution in path analysis to the placement of variables other than the explicit model set up by the researcher. Thus, there are a number of plausible models and a decisional dilemma that runs between the extremes of theoretical stubbornness and empirical opportunism. Regarding use of path coefficients, beta weights are used. Given differences in variances across the compared subgroups, the b values (unstandardized regression coefficients) have also been examined. These b values have no intuitive or "real" meaning here, given the variable transformations done. The important fact is that the picture provided by b values is not at all different from that derived from beta values.

FIGURE 5.1

A Plausible Path Model, Guatemala
(beta weights reported; N = 593)

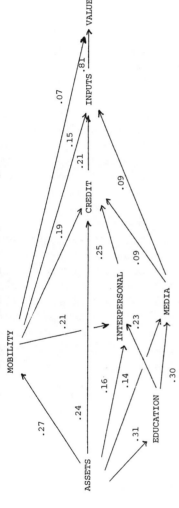

Variables	Mean	S.D.
Value per Unit	17.10	18.39
Inputs (Costs per Unit)	3.64	5.27
Assets	595.21	1061.76
Credit	0.37	0.48
Education	4.91	5.01
Mobility	4.62	4.02
Media	1.66	1.36
Interpersonal	0.74	1.13

Explained Variance for Value per Unit: 68%

Source: Compiled by the author.

127

volved in the process of examining even a few of the variables in a multivariate causal exercise. What the model seems to say is that having resources opens up a variety of opportunities, including access to credit itself. The farmer who is more mobile, educated, media consuming, and can interact with the change agent is bound to introduce modern inputs that make for better productivity.

The next step is to examine these relations for different subpopulations according to the question of structural constraints. Do high- and low-opportunity range farmers follow the same routes? Particularly, can it be established that communication has a differential role for the two groups, as we proposed earlier?

The above issues were examined for two subpopulations: one is the group of farmers that can be classified as high-opportunity range, the other group is an approximation for the typical highland farmer who makes up the low range. There were several procedures considered for adequate subdivisions of the sample. The selected criterion involves the use of two variables: sale coefficient and size of farm. The first represents a primary orientation toward subsistence or market agriculture and is derived as the ratio between what the farmer sold and what was produced.

The resulting curve (eta squared = 0.274) allowed for the discrimination of four quite distinct subgroups. For simplicity of reporting and presentation, only two basic groups are considered.* The first group, numbering 315, represents subsistence farming. At the lowest extreme, it includes farmers with less than one acre (0.56 manzanas) of land and virtually no sale activities. The upper limit for the group is set at two acres. Such a cutting point does not affect the primarily subsistence nature of the group but allows for some market activity. The second group represents the high-opportunity-range farmers—those whose land is five acres or more. These number 92 and have important market linkages.

Figure 5.2 presents the path model for the low-opportunity-range farmers. Means and standard deviations are also provided.† It will be noted that mobility and education are not determined by assets. This is not purely artifactual. There is enough variation of

---

*In fact, several other comparisons were made by alternative divisions of the sample. Results are surprisingly similar and add no new insights (or surprises, for that matter).

†These can be compared with those in Figures 5.1 and 5.3. The z-scores evaluating the differences among these means are not reported here, but all are highly significant—way beyond the 2.33 limit for an alpha of 0.01, with the exception of productivity values. This is a long and complex issue, discussed in Contreras (1979).

FIGURE 5.2

A Plausible Path Model for Low-Opportunity-Range Farmers, Guatemala
(beta weights reported; N = 315)

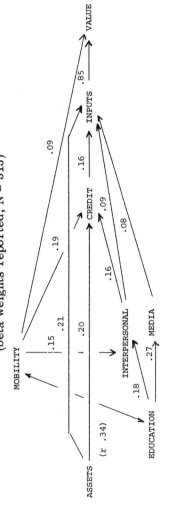

Variable	Mean	S.D.
Value per unit	17.45	22.93
Inputs per unit	3.14	6.78
Assets	172.75	93.69
Mobility	3.76	3.92
Credit	0.19	0.39
Education	3.74	4.57
Media	1.38	1.34
Interpersonal	0.43	0.87

Explained Variance for Value per Units: 77%

Source: Compiled by the author.

129

FIGURE 5.3

A Plausible Path Model for High-Opportunity-Range Farmers, Guatemala
(beta weights reported; N = 92)

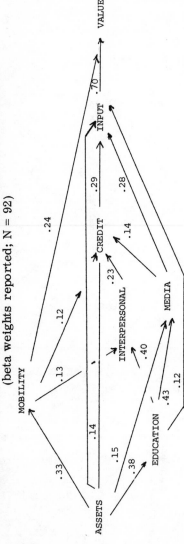

Variable	Mean	S.D.
Value per unit	17.08	8.87
Inputs per unit	4.86	2.87
Assets	2,153.44	2,022.07
Mobility	7.12	3.42
Credit	0.80	0.39
Education	7.86	5.10
Media	2.23	1.20
Interpersonal	1.49	1.38

Variance Explained in Value per Unit: 63.5%

Source: Compiled by the author.

assets—or of land if the reader prefers—within an admittedly restricted range so that, statistically, an effect was conceivable. In
practice, it is evident that under conditions of generalized poverty,
being extremely poor or very poor is not a useful discriminator for
the above variables. The interesting element, then, is that some
farmers make efforts to accede to second-order opportunity ranges,
and that type of effort seems to be rewarded, even if in a limited way.
Educated farmers (educated meaning literate and—very important—
that the Indian farmer is capable of functioning bilingually) develop
the ability to enjoy radio. This apparently has a slight effect on inputs. It also means greater chances of contacting the extension agent
and eventually obtaining some credit. Mobile farmers can be understood here to represent two groups: those few who have established
commercial links and those who travel to otherwise supplement their
income (for example, migrant laborers).

Figure 5.3 provides information regarding high-opportunity-
range farmers. It will be noted that media shows an important effect
on inputs and that education strongly affects media and interpersonal,
education itself being a clear function of resources (assets).

For those farmers who have the land and the resources, including credit if they need it, it appears that the informational path (edu-
cation/communication) is indeed of value in the decision to make use
of available modern products. If the comparison is made with other
groups, it can be inferred that it is only for the farmers who have
the resources to adopt costly innovative practices that an informational strategy makes sense. When credit is provided, farmers with
otherwise few or moderate economic resources can adopt.

Before closing, a brief recapitulation of the last part of this
section is in order (see Contreras [1979] for more detail on models).
Through path models for the sample, a subsistence-oriented group,
and a market-oriented group, attempts were made to uncover the
types of elements that were playing a part in the actual use of modern
agricultural practices and affecting productivity among low- and high-
opportunity-range farmers. Overall, having land is the crucial factor. This allows the farmer access to other resources, which then
play a role. Communication has a limited role for low-range farmers. The extension agent seems to play a part but, essentially, is a
link toward credit. Media do not lead significantly to modern outcomes (as expressed in this section), but they have a crucial impact
for bigger landowners—suggesting that when the economic resources
exist, media can play their informational and modernizing roles.

THE BRAZILIAN CASE ANALYSIS

The Minas Gerais state had, by 1966, a population of about 10
million. It has varied agriculture, the southern farms being more

commercially oriented (coffee, sugarcane, and tobacco), the northern ones primarily devoted to subsistence crops (corn, beans, and rice). Cattle operations consist mainly of beef in the western region and dairy in the central-southern regions, near the urban markets of Rio de Janeiro and São Paulo (Rogers, Ascroft, and Röling 1970).

Farmers in Brazil have more land than those in Guatemala. Half of the sample is beyond the maximum size (30 hectares) found in the Highlands sample. The relative distribution of land, however, follows a similar pattern: half the farmers have to make do with less than 8 percent of the land, whereas 5 percent of the landowners have access to one-third of the land. The distribution is not dissimilar to that of the country as a whole.

There is little schooling: 20 percent have had none and 60 percent have had one year. Functional illiteracy ranges between one-third and up to one-half of the sample (depending on how it is measured). Some 40 percent of the farmers belong to a cooperative. For one-third of those, it is the only organization to which they belong. Participation is also shared among other groups—clubs, societies, or charities. But for 40 percent of the farmers, there is absolutely no participation. They tend to be the poorest and smallest farmers. Farmers with the most land are members of several organizations.

While most of the farmers are positively oriented to credit, only half have ever asked for a loan. Loans are used primarily to buy land or cattle (60 percent) or to purchase equipment, fertilizers, and new seed (32 percent). Two-thirds of the loans are below U.S. $450. Sources for credit vary. Small farmers rely on private sources such as friends and neighbors; big landowners use banks. The ACAR is a source for medium-sized and large farms. Four-fifths of the smallest landholders have no credit.

There is considerably more mass communication availability and exposure in the Brazilian sample than what is true for the Guatemalan Highlands. Two-thirds have a radio; only 5 percent own a television set, but almost half are at least occasionally exposed to it; one-fourth of the sample receives newspapers or magazines regularly. No more than 50 persons in the sample are totally isolated from mass media. Although there is a tendency toward overlapping audiences across media, radio listening does act as a substitute for newspaper reading. Radio would seem to have an informational character. Half of the sample actually mention news and agricultural programs as their favorites. As a source for agricultural news, radio is mentioned by over two-thirds of the sample. Other media have less outreach as sources for agricultural news. Newspapers are mentioned by 20 to 30 percent of the respondents; magazines are slightly lower, excepting the biggest landowners, half of whom mention them.

Contacts with the ACAR extension agents are relatively widespread: 30 percent had no contact at all during the year prior to the survey; 33 percent had been contacted one to four times; 17 percent averaged some seven visits a year; and 20 percent had more than monthly contacts with the agent. These contacts, because of the nature of the ACAR, can be for credit or technical assistance help, and no clear pattern was found when the sample was divided by size of holding. Regardless of the purpose of the visit, the agent is considered a source of agricultural information by 40 to 50 percent of the sample—excepting the smallest landowners (the lowest 15 percent), of whom less than one in five considers the agent a source. In addition, the agronomist is the most trustworthy source by far (when competing with neighbors, radio, or newspapers).

The impression the author derives from an examination (not reported here) of all items related to attitudinal or cognitive modernity manifestations is that these farmers are far less traditional than the common stereotype for rural subcultures. Were it not for the lack of actual opportunities that allow for expression of behavioral modernity traits, these farmers could be much more than just attitudinally on their road to modernity, and extension activities focusing mainly on informational inputs would be indeed adequate. Such contention is now put to empirical testing.

The Brazilian data-set presents considerable analysis problems, because the relations uncovered reveal a very complex interaction of factors. The impact of land or assets is less categorical for outcomes, and second-order opportunity ranges are much more widespread than in the Guatemalan Highlands. The sample is better off in opportunities for modernization. The interrelationships between these series of opportunities are such that it is hard to establish some ordering of variables that represents a causal model homologous to the real causal processes in operation.* Thus, this analysis avoids the explicit presentation of path models, stopping only a step short with multiple regression analysis, for which coefficients are reported.

Two correlation matrices are presented to examine the relationships among opportunity ranges, communication, and modern outcomes. Data had been previously checked for nonlinear relations and transformed when necessary and justifiable. Table 5.4 is the correlation matrix for the opportunity ranges, communication included.

There is clear evidence for significant covariation of the set of predictors. To an important extent, opportunity ranges are cumulative for the farmers in the sample—a person high on one tends to be

---

*The author spent considerable time working out path models that could be both plausible and parsimonious. The price paid for simplification was, in his opinion, too high. It has been preferred not to present such models in the present work.

TABLE 5.4

Correlation Matrix for Opportunity Ranges, Brazil
(whole sample; N = 1, 015)

Assets	(1)						
Credit	42*	(2)					
Mobility	26	11	(3)				
Participation	50	36	29	(4)			
Education	29	21	24	41	(5)		
Media	42	29	31	55	54	(6)	
Interpersonal	22	29	14	35	34	35	(7)

*Critical value of r at 0.001 is 0.10 for N = 1,015; r × 100 is significant at 0.001.

Source: Compiled by the author.

high on the next. Inversely, the effect of structural constraints can be clearly inferred for a substantial number of farmers.

The relations between the set of predictors and modernity outcomes are examined next. Five modernity outcomes to be treated later in multiple regression analyses are shown in Table 5.5. They represent a cognitive or informational domain (political knowledge), an attitudinal-cognitive domain (empathy), two behavioral outcomes (innovativeness and adoption), and an ultimate effect representing an improvement in quality of life from a better income (residuals).

Table 5.6 presents the results of the multiple regression for political knowledge and two other outcomes. Modernization theorists contend that a modern person is in part characterized by being informed. The reader is referred to the betas, which will highlight the roles of education and media (specifically, as it turns out, newspaper reading) over assets for this information outcome. A similar situation occurs with empathy. Only 17 percent of the variance is accounted for, but over four-fifths of it is a function of communication variables, notably education.

Innovativeness is an important concept in studies of rural modernization. Hence, all factors that could legitimately contribute to its explanation were included in the regression. When 25 variables were first included, the total explained variance was 42.7 percent. The seven core predictors used here explain 39.2 percent, but, in fact, only three of them are needed to explain 38.2 percent. Such a result is consistent with the notion that being innovative is primarily the result of having resources available. Assets can account for 82

percent of the variance explained in innovativeness. Given the over-
riding influence of assets on innovativeness, there is little left for
the other variables to contribute. There is, however, an effect that
may be attributed to communication variables, as evidenced in the
beta weights for interpersonal (0.16) and media (0.09). There is a
temptation to take these results as confirming the optimism of the
communication factor. Further analysis, however, not reported
here (see Contreras 1979), seems to indicate the problems of regression analysis and the ordering of entry of variables. The conclusion,
when more careful analysis is made, is that there is a very modest
role for communication in innovativeness. Adoption, however, en-
hances communication's role through extension agent visits. Media,
in addition to providing a general environment for modernity, also
appear to be sources of agricultural information for some.

Two further aspects of communication deserve mention here.
From additional analysis it was found that two media were particularly adequate as sources of agricultural information in the adoption
process: the bulletin published by the ACAR and radio. The first is
a small and localized medium and it plays a role in adoption (r = 0.37),
just as newspapers and magazines seem to be good sources for the
earlier innovators. Radio's effect is, of course, captured by the

TABLE 5.5

Correlation Matrix for Opportunity-Range Variables and Selected
Outcomes, Brazil
(N = 1,015)

	Innova-tiveness	Adop-tion	Political Knowledge	Em-pathy[a]	Resid-uals
Assets	57[b]	43	37	17	0
Credit	30	32	24	19	21
Mobility	26	19	27	13	15
Participation	43	42	43	23	13
Education	29	34	56	39	20
Media	40	44	55	30	23
Interpersonal	33	44	27	33	23

[a]Empathy measured by an index of counterfactual behavior items.
[b]r × 100 is significant at 0.001, with the exception of assets-
residuals—which, by definition, correlates 0.00, as obtains here.

Source: Compiled by the author.

TABLE 5.6

Multiple Regressions for Political Knowledge, Innovativeness,
and Adoption, Brazil
(N = 1,015)

| | Percent of Explained Variance | | |
	Total	Explained	Beta
Political knowledge			
Assets	13.6	32.0	0.11
Education	22.5	53.0	0.34
Media	5.4	13.0	0.25
Other[a]	0.8	2.0	—
Total	42.3	100.0	
Innovativeness			
Assets	32.3	82.0	0.43
Interpersonal	4.4	11.0	0.16
Media	1.5	4.0	0.09
Other[a]	1.0	3.0	—
Total	39.2	100.0	
Adoption			
Interpersonal	19.6	55.0	0.28
Assets	11.3	32.0	0.21
Media	3.5	10.0	0.15
Other[b]	1.1	3.0	—
Total	35.5	100.0	

[a]Variables entered in single-step solution.
[b]Participation, 0.08 beta; credit, 0.06; education, 0.06; and
mobility, 0.02.

Source: Compiled by the author.

media index. Separate analyses that isolate media show that radio
seems to play some role in a later stage of adoption. Radio use as a
source of agricultural information correlates only modestly with innovativeness but 0.32 with adoption.

The comparative results for innovativeness and adoption seem
to suggest that different farmers are influenced at each stage of the
diffusion process—a matter that is well known—although little emphasis has been put on the resource constraints that inhibit innovations
for many.

The final outcome examined is farm income residuals. For the whole sample, only 10 percent of the variance is accounted for. The importance of residuals lies in the next comparisons.

It is time to examine subgroups and to see if different patterns of prediction obtain. This is done through a three-way division of assets. The three groups are fully characterized in Table 5.7, which provides means and standard deviations for outcomes and predictors. One should note the variability of assets, which is very low for the first group, presenting a statistical problem in the interpretation of comparative results. Besides betas, b values are also provided in the regressions because they differ at times, notably for assets.

New correlation matrices were examined for the groups and, overall, the opportunity range variables hold at least satisfactorily. For the 7 predictors and 63 correlations (21 correlations multiplied by 3 groups), 30 percent are not significant at the 0.01 level. Half of these concern assets. Thus, even with the restrictions in variability imposed by the division of the sample, one may still speak of an opportunity-range set within each group.

Regardless of the comparisons made across groups, the essential factors that are most influential in determining political knowledge are education and media. In an unreported analysis that added the educated/uneducated farmers division to that of assets, it was confirmed that educated but poor farmers have an important edge over their uneducated counterparts in poverty. Furthermore, even under limited resources, they manage to score higher on this information item (as well as in economic knowledge and other information-related variables) than farmers who have more resources but less education.

It thus seems that when low-assets farmers are provided with information opportunities, they can take advantage of them. In part, the results are an argument for the value of literacy skills, but mostly for the supportive environment that makes such skills necessary. It is clear that the question of modernizing forces must be understood as a multidimensional phenomenon. Acquiring and using literacy skills go together with a number of other variables; but if education were to be considered as an antecedent variable, a strong argument would be possible for its role as provider of some needed abilities that make farmers better users of other modernization opportunities, notably the mass media.

Providing information (understood both as the opportunities for using it and the message itself) has an important role to play in cognitive modernization. There are, however, two caveats. The first refers to the assumed importance of these results. What is of interest is not the score on a trivial scale but the process of education-communication in relation to a pure information outcome across several subdivisions of the farmers. The second reservation is

TABLE 5.7

Means and Standard Deviations for Modernity Outcomes and Opportunity-Range Variables for Three Assets Groups, Brazil

	Group 1: Low Assets (N = 306)		Group 2: Medium Assets (N = 403)		Group 3: High Assets (N = 306)	
	Mean	Standard Deviation	Mean	Standard Deviation	Mean	Standard Deviation
Outcome						
Political knowledge	-0.43	0.77	-0.05	0.94	0.49	1.07
Innovativeness	-0.47	0.68	-0.13	0.79	0.65	1.17
Adoption	-0.69	0.68	-0.03	0.86	0.65	0.99
Residuals	-0.09	0.66	-0.02	0.90	0.12	1.34
Opportunity ranges						
Assets	-0.67	0.11	-0.31	0.18	1.08	1.23
Education	-0.35	1.00	-0.02	0.94	0.38	0.95
Media	-0.44	0.83	-0.06	0.82	0.53	1.12
Interpersonal	-0.35	0.83	-0.01	0.99	0.33	1.05
Mobility	-0.20	0.63	-0.08	0.89	0.31	1.32
Participation	-0.41	0.66	-0.12	0.76	0.57	1.27
Credit	-0.37	0.23	-0.09	0.85	0.50	1.39

Note: Population (N = 1,015), mean = 0.00, standard deviation = 1.00.

Source: Compiled by the author.

more important, and it emerges from a comparison of several unreported analyses. Given a difference in assets, some farmers have wider opportunities for a fuller use of information channels, and this is reflected in a considerably higher score as an outcome.

Adoption and innovativeness were also examined for the three groups. There is a substantial difference among them in terms of explained variance. For innovativeness, variance accounted for is 13, 15, and 35 percent for low-, medium-, and high-assets groups, respectively. For adoption, the respective percentages are 32, 27, and 15. This has a methodological implication: the choice of one operationalization of practice adoption over another yields different results, which would not have become easily apparent if only whole sample analyses had been performed. By using both measures, the analysis is considerably enriched. Out of this methodological phenomenon, more interesting implications are derived.

Adoption seems to be an inadequate measure for high-assets farmers, just as innovativeness is for low- and medium-assets farmers. Thus, a better understanding of the process of practice adoption and the forces at play comes when innovativeness for high-assets farmers is compared with adoption for the other farmers. Such comparison is not faulty. The only distinguishing feature of both outcomes is the incorporation of the time-weighting factor. Furthermore, a "time" dimension is added to a static analysis in this way.

Finding that richer farmers innovate earlier is not a surprising result. Such finding is consistently reported in diffusion research, although the implications are not always set forth. What is of greater interest is the assessment of the processes and forces that influence early and late adopters, as well as whether some farmers simply stay as nonadopters.

As measured by innovativeness, lower scorers may well have as many adoptions as a higher scoring group, but they adopted later. Evidence points to poorer farmers as latecomers in the adoption process, if they adopt at all. By the time latecomers adopt, the early adopters are probably already innovating in another practice. Nonadopters are worse off. They are simply left behind. The agricultural practices plateau reached when an innovation is sufficiently diffused is now farther away from them.

Keeping in mind these conditions, what factors are mobilized by different groups of farmers regarding innovations and adoption? The examination of Table 5.8 provides some empirical evidence. The high-assets group, which is paramount to saying the innovators group, shows that the essential factor in being innovative is assets. It accounts for 28 percent of the variance in innovativeness, or 80 percent of the explained variance (35 percent). In general, there is a moderate effect of the other variables, of which contact with the change agent could be highlighted.

TABLE 5.8

Multiple Regression of Innovativeness for High-Assets and Adoption for Low- and Medium-Assets Groups, Brazil

| | Adoption | | | | | | Innovativeness, | | |
| | Low Assets (N = 306) | | | Medium Assets (N = 403) | | | High Assets (N = 306) | | |
	r	b	Beta	r	b	Beta	r	b	Beta
Assets	0.03	0.62	0.10	0.19	0.57	0.12	0.53	0.40	0.42
Education	0.29	0.02	0.03	0.19	0.00	0.00	0.30	0.08	0.06
Media	0.44	0.21	0.25	0.21	0.07	0.06	0.38	0.09	0.09
Interpersonal	0.44	0.21	0.25	0.44	0.30	0.35	0.25	0.16	0.14
Mobility	0.11	0.03	0.02	0.16	0.07	0.08	0.21	0.05	0.05
Participation	0.31	0.09	0.08	0.33	0.20	0.18	0.39	0.07	0.07
Credit	0.35	0.50	0.17	0.19	0.07	0.08	0.21	-0.02	-0.02
Constant		0.13			0.24			0.04	
Variance explained (percent)		32			27.3			35	
Adoption		-0.69(0.68)*			0.03(0.86)			0.65(0.99)	
Innovativeness		-0.47(0.68)			-0.13(0.79)			0.65(1.17)	

r = multiple regression coefficient

b = unstandardized regression coefficient

Beta = standardized regression coefficient

*Figures are mean; those in parentheses are standard deviation.

Source: Compiled by the author.

140

As one shifts from innovativeness to adoption, that is, from earlier to later stages in the process, two other factors become important. One is participation, particularly in cooperatives (it is the richer farmers who tend to be members of several organizations; participation for poorer farmers is virtually limited to being a co-op member). Participation proves to be an adequate channel in the adoption process of otherwise deprived farmers. Thus, the presence of a modernizing institution for the rural poor can help overcome some of the first-order constraints. Analyses not reported here show that co-ops make little difference in innovative behavior if material resources, such as assets and credit, are not also available. When resources and co-op interact, co-op members score higher than nonmembers in practice adoption.

The second factor that grows in importance as the innovation diffuses is communication. A first impression of the process can be inferred from the examination of the correlation and regression coefficients of media, interpersonal, and education to both outcomes in each group, as Table 5.9 shows. Having access to the extension agent and making use of the agent as a source of agricultural information and advice make an impact on the farmer's behavior. Less surprising than an assumed effect of the change agent for this sample (which can also be ascertained later on when residuals of farm income are examined) is an apparently similar effect across all groups, but particularly for some of the less resourceful farmers (medium assets).

Media appear to be very influential for the low-assets group, which is something of an unexpected finding. If the extension agent does not reach this group frequently enough, poor farmers seem to turn to alternative sources of information that can guide them in adopting what their limited resources allow.

In summary, given the series of results that have been presented in this section concerning the forces and processes that appear influential in determining practice adoption across groups, it can be suggested that information or communication strategies for modernizing rural life have a good chance as long as the adoption of the new behavior is not foreclosed by lack of resources. However, it is also apparent that, overall, access to resources results in higher scores on the new practices and that communication may very well provide information and persuasion, but it will not be able, even if the results of its intervention do succeed in effecting behavioral changes, to solve basic constraints that are not informational in nature, such as having land and resources.

An analysis of farm income residuals, that is, the income that could not be explained by land-related variables, shows some interesting results (Contreras 1979). As postulated, communication has

TABLE 5.9

Correlation Coefficients and Betas for Communication and
Innovation Variables across Three Assets Groups, Brazil

	Education		Media		Interpersonal	
	r	Beta	r	Beta	r	Beta
Low assets (N = 306)						
Innovativeness	0.13	-0.02	0.23	0.11	0.25	0.14
Adoption	0.29	0.02	0.44	0.21	0.44	0.21
Medium assets (N = 403)						
Innovativeness	0.14	0.00	0.17	0.07	0.26	0.16
Adoption	0.19	0.00	0.21	0.07	0.44	0.30
High assets (N = 306)						
Innovativeness	0.30	0.08	0.38	0.09	0.25	0.16
Adoption	0.27	0.09	0.33	0.18	0.27	0.16

r = multiple regression coefficient
Beta = standardized regression coefficient

Source: Compiled by the author.

effects, ultimately, on farm income for high-assets farmers over
and above the land factor effect. Yet, at the same time, farmers in
the low-assets group also appear to make beneficial use of communication, as reflected in their residual farm income. This result was
unexpected.

The policy question can be stated thus: Given a basic structural constraint primarily defined by land, and assuming that it cannot be altered (not that it should not be attacked), are policies aimed
at broadening second-order opportunity structures, particularly communication, effective? The critical balance between information provision and availability or provision of resources has been stressed
here repeatedly, yet it does appear that small farmers are willing
to receive information and exhibit openness toward it. The issue
seems to center more on the ability or inability to transform such
messages into innovative behavior and, in turn, to increased income.

It seems that farmers restricted on the basis of the amount of
land they have can, if other opportunities are available and they make
use of them, somewhat advance their station in life. Within the low-
assets group, some farmers characterized by participating more,
having access to some credit (which is not much for this group), and

being somewhat mobile (probably market links) are also higher communication consumers. That consumption appears to be instrumental for agricultural modernization, that is, one could speculate on active information-seeking behavior for these farmers. The clear implication is that (provision of material resources facilitated, as with credit or co-ops) there is a very important role for information strategies. Under such conditions, farmers are effective information-seekers, and such strategies seem to affect the quality of life of otherwise structurally constrained farmers. At the same time, their ability to catch up with the high-assets group is almost nil. Some manage to keep the gap from widening.

CONCLUSIONS

The object of this study has been to examine the role that communication plays in rural modernization. The starting premise was that communication has not played an important role because of a series of structural constraints. Negating the oversold role assigned in the optimist era for communication, some societal conditions have been established that are much more useful for understanding communication's role and for deriving more feasible communication strategies.

The first important lesson that emerges from the study is that to understand communication's potential, one must necessarily start with a serious examination of the societal context under which communication is to operate. That is, before accusing communication of not doing what it could not in fact have done, or of placing undue expectations on its potential, one should carefully examine not only the microsocietal environment but also the relations linking together the communication system with the macrosocial system of which it is part. It performs some important functions in the larger society, and it is from this society that the limits of communication are established.

Thus, there is a second point to be made, given that nobody would seriously object to an analysis of the social context for communication. It has to do with the fact that one has to theorize, to develop a model of society that somehow reflects the essential features of the complex realities one tries to comprehend. Communication, as a relatively young field, has mainly borrowed paradigms of society from other disciplines. Just as the field leaned heavily on a psychological basis, so development communication took the classical modernization paradigm too much at face value as a useful shortcut to the understanding of the societal context and for its insertion in the assumed directionality of the transitional process to modernism. The crisis of the modernization paradigm is not caused by communicators' frustrations, but the situation has forced communication researchers to look elsewhere. It is not this author's belief that a new paradigm exists that has the interdisciplinary variety and the empirical richness that one may demand beyond a necessary holistic viewpoint. Yet, the crisis must be faced, either from within (for example, Inkeles and Smith 1974) or from without, as with Marxist approaches, structuralism, or a systems approach.

The development of this work has aimed at uncovering some assumptions of the prevailing paradigm and the consequences that viewpoints have on "seeing" some parts but not others. It is hoped that the deeper implications of what structural constraints are have emerged.

Yet, important as a new conceptualization of society and communication is, one must also be concerned with policy implications, that is, what may be done today that is possible and worthwhile in the light of preferred value orientations and the image of society one holds. It was noted earlier that the conception of structural constraints was, ultimately, normative. Behind it lies a concern for the poor and their struggle.

Are communication projects worthwhile in this light? One must remember that this work did not touch upon the purposive use of mass media in the confines of a project, as others refer to in other chapters of this book. This is not the place, either, for even a summary discussion of communication strategies that are responsive to the rural poor, but many of the findings are relevant for them. They have been discussed throughout the analysis and no recapitulation will be made here. Only a few general remarks are pertinent.

Overall, it has been shown that one cannot think of rural societies, in general, or of a "typical" farmer. Distribution of resources in the countryside is very inequitable. Some farmers have objective opportunities to modernize, others face insurmountable constraints. More important—as a second step—is that even within the rural poor one must learn to make distinctions, as the analyses for Guatemala and Brazil suggest.

In the context of pure subsistence farming, there may be, in fact, very little to do, communicational or not, in piecemeal approaches. Evidence points (notably in Guatemala) to such rigid constraints that there is hardly room for any action that can conceivably alter the lives of subsistence farmers. Besides the societal structural constraints, it is furthermore true that subsistence farming tends to be located in the most hostile natural environments, which forces the point that one is not looking at an isolated or parallel farming situation, but that the whole arrangement of rural activities is such that there is a "functional requirement" for not altering subsistence farming—namely, the need for cheap and only temporary laborers in the coastal estates of Guatemala.

But among the rural poor there are also small farmers trying to compete in the marketplace. In general, there is among the rural poor some minimum flexibility in the provision of some opportunity structures, and it is in that wedge that communication strategies may be more feasible. An unexpected finding in Brazil was that small and constrained farmers did try to overcome the barriers to modernity through the use of mass media. This instrumental use of the media parallels a result of Whiting and Stanfield (1972). It is not an expression of optimism—the data are quite clear on how far these farmers would have to go—but evidence for a promising, though very difficult, new start.

This new start cannot forget that it is not communication alone that may produce some amelioration in the lives of the rural poor. There is a crucial role for resources. If adequate information is to be provided, conditions for the implementation of such information into practices must also be provided, along with a realistic appraisal of what societal and individual impact these new practices will have, given that the question of structural constraints will still be quite relevant.

Thus, a more fruitful perspective for communication strategies under structural constraints is to learn to work under them, and to work effectively. One task is thus externally oriented and has to do with assessment of the societal conditions impinging upon communication policies and activities. The other one is internal and has to do with maximizing the efficiency of communication strategies. This task includes what one may refer to as the "technical constraints," as McAnany calls them in Chapter 1, indicating that the task of implementing communication strategies for the rural poor is no less of a challenge than working one's way out of the societal structural constraints themselves through political strategies.

PART III

INFORMATION AND EDUCATION IN RURAL DEVELOPMENT: ECONOMIC ANALYSIS

6

ALTERNATIVE STRATEGIES IN THE ECONOMIC ANALYSIS OF INFORMATION/EDUCATION PROJECTS

Jacqueline Ashby, Steven Klees,
Douglas Pachico, and Stuart Wells

INTRODUCTION

This chapter explores the approaches that economics takes to make an evaluation of the impact upon agricultural development of the use of communication technologies for formal and nonformal educational activities. Economic analysis is increasingly viewed by public sector decision makers as a means by which to "rationalize" public sector activities. By weighing the costs of resource use against the benefits of the various impacts of an activity, it is thought that one can judge the value of undertaking that activity. Economic analysis, which usually emphasizes quantitative estimates of these costs and benefits, is believed to be able to provide some "hard" empirical evidence to guide decision making.

However, whether such a belief is warranted and, if it is, how to apply economics to the evaluation of education/communications technology (ECT) systems are both questions that need additional thought and discussion for several reasons. Policy makers and researchers in other fields usually have only a minimal idea of the premises that underlie various economic analyses. Furthermore, debates within economics, in general, and the economics of development, in particular, underscore the lack of consensus within economics itself. Finally, economic analysis applied to educational evaluation is a relatively new field of study, and economic analysis applied to communications technology for education—or communications, in general, for that matter—is really just beginning

Work on this chapter was initially supported by a contract from the U.S. Agency for International Development to EDUTEL Communications and Development, Inc., Palo Alto, California.

An understanding of the questions and issues relevant to the central topic of this chapter requires an examination, and, to some extent, a synthesis, of several related strands of literature. First, there exists a large body of economic literature concerned with development theory and practice (in particular, rural and agricultural development) that is relevant to understanding how educational technologies affect agricultural development. Second, there has been considerable work in the economics of education through which the particular role and consequences of educational activities have been studied. Third, the focus on the use of communication technologies brings in the whole relationship of communications systems to societal development, in general, and agricultural development, in particular. Economists have had something to say about this topic, but of at least equal importance in this area is the work of communications researchers. Furthermore, communications researchers rely as much on the societal development conceptions of other disciplines, such as anthropology, sociology, political science, and psychology, as they do on those of economics, and a review of such efforts provides interesting perspectives on the approach of economists.

Clearly, it is impossible to do justice to such diverse, yet related, bodies of literature. However, a synthesis of commonalities and differences from all the above points of view seems increasingly important if there is to be an understanding of how to approach questions of social policy that cut across many disciplines. Although this study is neither exhaustive nor definitive, it does try to clarify the dominant thrusts of the above approaches, the parallels between them, and their implications for evaluation by emphasizing theory and method, both of which are essential to evaluation. Some results of empirical studies are presented, but given the large array of studies that have been conducted, concentration is primarily on examining studies that contribute to understanding the application of theory and method. The aim is to contribute to the understanding of, and dialogue between, decision makers, economists, and researchers from other disciplines in order to apply economic analyses to the evaluation of the use of communications technologies for agricultural development.

The primary focus will be on the relationship of investment in human beings (commonly referred to in economics as the formation of human capital) to agricultural productivity and development. Human capital is generally thought to be augmented by the provision of education and information, and it is this perspective that provides a unifying theme to our analysis. The dominant approach in the Western world is based on the competitive market theory of neoclassical economists, which underlies most of the literature on the economics of development, agriculture, education, information, and communications. However, there are numerous iconoclastic deviations from this perspective, and a few more completely developed, coherent alternatives to it, the most preeminent of which revolves around the theories of Karl Marx and subsequent modifications. In this study, the human capital approach (based on neoclassical economic theory), as well as criticisms of it and alternatives to it, is discussed.

Across several disciplines two primary, contrasting, perspectives emerge that differ significantly in both theory and method. One parallels the dominant economics approach, with a focus on the behavior and attitude of the individual, whereas the other parallels Marxist economics, with a focus on structural, historical, systemic characteristics. These two perspectives have their counterparts in both theory and method; and, in conclusion, the authors of this chapter will contend that, in many senses, the perspectives represent different paradigms (in the sense that Kuhn [1962] used the term) for the social sciences, which cannot be compared through empirical research. The selection of particular education and communications policies for agricultural development thus, in many important respects, reflects an explicit or implicit philosophical commitment more than the results of some rationalistic, empirical judgment.

In "Theoretical Perspectives," the reader is introduced to the theories that are most relevant to an economic analysis of development, education, and communications strategies. Then, in the following section, the methodological approaches that these theories use to evaluate real world phenomena and policies are investigated. Also, to understand the empirical methods that most economists advocate, some aspects of economic theory relevant to the analysis of agricultural production relationships are reviewed. References to the results of empirical studies will be made wherever relevant throughout these sections. Finally, the main points of the chapter are reviewed and some concluding observations are presented.

THEORETICAL PERSPECTIVES

Perhaps the most significant component of any evaluation is the explicit or implicit theoretical perspectives that guide it. In this section, some of the theories relevant to three areas of study are reviewed: the approaches taken to national development, in general, and agricultural development, in particular; the approaches taken to the evaluation of the impact of educational sector activities on agricultural development; and the approaches taken to the evaluation of the impact of communication sector activities on agricultural development. Finally, there is a summary and discussion of the implications of the analysis for the evaluation of ECT strategies relevant to agricultural development.

Development Theory and Strategies

Underlying most economic analyses of development strategies is the theoretical framework of conventional economics; therefore, to understand such applications it is necessary to have a basic understanding of this framework. What is usually termed economics is one version of the subject of economics that would be more accurately labeled by any one of a number of expressions: "competitive market theory," "free market theory," or "neoclassical economics." These labels are used equivalently to refer to a body of literature, theory, and applications that traces its intellectual history from the work of Adam Smith's The Wealth of Nations (1776) and has devoted considerable attention to the workings of the "invisible hand" of the market economy. Although primarily directed toward analyzing a capitalist system based predominantly on the private ownership of resources, it has also been applied to the workings of socialist systems with public ownership that bases resource allocation on public profit-oriented market operations (Vanek 1970).

Competitive market theory begins with some assumptions of how the economy operates. Chief among them are:

1. Firms that produce goods and services are out to maximize their own profits.

2. People who consume goods and services are out to maximize their own utility (economist's jargon for happiness).

3. These profits earned from production, and utility gained from consumption, are unaffected by the production or consumption of others.

4. There are many buyers and many sellers of each type of good or service, among which competition is solely on the basis of price.

5. None of these individuals or firms can affect the market price by themselves.*

6. There is complete information available to producers and consumers concerning prices, market opportunities, and the alternative technologies of production.

Assuming that these conditions hold, a number of conclusions have been shown to follow that many persons would deem desirable.

---

*Actually, item 5 and the last part of item 4 are not assumptions but are conclusions that can be shown to follow if the other assumptions hold. See any standard microeconomics textbook for more detail on these and other points in this subsection (for example, Henderson and Quandt 1971).

Under such a system firms would produce those goods and services most valued by consumers. These firms would produce and sell these goods and services at the lowest possible cost. Human labor and other inputs would be paid at a rate equivalent to what they add to the value of the firm's output. An economy operating according to the above assumptions would not "waste" anything, because no reallocation of resources could yield an improvement in such a way as to make even one person better off without making someone else worse off. Economists would label such a society "Pareto efficient."

The behavioral dynamic that gives rise to this state of affairs is individual self-interest, motivating both the producers' and consumers' choices. Perfect competition relies critically on prices to act as signals that convert this private self-interest into social gain. The price of a good or service reflects both the relative value that consumers place on a good (demand) and the relative value of resources that go into producing that good, given our knowledge of production techniques (supply). Prices are thus viewed by market economists as measures of social value, or, more precisely, as societal opportunity costs. In a market system, they are a measure of the value of the resources that society had to use or employ to produce a particular good or service. Given competitive forces, if those same resources were more highly valued by consumers in another endeavor, then profit-maximizing entrepreneurs would bid the resources away from the production of the less-valued good or service.

Unfortunately, the competitive market-theory focus on a static, stable, equilibrium economy is not well suited to examine questions of economic growth, because these questions must deal with the dynamic behavior of an economy over time. Competitive market theory does allow for some changes over time, but changes are usually considered to be exogenous.

Neoclassical economists generally view development as synonymous with economic growth, referring to increases in the total goods and services produced, as generally measured by the gross national product (GNP). The presence of a competitive, market-based economy is essential to such measures of development or growth, because they rely on prices to aggregate the total value of goods and services produced. The source of economic growth is seen by neoclassical economists to be a function of societal savings and investment (see Ranis [1968] for a succinct review of this approach).

Post-World War II governmental policies reflected the development strategies implied by such a theory. To break out of poverty, a poor nation needed to tighten its belt, forgo some present consumption, and invest its resources in new technologies. Alternatively, an infusion of foreign aid might create growth. The locus of economic growth was thought to be industrial development, and this depended on investment in physical capital. In the late 1950s and early 1960s, disappointments with the apparent effects of loans and gifts from rich to poor nations for dams, factories, and physical machinery —combined with the development within the neoclassical perspective of theory that focused on the critical importance of investment in human resources to economic growth—yielded a marked concern with the formation of human capital through education and training as a necessary complement to physical capital investment.

From this overall perspective, rural development and agricultural productivity were of secondary importance. Industry, especially capital goods industry, was viewed as the leading growth sector of the economy (Hirschman 1958). Rural society in low-income countries was viewed as economically stagnant and culturally tradition bound. Agriculture was seen as economically inefficient in using available factors of production and characterized by a low propensity to save and invest. From this view, agriculture is important primarily in that it provides a pool of surplus labor that can be rapidly transferred to the industrial sector without affecting levels of output in agriculture (Kao, Anschell, and Eicher 1964). The growth of agriculture is of importance only in that a more productive agriculture may be needed to feed a growing industrial-urban population.

For this strategy of development, explanations of rural poverty and low levels of agricultural production are ultimately rooted in cultural explanations of persistent inefficiencies in agriculture. The individual farmer was perceived as a prisoner of traditional culture; irrational and unresponsive to economic incentives; at best, ignorant of the possibilities of change; and, at worst, "lazy" and resistant to change—in that the farmer would do only the work necessary to satisfy traditional levels of consumption (Reynolds 1969). The solution to the problem of agricultural stagnation was, in the first place, seen to lie in uprooting traditional society, which would happen over time as a consequence of the forces of industrialization, as it had in the wealthier nations. The process could perhaps be speeded through the spread of education and mass communications. Both were seen to be of key importance in remolding traditional values and attitudes, particularly in teaching rural people to perceive their economic self-interest and in motivating them toward change (Myrdal 1968). Second, technological inefficiencies in agriculture could again be solved by direct transfers of technology from the industrialized countries. This approach emphasized the utility of extension education to teach farmers the advantages of innovation and to facilitate the spread of technology.

More recently, a strategy of development based on expanding the GNP through investment in heavy industry has appeared to many as increasingly unacceptable. Concerns with equity, brought on at least in part by rising and often frustrated expectations of the poor,

have brought into question the uneven growth policies of the past.
Food shortages have, in some cases, proved too stringent a constraint to permit a continued bias of investment against agriculture
in favor of industry (Schultz 1965). Even in countries that have not
found growth inhibited either directly by food shortages or indirectly
through a foreign exchange constraint imposed by the need to import
food, industry-based growth has frequently manifested undesirable
equity and employment effects (Mellor 1976). Moreover, even where
industrial growth has been most rapid it has not usually expanded at
a rate sufficient to provide employment for an exponentially growing
population, let alone a population migrating out of the countryside
into the cities. Furthermore, given the relationship between low income and high fertility, a high unemployment rate appeared increasingly intolerable, if only because of its accelerating effect on population growth (Kocher 1973). In the agricultural sector, the benefits
of technology transfer have accrued in many cases to the larger and
more prosperous farmers, while small farmers appear in some instances to be relatively or absolutely worse off than they had been a
decade before (Freebairn 1973).

However, while the industrial-based growth strategy appears
ever more unsatisfactory, the potential of agriculture-led growth has
been perceived to increase. This is due, in part, to the technological
successes in discovering new high-yielding seed varieties and agricultural practices that have, in some cases, led to spectacular improvements in agricultural output—the so-called Green Revolution
(Brown 1970)—and, in part, to the development of economic growth
models in which agriculture plays a leading role in increasing output,
employment, and investment (Mellor 1976).

Earlier views of traditional agriculture as inefficient, and cultural explanations of persistent poverty, have been increasingly chal-
lenged. A number of studies have indicated that investment in traditional factors of production showed a low rate of return, thus offering
a weak incentive to save and invest in agriculture (Schultz 1964).
Farmers using traditional technology were found to be relatively efficient in using available factors of production and to be responsive to
prices and opportunities for change when innovations were profitable
(Wharton 1976). A conception of the peasant farmer as a rational
economic decision maker, similar to farmers in modern agriculture,
emerged.

Concomitantly, the limitations of direct transfer of technology
were recognized, as the failure of borrowed technology to diffuse
among farmers in the developing countries could be explained in terms
of the shortcomings and unprofitability of the technology itself (Frankel
1971). A key source of productivity growth in agriculture was identified as the ability to develop technology innovations using available,

less costly factors of production, usually with more labor-intensive techniques of production (Hyami and Ruttan 1971). The strategy of development based on increasing agricultural production necessitates a supply of new factors of production that must be appropriate to specific economic and agronomic conditions, and thus profitable for farmers to use. Consequently, of crucial importance to this strategy is investment in regional and national research systems for agriculture (Arndt, Dalrymple, and Ruttan 1977).

A key factor in determining the rate at which farmers can successfully use technological innovations to increase production is seen to be the abilities of farmers to process and use information and to adapt decision making in the face of new elements of risk and uncertainty introduced by new factors of production. Consequently, an important feature of an agriculture-based strategy of development from this perspective is investment in farmers' abilities through expansion of education and information dissemination. These factors will be discussed more extensively later in this section.

Significant changes have taken place over time in the focal points of mainstream development theory and strategies. Neoclassical economic theories have fostered, and even generated, some of these shifts. The perspective taken by these economists is seen to be as applicable to agricultural productivity and development as it is to the industrial sector. At the macrolevel, economic models give rise to recommendations for various savings, investment, taxation, and employment policies that can promote economic growth. At the microlevel, which will be of critical interest to the evaluation of specific ECT policies, the criterion of economic efficiency can guide the selection of the most socially valuable production activities and the techniques of production. Given that prices reflect the social value of resource inputs and outputs of a system, if private and public sector decision makers choose their activities to maximize profits or net monetary benefits (that is, benefits minus cost), the total value of society's output of goods and services will be maximized. As will be shown in "Methodological Approaches," considerable economist effort has been focused on determining what contributes to efficient decision making by an individual producer.

Despite the predominance of the approach discussed thus far, there are some fundamental problems that raise serious questions about the validity of the neoclassical perspective of social efficiency and development. First, the neoclassical approach depends on a certain few assumptions about both individual behavior and the structure of the economy for its conclusions that prices reflect social value, that competitive markets allocate resources efficiently, and that the public sector should be guided by cost-benefit analysis. Since it is clear that no real economic system operates strictly according to the few, but rather stringent, assumptions of perfect competition, a critical question is, What happens when the behavior of the system deviates from these assumptions? Some theoretical arguments (Baumol 1972) imply that even when small deviations occur there is no saying whether the system operates at a state close to efficiency. In an interdependent economy, one distorted price creates ripples, distorting other prices. In this situation, where prices do not reflect measures of social value, private or public sector decisions based on monetary analysis of costs, benefits, or profits have no necessary relationship to wise social choice.

Second, competitive market theory assumes that the tastes and preferences of consumers of goods and services (demand) are what guide resource allocation, and it also assumes that these preferences are outside the influence of economic activities. Education and communication systems, which can be viewed as an economic activity that may change individual preferences as much as inform them, contradict this latter assumption, and the same could be argued for other aspects of our economic system (Gintis 1974). Under these circumstances, the question then becomes, Whose preferences, and preferences at what point in time, will guide resource allocation decisions?

A related issue concerns the weighing of these consumer preferences that are guiding production decisions. How do these preferences become aggregated? The theory of perfect competition essentially yields the rule of "one dollar, one vote." The preferences of those who have the most money influence the goods and services produced by society in direct proportion to their greater wealth. To a large extent, competitive market theory ignores equity issues.

These latter points raise questions that are difficult for neoclassical economic analysis to deal with. Economists' concept of "society" as some abstract entity that receives all the benefits and incurs all the costs of any particular investment activity is called into doubt: first, because "society" as an aggregate of individuals has different preferences at different points in time that are affected by its earlier resource allocation decisions; second, because "society" consists of individuals and groups with unequal power and thus total benefits exceeding total costs will not necessarily prevent some individuals or groups from being hurt by a decision; and, third, in a more realistic view, because unequal power exists, decisions may be made for which total benefits are less than total costs as long as the costs are imposed on a group other than the one receiving the benefits.

The problems discussed above, taken together, form a critique that questions the basis of most Western economic thought and, consequently, that of the cost-benefit analytic framework that is most commonly used. It is not clear that monetary values represent societal values; nor is it clear what "society" as an aggregate concept really means. Alternative economic viewpoints have been advanced, perhaps the most coherent centering around the works of Karl Marx and subsequent additions to his theories. It is perhaps even more difficult to summarize justly this body of literature than that of neo-classical economic theory. Nonetheless, the basics are essential to understanding an important alternative view of the economics of development, as well as education and communications.

Fundamentally, the Marxist economist views resource allocation in most societies as a struggle between competing groups with unequal power. Under capitalism, from this perspective one can usefully analyze social resource allocation by examining the conflict between two simplified classes: capitalists, who own or control the nonhuman productive resources, and workers, who must sell their labor to capitalists for survival.

Marxist theory argues that although capitalists are motivated to accumulate wealth, they are not profit maximizers. Equally important to them is the maintenance of their position over time, and with it a whole system of social relationships. Thus, there are hierarchical organizational forms, not because such forms are necessarily efficient but because such forms maintain social distance between and within classes and act as a legitimation mechanism for status and wealth differences. Thus, capitalists favor capital-intensive technologies (over the most profitable technology) using fewer workers, because fewer workers are easier to control. Systemically, this behavior gives rise to the maintenance of a body of unemployed and underemployed workers (what Marx called a "reserve army") whose very existence acts as a threat to keep employed workers in line. Such a perspective explains the persistence of sexism and racism over time, which to neoclassical economists is "irrational." Everyone could be better off by hiring the best person for each job, but prejudice is useful to capitalists because it fragments the working class (Gintis 1976).

The capitalist class has had considerably greater power than the working class in the past. Workers are seen as alienated from the product of their work, from the work process itself, and in their daily social relations with others. However, this does not mean that the working class is powerless; indeed, major social change from this perspective occurs from class conflicts brought about by the contradictory forces emanating from within the capitalist structure itself. One major contradiction is that the capitalist accumulation process and the situation in which workers find themselves is sufficiently contradictory to human desires that workers' consciousness of their situation will increase, and with it their power. Most Marxists do not view social change as economically or historically deterministic, as they are often caricatured, but as susceptible to collective, political actions (Ollman 1973).

The Marxist view of national development is explicated within a global structure dominated by monopoly capitalism (Baran and Sweezy 1966). A key weakness of both industrial and agricultural growth-based development strategies is seen as the failure to take into account the implications of the institutionalized maldistribution of power and wealth between and within countries. Capitalists in advanced industrial nations, it is argued, who are searching for profitable investments and the ability to maintain the high level of consumption of luxury goods at home, have expanded across the globe to exploit cheap labor in obtaining raw materials. The limited industrial expansion and relative agricultural stagnation in poor countries is seen to have evolved historically from international relations of colonialism and unequal power, and hence exchange, between producers of raw materials and industrial capital goods. These relations have sustained a distribution of wealth and power within poorer nations that has made it possible for elites to adopt patterns of consumption similar to those in wealthier countries, and which are therefore dependent upon imports. These consumption patterns, and related import and capital goods dependencies in such economies, distort industrialization to the production of luxury goods, yielding internal terms of trade and returns to investment disadvantageous to food production in agriculture (de Janvry 1975). As a result, agriculture in such societies has historically undergone a process tending toward stagnation.

The major constraint to increasing agricultural production to its full potential is identified as the distribution of power and wealth that underpins traditional modes of agricultural production. Large, landlord-dominated farms tend to underutilize land and labor compared with small labor-intensive farms, which often achieve higher production per unit of land. The power structure distorts markets for inputs, including capital and credit and new technologies, in favor of larger, more prosperous, and more powerful farmers. From this perspective, the conservatism of small, poor farmers is a reflection of their limited control over and access to scarce resources. Moreover, the capitalist and/or landlord elite is hypothesized to wish the reduction of labor management problems through the creation of a reserve army of unemployed or marginally employed workers, and, consequently, technology development tends to be oriented toward capital-intensive, labor-saving, and often land-extensive techniques. The research-technology solution to agricultural stagnation is thus seen to have severe limitations imposed by prevailing political and bureaucratic structures that determine the supply of new technologies.

Investment in individual capacities through education and information provision is seen as subject to the same limitations. From this perspective, education and communication systems (whether formal or nonformal), which are controlled by elites, function primarily to socialize in, and select for membership from, various status groups, rather than to provide individuals with the opportunity for learning and utilizing economically productive skills (Carnoy 1974). Furthermore, regardless of the effectiveness of education in generating individual skills, the capacity of education systems to alter power structures that constrain opportunities to utilize such skills is limited (Carnoy and Levin 1976).

Thus, from a Marxist perspective, the possibilities of autonomous national development are seen to be constrained by this center/periphery model by which the structure of monopoly capitalism places the poorer nations in a peripheral state of dependency and uneven development, revolving around the demands of the wealthier centers. Profits and monetary benefit-cost analyses are rejected as legitimate measures of social value, because the neoclassical economics framework on which they are based is seen as both incorrect in theory and inapplicable to real world economic systems. Although the potential of governmental actions to achieve significant system change is argued among Marxists, many would advocate policies directed toward strengthening workers' control over, and consciousness of, production. From this perspective, proposals for industrial democracy, labor-managed farm cooperatives, Freire's (1973) emphasis on "conscientization" in education, and economic and political alliances of Third World countries are examples of strategies that can perhaps lead to more equitable and nonalienating societal development.

The Role of Education

The role of education in national development, in general—more specifically, in agricultural development—is conditioned by the development theory context within which education is viewed. Although the early industrial-based development strategy discussed above recognized that some gains might be possible from educating farm populations into modern values, among the most important of which were considered to be willingness to innovate and responsiveness to economic incentives, it was nonetheless felt that education of the rural masses was not essential for economic growth. An early challenge to this view emerged in the early 1960s as economists tried to account for the historic growth of the developed countries. It was generally found that increases in the amounts of capital and labor over time were not sufficient to explain the rate of growth of the GNP. Denison's (1962) work was seminal, suggesting that schooling, by improving the quality of the labor force, was an important economic growth factor that had hitherto been ignored.

The importance of education as an investment received considerable support in the elucidation of the theory of human capital (Becker

1964). Attendance at school, participation in nonformal or on-the-job training programs, and learning by doing are all activities that involve immediate and real costs of learners' and teachers' time as well as material resources. As a result of these costly investments, the productive skills of the learners are thought to be improved, so individuals are hopefully more productive than they were before the training. These productive skills, acquired through some learning experience, may be viewed as a capital good—human capital. Like physical capital, human capital is formed by an initial investment and is a factor of production that earns a return for its services. Expenditures on education or information can be seen, therefore, as investments, and economic analysis can be applied to the examination of these investments, both to ascertain whether efficient use is being made of resources invested in human capital and to compare the returns to alternative investments.

Early work emanating from this perspective gave rise to the field of manpower planning, which has pervaded the approach taken in low-income countries to educational system planning. Gross associations between educational levels and sectoral productivity, combined with rather rigid assumptions about the structure of industry and agriculture, gave rise to educational strategies recommending specific ratios of investment and student output among the various levels of educational services. However, the poor theoretical basis of the manpower planning approach and its dubious historical application have convinced even the most neoclassical economists that it is, at best, inadequate (Blaug 1970).

Perhaps the most common approach used by economists to evaluate the worth of an educational activity is to examine its relationship to the subsequent earnings of students who undertake that activity. Sometimes, the gross association between education and earnings that is observed is used as an estimate of the impact of future education on earnings. This result is then taken as a measure of the benefits of education and compared with the costs of education in order to yield various cost-benefit measures that can guide educational investment. Improvements in statistical and data analysis techniques, combined with the knowledge that gross association between two factors—such as education and earnings—are unlikely to be representative of causal influence, have led to the use of more sophisticated approaches to uncover the impact of education on earnings. In particular, economists often try to estimate earnings functions, that is, the relationship between individual earnings and all the various factors that affect it, including education. If this functional relationship is estimated properly, it supposedly allows the determination of the causal impact of education on earnings, as will be discussed more fully in "Methodological Approaches." It should be clearly noted that this approach to investigating the societal benefits of education rests solidly on the assumptions of neoclassical economic theory. The earnings of workers are the prices of labor resources and, under perfect competition, are measures of the value society attaches to the skills of workers. For economist cost-benefit measures to be valid guides to wise social (as opposed to private) investments, this assumption is necessary.

Most recently, economists have paid greater attention to another approach to evaluating the benefits of education, especially relevant to questions of agricultural productivity. Through theoretical and statistical modeling of the production process, it is thought possible to obtain direct estimates of the impact of education on production output. This approach has two distinct advantages over the earnings function approach discussed above. First, theoretically it allows one to look directly at the impact of education on economic output without necessarily having to assume that the wages of workers are measures of their social value. Second, economic theories have been better developed to model production processes than to model the process by which individual earnings are determined. Traditionally, economists have viewed production functions as engineering-determined relationships showing the maximum output that can be obtained for varying input combinations, given the technological state of the art. Within this conception, education may have an impact on output in that better- versus less-educated or -trained workers can be viewed as different types of resource inputs that may have differential impacts on the output produced. However, recent theoretical emphasis on the potential of education to influence production output by improving the abilities of production managers and decision makers to make more efficient production choices has led to additional tests of the impact of education. This is especially important in agriculture, where the developing view of the farmer as an economically rational decision maker fits well with this model. Education is theorized to be of particular importance under conditions of agricultural modernization and technological change, because the ability to allocate resources efficiently can have considerable economic payoffs in this new, more dynamic, and complex economic environment (Schultz 1975).

The work of Welch (1970) has been particularly influential in this area by probing at least somewhat into the mechanism by which education is supposed to affect productivity, and by examining empirical approaches that allow the measurement of the different types of such impact. Welch distinguishes between three potential effects of education: the improvement of the skills of workers that make them more productive; the improvement of managerial knowledge and ability fostering the purchase of those inputs associated with efficient, least-cost technologies; and the improvement of managerial knowledge and ability to take purchased (and also unpurchased) inputs and organizationally combine them into the most efficient, least-cost production techniques. The first component is termed the worker effect; the latter two, combined, the allocative effect. Thus, education is viewed as producing certain skills that may enhance ability on the job as well as providing certain aptitudes and attitudes, usually undefined by economists, that enable industrial or agricultural decision makers to better process and evaluate information relevant to production, and thus better allocate their available resources. The translation of this theory into empirical methodology and results will be discussed in the final section of this chapter.

It is also important to point out that economists evaluating education do not always attempt to translate educational process outcomes to monetary measures of benefits. Economists generally consider a monetary measure as a preferable criterion to use for evaluation, because it can be directly compared to the monetary costs of investment. However, it is usually recognized that money values may not be able to capture theoretically or empirically all the positive outputs of educational activities. Furthermore, the data to analyze impact on earnings and productivity are usually not available, especially for different types of education (as opposed to different amounts of education), because it requires long-term observation of what happens to graduates (and dropouts). For these reasons, economists often look at the effectiveness of education as measured in terms more directly relevant to the process, such as skill and attitude formation. Most often such analyses examine education as a type of production process, similar in conception to those in industry or agriculture, by which educational inputs are translated into educational outputs. Considerable effort has been expended on the investigation of these educational production functions (Klees and Wells 1977). They allow the examination of a more limited, cost-effectiveness concept of efficiency through which one can choose the least-cost means to produce desired effects, although the benefits of the effects must be assumed without some explicit criterion, such as price, by which to judge them. This approach may be of interest to policy makers who wish to ascertain the impact of ECT interventions on farmer knowledge, attitudes, and behavior, as well as on production.

The exposition above is based on the neoclassical view of education as human capital. Objections to the human capital approaches to educational evaluation have been numerous, often reflecting the basic objections to neoclassical economic theory discussed earlier. Association between education and economic growth may easily imply the reverse causality: growth yields a society that consumes more education (Blaug 1970). Associations between education and earnings may be caused as much by education acting as a filter to screen out less productive individuals, or as a status selection mechanism for productive positions, as by education delivering any productive skills (see Arrow 1973). Moreover, earnings may bear no relationship to productivity if perfectly competitive markets are not in operation throughout the economy. Alternatively, associations between education and earnings may reflect more the development of a set of affective worker characteristics, such as punctuality and motivation by external rewards, than cognitive skills, which feed into a capitalist hierarchical system of production bearing no necessary relationship to social economic efficiency, even within the terms of the neoclassicists (Bowles and Gintis 1976; Gintis 1976). Associations between education and physical output may be less the result of any intrinsic value of education than of a structural system that rewards the children of high-status families and the larger, wealthier landholders who consume more education.

From a Marxist economic perspective, education is seen primarily as part of an ideological superstructure that, over time, reinforces the attitudes necessary for the maintenance of capitalist production and the legitimacy of elite control. Although education may have productive value in that it can increase the ability of human beings to produce various goods and services, such productivity is confined to a very narrow capitalist conception of growth, development, and social value, all reflecting a price structure that is primarily a tool of those with wealth and power. The focus of these economists is more on questions of equity and control of the work environment than on questions of productivity and efficiency, although it is often argued by Marxist economists that greater equity and worker control will generate more, not less, efficient production of system outputs (Bowles and Gintis 1976; Carnoy 1974).

With specific reference to the association of the education of farm workers and managers with agricultural productivity, alternative explanations to a causal impact are possible. The productivity of the farm may depend on the political power and influence of the farmer and the farmer's family in situations where inputs to agriculture—such as water, fertilizer, and seed—are distributed through a political process (Frankel 1971). Extension programs in developing countries often use the strategy of channeling contact through progressive, leader farmers, who in many cases are also the wealthier and politically more powerful farmers. Political power is likely to be associated with size of holding, caste or ethnic group, and position in the tenure structure, as well as with education. Thus, the use of an efficient combination of inputs may depend as much on the farmer's command of resources, including political power, which structure access to inputs, as on the ability to choose correctly between alternative combinations of inputs.

Small, poor farmers often face severe liquidity problems and are compelled to sell output when prices are lowest and to purchase when prices are high (Griffin 1974). Efficiency may, in this situation, depend more on the farmer's resource base—reserves of cash and agricultural surplus, which may be correlated with education—than on decision making or other skills. Most fundamentally, from this perspective, even if education can yield increases in agricultural output, such growth does little or nothing to help the poor farmer or the poor country, the condition of both of which result from an internal and external historical structure of exploitation that inherently needs individuals and nations in marginal subsistence positions. True national development can only result if the contradictions within such a global, monopolistic, capitalist system eventually lead to its own demise.

The Role of Communication

By and large, economists have neglected any specific examination of the role of communications in the development of economic systems. The economics of communications is scarcely recognized as a field of study; it certainly has not received the considerable attention devoted to the economics of education (for a more detailed discussion, see Klees and Wells [forthcoming]). However, clearly related is a large body of literature concerned with the economic role played by information. Neoclassical economic theory generally assumes that accurate and complete information relevant to market conditions and productive techniques is available to all system participants. Given the obvious lack of realism of this assumption, many economists have examined various conditions about which less-than-perfect information is available and their impact on production and economic efficiency (Lamberton 1971). Also, from this perspective, an argument is sometimes made for the free flow of ideas and information as essential to efficient production, as well as beneficial to social development and individual opportunities (Coates 1973).

Despite this relative lack of specific attention, investment in communications systems fits well into the human capital framework. The dissemination of information relevant to market conditions, opportunities, and new production technologies should increase the allocative ability of the industrial or agricultural decision maker to purchase more cost-effective inputs and to organize them so they produce efficiently. Moreover, such information provision may also directly increase a worker's productivity. Thus, communication systems may enhance the productive value of human beings, and investment in them can be seen as adding to the stock of available human capital, quite similar to the manner in which Welch (1970) viewed education. Indeed, any distinction between information and education blurs as one examines the informational nature of much education and the affective and cognitive learning that results from most communication systems.

While economists have not paid much attention to communications, communication theorists have paid at least some direct attention to economics, in particular to the role of communications in national development. The approach taken to development, however, relies as much on the conceptions of other disciplines—such as anthropology, sociology, psychology, and political science—as it does on economics (Rogers and Shoemaker 1971). Most generally, this approach views the essence of development as a process of technology transfer, similar to the perspective of neoclassical economists. However, the focus is on an aspect of this technology transfer process usually neglected by economists, namely, how such innovations spread. Economics, with its assumptions of free and perfect information and rational maximizing economic factors, mostly sidesteps this whole question of diffusion of innovations.

Part of this literature theorizes that the adoption of new technologies requires institutional and structural changes in traditional societies to alter the role of the family, religion, and culture in a way that will yield the specialization, mobility, and rationality necessary for a market economy and growth (see Golding [1974] for a critical view). Communications systems are again seen in this light as quite similar to educational systems in that they provide information and produce attitude changes that are thought to be conducive to what is viewed as the necessary modernization of societies. The work of Lerner (1958) has been most influential and centers around an elaboration of the relationship of urbanization, literacy, and mass media exposure to development, which is conceived of as some aggregative societal participation concept involving political, economic, and psychological manifestations. Lerner hypothesizes that the urbanization process leads to a rise in literacy, which, in turn, fosters the development of mass media (exposure to which may increase literacy). Lerner argues that the oral-based traditional communication system, characterized as hierarchical, status-based, prescriptive, and small-group oriented, must give way to modern ones, which can be characterized more as professionally based, descriptive, and mass oriented. Social development in the form of greater GNP per capita, political participation, and other indicators of modernity then follows from the diffusion of innovative ideas and attitudes via urbanization, literacy, and mass media exposure. Within this framework, the rural, agricultural sector of the economy exists primarily as the population and food source for growing urban areas.

The perspective above closely parallels that of the industrial-based growth economist framework described earlier, with a similar role envisioned for the rural populace. Those economists who argued that development needed human capital in the form of threshold literacy rates and specific ratios of enrollments among primary, secondary, and higher education (Bowman and Anderson 1965; Blaug 1970) were matched by communications theorists who argued for threshold rates of urbanization and literacy as necessary to mass media growth and consequent development.

The process Lerner describes can be viewed as operating not only at the societal level but also at the individual level. The focus in much recent communications research is thus directed to the individual level, looking at the process by which individuals adopt innovations. This literature has been influenced considerably by supporting sociological and psychological theories; the former (Rogers and Shoemaker 1971) looking at stages in the adoption process (for example, awareness, interest, evaluation, trial, and acceptance) and the latter looking at the operation of role models and personality attributes that foster innovative behavior (McClelland 1961). Communications researchers in this area focus on the impact on innovation adoption of sets of variables that describe either types of communications contacts or types of individual psychological orientations—such as empathy, cosmopolitanism, or the number of newspapers in the home. With the more recent interest in agricultural development, the focus of study for the communications researcher was easily shifted. Given an approach that examines the adoption of innovations by individuals, one can as easily study the communications system properties and psychological traits that foster the adoption of agricultural innovations as innovations in other sectors (Rogers 1969).

This approach to the role of communications in development fits well with that of human capital theorists and with early neoclassicists who pointed to the important role of entrepreneurship, but who never began to examine the process by which entrepreneurs arise. The more recent economist focus on the effects of an individual's allocative abilities on productivity and development (Schultz 1975) is clearly supplemented by a communications literature that investigates the characteristics of successful allocators, assumed to be those who are early adopters of new technologies (see Chapter 5).

Again, the critiques of this literature have been many, and in a number of ways they parallel very closely the critiques of neoclassical economic theory as applied to development, agriculture, and education. Perhaps foremost, the increasing concern with equity has had its counterpart in communications research. The recent emphasis on the "communications gap" effect, the result of studies that report larger gains for higher-socioeconomic-status individuals from mass media systems (Donohue, Tichenor, and Olien 1975), has close parallels to the economic critiques of uneven, inequitable development, and to educational research showing larger knowledge gains and rates of return to education for students from higher-income families.

Concerns with the persistence of inequitable development and the lack of rapid social change predicted by communications specialists who promoted technology transfer have led many of these same researchers to question the traditional wisdom. Schramm and Lerner (1976) reflect on the disappointing performance of the dominant paradigm over the past decade. Rogers (1976), in an article titled "Communications and Development: The Passing of the Dominant Paradigm," examines the historical development of this conventional wisdom. He sees past mainstream communications research and policy in national development as reflecting the interrelated development of four principal forces: the industrial revolution in the United States and Europe; the extensive colonization of Latin America, Africa, and Asia; the quantitative empiricism of North American social science; and certain aspects of capitalist economic/political philosophy. Rogers views the primary failings of the dominant paradigm as rooted in its Western intellectual ethnocentrism, which is manifested in several assumptions: the inferiority of "underdevelopment," the universal applicability of development concepts, and the individual-blame logic that accompanies the communications research and policy focus on the new characteristics assumed to be needed by individuals for development.

These criticisms reflect the same changes that appear to be taking place in the orientation of the dominant view of the development process that was discussed earlier in this chapter. The literature is currently abounding with discussions of an emerging new model that is supposed to be "increasingly decentralized and user-oriented, one that pays attention to the needs and preferences of rural families, as well as to national production goals" (Kearl 1978, p. 3). Whyte (1977) argues that the new approach to the diffusion of innovation must begin with exploratory field research of what farmers do locally, not start with a technology to diffuse; integrate recommended new technologies with a total development strategy that pays attention to the access of farmers to new inputs to credit and to markets; reflect joint planning by agronomists and social scientists, not relegate the latter to the separate task of explaining "resistance to change"; and be predicated on active participation of farmers. From the perspective of what we may think of as this new orientation of the dominant paradigm, the inequities in past development strategies can be countered rather simply by directing interventions solely toward those in most need: that is, small farmers, slow adopters, or those with the least knowledge of new technologies. Indeed, in the same volume in which Rogers talks about the passing of the old paradigm, Röling, Ascroft, and Chege (1976) and Shingi and Mody (1976) present examples in Kenya and India of how such diffusion strategies may proceed more equitably.

The critiques and reorientation of the dominant paradigm have reflected the generally more fundamental criticisms voiced by a growing body of literature generated from Marxist and assorted "new left" perspectives that question the ahistorical concentration on the individual effects of communications interventions. Golding and Murdock (1976) present a scathing view of the standard communications research approach:

> How many chain diagrams linking sender-message-receiver have been presented as insightful theories, with the occasional addition of a loop going in the opposite direction called "feedback" as a sophisticated refinement? The more advanced of these "models" have a dotted line round the edge called "social context." Model building is not theory building, and basal sketches of this kind are not even adequate as models. [P. 8]

From this perspective, Lerner's theory is viewed as a mechanistic manipulation of structural variables with little, if any, understanding offered of the forces that affect urbanization, literacy, and the rise of mass media (Golding 1974).

Marxists point to the basis of the dominant communications paradigm in the functionalism theories of sociology (combined with a little behaviorist psychology) that view social institutions from a conservative bias. Such institutions are seen as functional to the extent that they contribute to the maintenance of a societal equilibrium. Thus, communications media are conceived of as a functional institution of socialization, as opposed to a legitimation device of an inegalitarian social system. From this perspective (which occurs in many respects with the conflict theories of sociology), Beltran (1976a) critiques the elitist bias of the diffusion theorist's two-step flow model in which innovations trickle down from "leaders" or "early adopters" to the masses.

Perhaps most fundamentally, Marxists criticize the dominant focus on audience response to communications systems as based on an unrealistic, idealist theory of social change, in which ideas are the motivating force for "progress." Change is seen as exogenously induced by new techniques and their transfer, and, therefore, the effects of communications systems can be studied independently of the generation of these motivating forces. To the contrary, Golding and Murdock (1976, p. 13) contend that "the primary task of mass communications research is not to explore the meanings of media messages but to analyze the social process through which they are constructed and interpreted and the context and pressures that shape and constrain these constructions." From a Marxist perspective, communication, like education, operates to maintain an ideological superstructure supportive of the vast inequalities between and within nations, as required by monopoly capitalism—any development such a structure can yield will likely be to the interest of the controlling elites.

The same authors argue that the Marxist framework above is "only a starting point":

> It is not sufficient simply to assert that the capitalistic base of the "culture industry" necessarily results in the production of cultural forms which are consonant with the dominant ideology. It is also necessary to demonstrate how this process of reproduction actually works by showing in detail how economic relations structure both the overall strategies of the cultural entrepreneurs and the concrete activities of the people who actually make the products the "culture industry" sells. [Pp. 18-19]

Thus, for example, the impact of communications systems can be better understood by studying the sources of media messages, reflecting the concentration of power and wealth and the accompanying control of the structure of the national and global communications industry. The value of the free flow of information implicitly assumed within much communications research is seen primarily as a tool by the powerful to maintain a structure of dependency.

Again, the Marxist paradigm should not be seen as a deterministic view of the influence of the materialist, capitalist organization of production. Williams (1973, p. 4) argues that the production relationships of capitalism determine cultural forms only in the sense of a "process of setting limits and exerting pressures." Nor should this view be seen as denying the individual a role in social change and development. The development of an individual's consciousness of the societal forces affecting that individual is seen as critical to social change. For example, Bordenave (1976), in an article specific to the communications of agricultural innovations, after rejecting the simplistic "transmission mentality" farmer, innovation, communication system model most researchers use, argues for the need to develop approaches of individual development more similar to that of Freire (1973). The outcomes of private and public sector policies, in communications or any other field, are not seen as predetermined in favor of the controlling capitalist (and landlord) but reflect the outcome of a struggle between competing classes, albeit ones with unequal power. Nonetheless, most of these critics would argue that the emerging reorientation of the dominant paradigm toward local needs and participation, although perhaps well intentioned, is unrealistic. Primarily, it is still idealist in conception; does not take into account the root causes of the situation of the poorer, smaller farmers; and implicitly assumes the goodwill of the more politically and economically powerful classes in allowing the more impoverished classes to "catch up."

Summary and Implications

This review was begun to examine the approaches that can be taken to evaluate the economic benefits that result from the efforts to promote agricultural development using mass media communications technologies for formal and nonformal educational system activities. In this section, the principal theoretical perspectives that bear on this issue have been explored. It has become clear that such issues are not simply the domain of economists but involve the theories that have been generated from a number of social science disciplines and fields of study. What is most striking to the authors from this review is that two contrasting, but rather internally consistent and coherent, perspectives emerge across a wide range of literature dealing with economic development, education, and communications, each of which has quite different implications for studying the effect of ECT interventions on agricultural development.

The dominant paradigm reflects the relatively parallel conceptual frameworks that underlie most economic, education, and communications development research and policies. From this perspective, educational uses of communications media can contribute positively to societal development to the extent that they promote the productive abilities of the individual. Neoclassical economic theory makes explicit the connection that individuals' earnings and profits are measures of social benefits, but most other theories discussed at least implicitly rely on this belief.

The approach that mainstream economics takes to the evaluation of ECT efforts related to agricultural development complements that of the psychology/sociology-based communications research. The traditional, rather deterministic, economics view of input-output relationships in production processes has been supplemented in recent years by the realization that the decision-making role of human beings in such processes introduces uncertainty of production outcomes and the possibility of increasing output by making people better decision makers. Communication theorists' study of the process by which individuals adopt new ideas and techniques is clearly relevant to this approach.

There appears to be considerable room for further integration of these complementary approaches. It is likely that future research will see more communications theory in economics and more economics theory in communications. Although not done at present, it is easy to conceive of economists replacing or supplementing their educational variables in agricultural production functions by communications variables that reflect, for example, exposure to mass media rather than exposure to education alone (see Harker [1973] and Klees and Wells [1978] for preliminary efforts in this direction). It is also quite sensible to expect that communications researchers, in their efforts to make the rather simplistic models of the innovation adoption process currently in use more realistic, will include more economic variables as measures of motivating factors (Benito 1976). Even when the outcome of interest is knowledge gained (as opposed to agricultural output and profit), the economists' perspective that has resulted in the extensive analysis of knowledge production functions in education can clearly supplement existing analyses. The usual approach of policy makers to evaluation that asks economists to analyze costs and benefits and asks other researchers to study system effects is thus most likely dysfunctional to the interdisciplinary needs suggested by the above review. From the perspective of the dominant paradigm, promotion of these integrative efforts should improve our ability to evaluate the societal benefits of ECT strategies for agricultural development.

The other paradigm that emerges from our review reflects the base in Marxist theory underlying the critiques of traditional approaches to economic development and the specific role of education and communications systems. From this perspective, educational uses of communications technology for agricultural development must be viewed within a historical context in which conflict between classes with unequal power has led to uneven societal development. Marxist economists point out the basic failings and hidden-value assumptions of theories of economic efficiency that make the criteria generated to evaluate private and public sector activities of quite doubtful validity and legitimacy for deciding what represents societal benefits. Efficient for whom? is the question raised in a world where there are gainers and losers from every decision. This view is paralleled by Marxist sociologists and communications theorists. Elliott (1974) argues:

> "Society as a whole" or "basic human needs" are devices for obscuring or ignoring the issue of who controls society and who defines the way in which such needs are experienced and learned. The problem can even be formulated within the language of functionalism if we ask, functional or dysfunctional for whom? [P. 261]

It should be clear that Marxist theorists do not deny the possibility that individuals may privately gain from various education and communications policies and programs. Indeed, it is even possible that poor rural farmers may increase their output, income, and earnings through some interventions. But to sum up the monetary costs and benefits resulting from an intervention will not yield a measure of societal costs and benefits—if prices, wages, and profits do not reflect social value, it is not at all clear what such a sum signifies. Moreover, the conventional approach that evaluates the impact of ECT interventions within a framework that usually places boundaries around the intervention, isolating it from interaction with most of the rest of the social system, is likely to miss the most important facets of what is actually happening. In looking at such interventions, Marxists would argue that the central concerns must be the position and orientation of sponsoring agencies, the historical causes of the plight of the rural poor, the industrial and landed class interests that may be served by the intervention, and the long-term impact on the consciousness and relative position of the individuals and classes affected.

According to the predominant wisdom of science (social, natural, or physical), the mechanism for resolving the truth of competing theories is empirical investigation. The contrasting perspectives on the economic costs and benefits of ECT systems offered by the dominant and Marxist-based paradigms should, therefore, also be amenable to such resolution. The primary methodological approaches and tools that are available and have been used for empirical study will be examined in the following section.

METHODOLOGICAL APPROACHES

The basis of most empirical research is the scientific method, beginning with theory that leads to the formulation of testable hypotheses; these are then empirically tested, yielding results that may or may not support the initial theory and hypotheses. Within this framework, theory and method may be examined independently. Theories and hypotheses about social and natural phenomena can be generated from any disciplinary, group, or individual perspective. How best to test those hypotheses against real world data is a separate issue. This philosophical perspective on theory and method has therefore led to the development of research methodology as a separate field of study. To be sure, almost every discipline or area of study has its own specialists in research methodology. However, all are quite similar in approach; the major difference lies in the problems studied. Thus, although an investigation of the methods that can be used to evaluate ECT policies and programs involves the methods of many disciplines, the commonalities among these methods make the task more manageable. The primary interest here is in analyzing substantive questions, so the discussion of methods will not remain in the abstract. To understand the specifics of the methods most frequently used by economists, it is necessary to elaborate, in somewhat greater detail than undertaken in the previous section, the theory economists use to examine social benefits and costs.

Methodological Tools

Theories are basically explanations of cause-effect regularities that are hypothesized to exist in the world we observe around us. The theories discussed in the previous section are explanations of the relationships between education and communications activities and various aspects of rural development. The question of how to test a theory or hypothesis is the central question here. That is, for example, What constitutes evidence that education and communications activities improve agricultural productivity or individual well-being in rural regions? By and large, the current dominant scientific wisdom argues that most theories relating to the physical or social sciences can be examined by relatively objective, quantifiable procedures. Although quantification may not be required from this perspective, in recent years most social science disciplines have increasingly identified it with objectivity and rigor. This has certainly been true in economics, sociology, communications, and education, and this trend seems to be underway even in such fields as history or anthropology. Here and in the next section of this chapter, the focus will be on quantifiable empirical research; further discussion of this question will be presented later.

Most scientists would argue that the best way to establish the truth or fallacy of a particular hypothesis is through a carefully controlled experiment. However, it is practically difficult and often morally problematic to "control" all variables other than the desired manipulation. Moreover, even when controls are feasible, the political significance of the results of a controlled experiment is usually doubtful, because the policies recommended are implemented in uncontrolled environments. Although quasi- and "natural" experimental situations have been the basis for some ECT evaluations, such designs usually lack the ability to discriminate what it is about an ECT package that has an effect. Furthermore, in most cases there are nontreatment factors that intervene between the initial and the end treatments, calling into doubt any conclusions of effectiveness. Thus, despite the theoretical utility of experimentation, given the difficulties discussed, the development issues need to be, and usually are, examined by other means.

Perhaps the most common method of making causal inferences is based on the observation of association between different variables of interest. In the world around us we observe individuals with differing amounts and types of formal and nonformal education, with access to different types of media, with different occupations, different knowledge and attitudes, and earning different incomes. We observe different countries and manufacturing firms or farms with different output and productivity, employing or run by people with different attributes. Associations between any two or more of these variables may form the basis for inferring that one, in fact, caused the other. Early development theories oriented toward industrial growth reflected, at least in part, the casually observed historical association of the industrial revolution with economic growth. Similarly, the belief in the influence of education on development reflected the associations observed between higher education and higher income and productivity among individuals and nations. Whole and partial linear correlations have been the primary tool in the study of such empirical associations. However, the oft-repeated dictum that correlation is not causation, and the almost infinite number of alternative explanations of the data, has led most economists to dismiss such simplistic evidence as a source of theoretical support. Relying on improvements in statistical theories, methods, and data processing, economists focus most heavily on the techniques of regression analysis that are believed to be able to separate various causal influences if a complete, valid model of the system being studied is specified and adequately operationalized.

Communication theorists and researchers in other social science disciplines would likely be characterized by economists as somewhat lacking in methodological sophistication. For the most part, such research relies on correlation techniques, partialing out the effects of intervening variables and assuming that a statistically significant partial correlation can provide meaningful support for a theoretical hypothesis. Econometrics—the study of empirical methods by economists—generally argues that such an approach cannot accurately separate causal influences within a complex system. Variables omitted from consideration will likely bias the results, and the correlation measure is considered a very inadequate estimator of effect (compared with a regression coefficient) when, as is often the case, included variables are related to one another. Even strong partial correlations usually have a multitude of conflicting causal explanations. A small partial correlation may be masking a strong, even linear, causal input. Furthermore, nonlinear relationships will either not be measured or will be distorted.

Almost all of the diffusion of innovations literature can be critiqued extensively from this perspective. The path analytic approach of the sociologist, now diffusing to other disciplines, is considered more reasonable because it parallels the causal modeling of economists. Again, the focus of this critique of correlational empirical approaches (several examples are included in this book) is not that they pay no attention to theory but that if social process theories are available in these disciplines, they cannot be examined by purely correlational analysis—a model that includes all important factors, hypothesizing the specific causal pattern theorized, must be estimated by regression techniques that allow all relevant variables to be included simultaneously.

Clearly, there are significant problems with regression analysis as well, which economists have long recognized and studied; the point of view generally taken is that, despite the problems, it is the best procedure around. However, the ability of regression analysis to separate causal influences from observed gross associations has severe limitations, because the resulting measures of impact will be inaccurate unless many rather unrealistic conditions hold. For example: a theory is elucidated that includes not only all the major causal factors but also their interrelationships; the theory is operationalized accurately in that the variables measured are valid proxies of the conceptual causal factors; the measured (nondummy) variables have certain mathematical properties that make quantitative differences meaningful; the quantitative, operationalized, functional relationship estimated must be an accurate reflection of the true interrelationships between variables; and any factors that do affect the phenomenon of interest but are not included in the model have no association with any of the included variables. Clearly, this list of conditions foreshadows some of the failings of the dominant paradigm's approach to social science that was discussed earlier. These limitations will be comprehensible after discussing, below, how economists attempt to use regression analysis methods to study ECT-related issues.

Economics Applications

As was discussed in the beginning of this chapter, neoclassical economics focuses its attention on the efficiency with which resources are allocated in a society. The role of education and communications activities in development is examined through empirically investigating certain types of resource allocation questions. How do educational resources affect such educational outcomes as cognitive achievement, attitude formation, and adoption of new behaviors? How much of the productivity differences between workers or farmers with different educational levels are actually caused by educational differences? What specifically does education do that can yield income or productivity differences? Although this chapter has focused this illustrative set of empirical research questions on the role of education, the same questions could be posed for communication. Substituting "types of communications activities" or "access and exposure to media" for "education," the question would concern the impact of resources allocated to different types of communications activities and their effects on economists' criteria of individual and societal well-being.

It should be noted that there are two levels of focus that economists apply to these development issues—a macro look at the impacts of education and communications policies on overall societal development, and a more micro look at such impacts on individual units operating within the society, such as individuals, firms, or farms. This section concentrates on the microanalytic aspects of economic theory and empirics, because these are most directly relevant to the evaluation of specific ECT programs. Nonetheless, the two perspectives are both important. Indeed, questions of national economic growth have to be looked at almost on a more aggregate level, because the efficiency of individual operating units within an economy does not necessarily guarantee a high rate of economic growth. All micro units may be efficient, but, if resources are largely devoted to producing goods and services for present consumption instead of investment, the rate of economic growth may be low.

This section, then, examines how neoclassical economists apply their theories to the study of three specific topics relevant to the impact of ECT projects and policies on agricultural and rural development: the determinants of individual earnings, the determinants of agricultural productivity, and the determinants of agricultural knowledge, attitudes, and practices. Prior to examining these specific topics, however, a closer look must be taken at neoclassical concepts of efficiency, cost-effectiveness, and cost-benefit comparisons, as these form the underpinning for all three issues.

As discussed earlier, neoclassical economics is concerned mostly with the efficiency with which resources are allocated between competing possibilities. Although economists have differentiated between several types of efficiency, the most all-encompassing concept of efficiency is labeled <u>Pareto efficiency</u>. If a society is Pareto efficient, the resources it has at its disposal cannot be reallocated to make one person better off without making someone else worse off. That is, there is no waste in production, for, if there were, production could be increased without incurring any resource costs and the additional output could improve the welfare of at least some individuals without taking anything away from others.

No waste in overall societal production really means that individual decision makers, in their private and work-related decisions, try not to waste resources. In a competitive market economy, which is usually the assumed state of affairs for neoclassical economists, the prices of all goods, services, and resources represent their societal value, and profits represent net social benefits. Thus, if manufacturers or farmers operate their businesses to produce the maximum value of output for the least cost—that is, they maximize profits—they are contributing to the achievement of a Pareto-efficient societal state. Although the public sector does not ordinarily have profit maximization as its motivating directive, economists argue that public sector decision makers should substitute an explicit analysis of the benefits and costs of any activity as its means of evaluating the alternative activities that it might undertake.

This type of efficiency reasoning underlies the neoclassical economic approach to an evaluation of educational activities through its impact on individual earnings. Private individuals are viewed as undertaking education to maximize their private returns on the investment, an important component of which is the monetary benefits that accrue to them through increases in earnings. The public sector can evaluate the worth of its investment in education by comparing the earnings benefits resulting from education with the costs incurred (which are considered the total of all private and public costs incurred, including forgone earnings). Private earnings are viewed as a measure of social benefit because, under competitive markets, prices reflect social value; thus, wages are a measure of the social productivity of labor.

This evaluation approach to the economically efficient use of educational resources requires that one estimate the impact of different amounts and types of education on earnings to compute benefit measures that, along with cost information, should guide social policies. The preferred method for determining education's impact on earnings is regression analysis applied to data gathered from longitudinal or cross-sectional surveys. Experimentation is unlikely to be socially or practically possible, and various correlational techniques do not permit a reasonable determination of causal impact, as was discussed in the previous section. To use regression analyses to examine education's impact on earnings, one needs to elaborate a theoretical model that includes all the relevant variables that cause earnings variations, quantify all these variables, hypothesize the correct mathematical form of the functional relationship between these variables, and then gather data on which to estimate the model. Unfortunately, social science's present grasp of why most individual characteristics vary in a society—be it income, education, personality, preferences, and the like—is quite rudimentary, and the ability to rigorously quantify them and theorize their precise functional relationship is almost nonexistent.

As a consequence, most studies of earnings functions use a single linear-form equation, with individual earnings or income in a particular year as the dependent variable and a grab bag of assumed independent variables—such as the number of years of education attained, the educational level and income of the student's family, some measure of ability or intelligence, marital state, and years of work experience. The regression coefficient of the education variable is the measure of the benefits impact of additional education on earnings in a given year. If the data could be gathered on the same sample of individuals over the entire working life, one could run similar regressions for each year and examine the impact of education on earnings over time, which is simply the succession of resulting regression coefficients. Some measure or guesswork concerning this trend in education's impact is necessary, because to compute the rate of return (to the individual or to the society) of educating individuals, its influence must be projected over the entire working life of the individual.

One can also use this approach to evaluate different types of education programs by gathering earnings and other variable data on individuals who did or did not attend any particular type of program, such as vocational education or a nonformal education program. Usually these types of education variables are treated as zero-one, attend-not attend, dummy variables; again, the regression coefficient is viewed as a measure of the causal impact of education after controlling for all other relevant differences between individuals.

Although the examination of education's influence on earnings is perhaps the most popular method used to study the economic benefits of education, it is most frequently used within urban labor market settings, rather than within rural farming regions. This is not to say that this approach is irrelevant to the evaluation of education and communications policies in agricultural and rural development. For example, rural education may develop and select those individuals who can contribute to the expansion of urban industrial activity. Part of the benefits of rural education can then be examined in terms of its impact on rural-urban migration, and the success in the cities of its graduates. Also, one may use this approach to educational investment evaluation where there exists a rural wage-labor market. Many small farmers supplement their farming income through other work, and education and communications strategies may influence the earnings of these individuals. Hence, this may be an important area for study and policy.

The above discussion notwithstanding, recently economists have considered it preferable to examine the benefits of education through a direct analysis of its influence on productivity. This is the result, in part, of economists' having a more well-developed theory of the determinants of production than of the determinants of earnings. Also, it allows one to sidestep the questions of whether earnings measure productivity. Moreover, it is most relevant to this study's central topic of interest, because many agricultural development strategies have been oriented toward improving the productivity of farmers. To understand how this agricultural production function approach has been applied, the discussion of efficiency with which the examination of earnings functions was introduced must be continued.

Given that the goal of policy derived from neoclassical economics is primarily to ensure the achievement of a Pareto-optimal societal state, economists become concerned with the extent to which the behavior of individuals and firms contributes to this goal. Firms or farms that maximize their profits will foster this state of societal efficiency, given that the other assumptions of the perfectly competitive world hold. To profit maximize, firm and farm managers must know two things: the technical and organizational combination of inputs that will yield the maximum combination of the outputs they are producing and the prices of those inputs and outputs, so they can choose the alternative that yields the most profit among the feasible input-output possibilities. This distinction gives rise to the analysis of primarily two types of efficiency (specific to the firm level, as compared to the global criterion of Pareto efficiency) that relate to the ability of the enterprise to achieve profit maximization: technical efficiency and allocative efficiency.

A firm is technically efficient if it produces the maximum feasible output given the set of inputs it uses. Technical efficiency is often considered an engineering problem in that it pertains to the knowledge of particular techniques for converting inputs to outputs. Leibenstein (1966, p. 407), in his pioneering article on technical efficiency, gives four reasons why firms may not be technically efficient: "(a) contracts for labor are incomplete,* (b) not all factors of production are marketed, (c) the production function is not completely specified or known, and (d) interdependence and uncertainty lead competing firms to cooperate tacitly with each other in some respects, and to imitate each other with respect to technique, to some degree." Moreover, firms may not be technically efficient if the motivation to maximize profits is absent or weak.

The allocative (or price) efficiency concept is concerned directly with the firm's relationship to the market for inputs and outputs. A firm is allocatively efficient if it chooses to purchase that set of inputs and outputs that maximizes its profits, given whatever knowledge it has with regard to production function relationships (that is, regard-

---

*This realization forms the basis for the distinction between Marxist concepts of labor and labor power and their view of the necessity for particular organization forms to control alienated workers under capitalism (Gintis 1976).

less of whether it is technically efficient). Neoclassical economics demonstrates that, given certain assumptions, a firm is allocatively efficient if it employs each input up to the point where the value of its marginal product (the output produced by the addition of the last input unit purchased) equals the price of that input. For example, consider a firm with two inputs, capital and labor, combining them in such a way that the value of the marginal product of labor is greater than the price paid. If this were so, a firm could hire another laborer for a cost lower than the amount that worker would contribute to profits; and if it were rational and profit maximizing, it would do so. If, as economists generally argue, the marginal product of any single input diminishes as more is added, eventually the firm would stop hiring additional labor (or capital) at just the point where the wage equaled the value of the marginal product (going beyond that point would mean that hiring a worker would reduce profits). Both allocative and technical efficiency are required for a firm to be maximizing profits— this is sometimes referred to as "economic efficiency."

To determine whether firms are economically efficient, it is necessary to estimate the production function for the particular process in which they are engaged, then noting the extent to which the firm operates on the production function and the extent to which they choose to operate at that particular point on the production function for which the prices of inputs and outputs they face yield the maximum profits. The empirical key to this analysis is the correct estimation of the true production function.

Realistically, one can expect that not all firms will be technically efficient. Differences in motivation and other usually unmeasured inputs (for example, managerial talent), differences in knowledge, and differences in nonmarketed firm outputs (for example, working environment) will all likely lead to the production of different output from the observable inputs. Recognizing these sources of real or apparent technical inefficiency, a methodological procedure sometimes used by economists is to estimate the production function for an industry or particular process by examining separately the data for "best practice" firms, that is, those firms that seem to be getting the most output out of their inputs.

Regardless of whether one tries to discern this production frontier (the term used to refer to the true production function, by which technically efficient firms maximize output for given inputs) or the average production function of all firms being studied, the primary methodological tool economists use is, again, regression analysis. As before, one must begin with a theoretical model of the process, the variables involved, and their interrelationship. Although, sometimes, it is possible to utilize engineering knowledge of technological interrelationships to construct such a function, most processes are usually too complex to allow for this detailed, a priori specification. Thus, in most cases, economists rely on their general constructions of theories of the production process, which, as mentioned earlier, are considerably more developed than their theories of the process by which individual earnings are determined. Most generally, economists view the production of any output, especially in agriculture, to be a function of the land, labor resources, and other nonhuman resources, generally termed capital.

The work of Welch (1970) has been very influential in elaborating the role of education in production and how to look at it methodologically. Although Welch's analysis of what he calls the "worker" and "allocative" effects of education was described earlier, that approach will be reviewed here in the context of how to examine these effects empirically, because this is probably the major specification of neoclassical economics' view of how to evaluate ECT activities. First, Welch suggests that one may simply want to look at the direct effect of better-educated workers and managers on output produced (his "worker" effect). In this case, one may estimate a production function, as discussed above, with education included as a specific variable, of the general form

$$Q = q (X, E) \tag{1}$$

where Q is output, E is education, and X stands for all other resource inputs (which, of course, must be individually specified when estimating the function). Once specified and estimated, the resulting marginal product of education represents the "worker" effect.

However, according to Welch, this formulation does not capture all the effects of education on output. In particular, it misses what might be thought of as the increased managerial ability, which may accrue to better-educated firm managers, to purchase the best combination of inputs, to use them most effectively, and to allocate them among competing uses. To get at the effect of education on the ability to allocate resources among competing uses, Welch considers the case of a firm that produces two or more outputs. One can then estimate the total revenue (R) function, where

$$R = r (X, E) \tag{2}$$

If the X's are not specified according to how much of each input is devoted to the production of each different output (for example, one just specifies the total amount of labor used for producing all outputs), the resulting marginal product of education, in effect, picks up interfirm differences in the ability to allocate each input between the outputs produced so as to maximize total revenue (one aspect of Welch's "allocative" effect of education), in addition to the direct worker effect of education.

Finally, to get at the remaining aspects of education's influence on productivity, one may estimate a value-added function, where value added (V) refers to the total revenue of the firm, less the costs of purchased inputs. Welch argues, in effect, that one should intentionally misspecify this function as

$$V = V (Z, E) \tag{3}$$

where Z is a subset of all inputs (X), other than education, composed of those inputs at the disposal of the firm that are not purchased in the short run (for example, in agriculture one might consider land and some portions of capital as fixed inputs in the short run). By eliminating purchased inputs from this value-added function, Welch reasons that the marginal product of education will pick up, in addition to the two effects discussed above, differences in the ability to purchase the correct amount of inputs to maximize value added.

Thus, Welch's total estimate of the "allocative" and "worker" effects of education can be seen as picking up the contribution that education makes to the total ability of firms to be technically and allocatively efficient (that is, to maximize profits). Welch points out that moving beyond the simpler, direct effect of the educated worker on production is especially important in looking at agricultural situations that are in a state of flux, where allocative skills strengthened by education may be very important (Schultz 1975).

Although Welch's formulation is not the only approach neoclassical economists use to examine the productive impact of education, it gives a picture of the type of theoretical reasoning employed. To use regression analysis to estimate such effects empirically, there is the need for theory to specify not only which variables are to be included but also how they are interrelated and how they should be measured. The linear functional form most common to earnings function estimation is generally rejected for production function analysis, because it assumes that inputs operate independently and that the marginal product of any input is constant (that is, one more unit of any input, regardless of the amount already employed of that and other inputs, will always yield the same increase in output). Most common is the use of a multiplicative functional form, which allows for the economist's usual assumption of diminishing marginal products for increases in any input and for interaction among the inputs included, as exemplified by

$$Q = A K^{B_1} L^{B_2} E^{B_3} \tag{4}$$

where Q is the quantity of physical output produced; K is the amount of capital used; L, the amount of labor employed; and E, the laborer's level of education.

Of course, whether this particular functional form truly describes any particular production process is an empirical question. A number of economists have questioned the general applicability of the Cobb-Douglas function (as this multiplicative form is often termed), because, although it allows for diminishing marginal products, it forces the output elasticities of each input to be constant. (The elasticity between two variables is defined as the percentage change in one variable resulting from a 1 percent change in the other. In equation 4 the B's represent the respective output elasticities of each input, and they are constant regardless of the level of any or all inputs. For example, if $B_3 = 0.40$, it would mean that a 1.0 percent increase [or decrease] in the amount of educated labor would yield a 0.4 percent increase [or decrease] in the amount of output produced, given any value for K, C, and E.) Moreover, critical to theory of the ability of the firm to respond to price changes in input factors is the ability to substitute one input for another. It can be shown that the Cobb-Douglas form assumes that the elasticity of substitution between any two inputs equals one (that is, a 1 percent increase in one input yields a 1 percent decrease in the other). This assumption has little theoretical basis, and empirical evidence often seems to contradict it. For these reasons, some economists argue that a different functional specification should often be used—a constant elasticity-of-substitution function. In practice, this form is difficult to estimate when more than a few inputs are specified.

Many empirical studies of agricultural and industrial production have been undertaken from these perspectives. Lockheed, Jamison, and Lau (forthcoming) provide a recent review of this literature. They generally conclude that the weight of evidence indicates that both formal and nonformal education activities are an important input to agricultural production. Nonetheless, it should be noted that the considerable variety exhibited by these studies, in terms of which inputs are specified and how they are measured, is an indication of a lack of ability to quantify precisely the production process relationship. Moreover, although a number of studies do use physical output as the dependent variable, many of them use cost measures of inputs, instead of their physical quantity. This adds to the chance of misspecification of the function, because the theory described above bases its specification of the production function on the relationships between physical inputs. Further, despite the reasonableness of Welch's general theory, when revenue or value added is used as a dependent variable, we cannot expect the same Cobb-Douglas function to apply, because it is based on physical output.

Some economists have derived the functional form that a profit or value-added function would take, given that the production function is of the Cobb-Douglas type, and have used this to examine directly the impact of agricultural inputs on profits and questions of relative technical and allocative efficiency (Lau and Yotopoulos 1971). However, the additional information necessary to estimate such profit functions (in particular, the different prices that different farmers face), the additional assumptions required to use the profit function form (for example, that all farmers try to profit maximize), and the very specific and probably unrealistic assumptions of the type and form of inefficiencies that do exist between farms—all serve to make such an approach, difficult empirically and conceptually, of uncertain validity. Nonetheless, because all approaches suffer from similar defect, it is likely that there will be increased use of production, revenue, and profit functions to evaluate education and communications activities.

The third and final type of economist evaluation that will be mentioned in this section is that related to the impact of education and communications on individual knowledge, attitudes, and practices. The two previous approaches have been oriented toward translating such activities into a monetary benefit measure of their individual and societal impact, through either earnings or production. Economists strongly favor monetary benefit analysis, because, when compared with monetary costs, such evaluation offers a relatively unambiguous guide to policy formulation. Nonetheless, a project is often evaluated before it has had sufficient time to have an impact on individual earnings and productivity, and, also, there is often an interest of policy makers in evaluating the impact on what economists would mostly consider intermediate outcomes of the program—the resulting change in knowledge, attitudes, and practices of individuals.

Over the past decade and a half, economists have conducted a considerable amount of studies with this orientation, mostly concerned with the production of cognitive knowledge in formal schooling situations. This approach is generally applicable to an examination of attitude and practice change and is equally relevant to nonformal educational activities or communications system effects. Essentially, economists have viewed the school's production of cognitive knowledge in the same manner they view a firm's production of marketable outputs. In this country, there is a rather extensive educational production function literature that has examined this topic in both theory and practice. Unfortunately, this has led to a grab bag of measured factors to be included in such studies as input measures: IQ and various teacher and school characteristics—such as teachers' years of experience, teaching style, the age of the school building, the type of facilities provided, and various background measures of the students' environment. A linear relationship between these variables is usually hypothesized, although other functional formulations have been occasionally tested. Given the imprecise formulation, the inconsistency of the results obtained should not be too surprising. Few, if any, specific factors have shown a consistent relationship to educational achievement.

Although in all three theoretical and methodological approaches reviewed in this section the focus has been on the evaluation of educational activities, it should be apparent that they are equally applicable to the study of communications and ECT activities. If one believes that communications systems can be as much a source of human capital formation as can education systems, the former will have an impact on earnings and production. Therefore, earnings and production functions studies could include variables that describe access and exposure to those aspects of a communications system or program being evaluated. Similarly, the educational production function approach can be applied to any type of program that affects knowledge, attitudes or practices. In the following section, a more critical view of these approaches will be taken.

Critiques and Alternatives

Earlier in this section the authors described the experimental, correlational, and regression-analysis-based approaches most common to social science research; later, the specifics of economists' use of regression analysis for educational evaluation were elaborated. The authors then discussed difficulties with using the experimental method to examine most educational issues. Next considered were the correlational approaches that are used to study phenomena observed in uncontrolled environments and to correct for "intervening" variables in quasi-experimental field research. The quite significant theoretical inadequacies of this approach were highlighted: it yields no measure of impact, which is what is needed for evaluation; and there are compelling reasons to believe that the measures of association used are almost always biased upward or downward. With these criticisms in mind, the primary focus was on the methodological basis and economic theory necessary to utilize regression analysis for educational evaluation, because most economists consider it to be the best practical tool for separating and estimating the causal impact of variables in which they are interested. Although there was reference in the discussion to some of the limitations of this analysis, this section will begin with a more complete and systematic look at the problems with regression analysis and its specific application to education and communications system evaluation. Some alternative approaches to empirical research will then be looked at briefly.

As was described earlier, for regression analysis to generate accurate estimations of any causal impacts, at least three principal conditions must be met. There must be a theory that specifies a complete causal model, including all relevant causal variables. The variables must be quantified in a rigorous manner. Finally, theory must indicate the manner in which these quantified variables are related to one another. If these conditions are not met, the question that follows is, How inaccurate will the results be? Unfortunately, there does not seem to be a clear-cut answer. For any study, there are always reasons to support the arguments that the regression coefficients are both overstated and understated. There appears to be no reliable means in any particular case to resolve the direction or the magnitude of the bias. To understand more fully the potential sources of this bias, the use of regression analysis in agricultural production studies is critically examined below. This discussion does not consider earnings and educational production studies, but the same types of criticisms apply.

In judging the applicability of regression analysis to agricultural production function estimation, there must be a return to the question of how adequately the economic theory allows specification of the model. First, the common use of a Cobb-Douglas function to relate inputs to outputs is likely to represent the exact production process specification for few, if any, particular agricultural systems. Alternative functional forms have been posited, but it is unclear how to choose between them other than by goodness of empirical fit (highest R^2)—a poor criterion, because the choice is supposed to be made by a priori theory. It is probable that forcing the estimation into one of the few general functional forms used yields biased estimations of impact, although the extent and direction of bias is usually unclear.

Second, the selection and measurement of the input and output variables are generally not rigorously defined a priori. Yet, according to regression analysis theory and economic theory, these judgments may not be made arbitrarily or biased regression coefficients will be obtained. For example, if the economic theory specifies a Cobb-Douglas relationship between total physical inputs and outputs, the same functional form cannot be used (without making additional assumptions) to look at dependent variables, such as output per acre, revenue from several crops, profits, and profits per acre, as many studies have done.

Input variable specification is an equally difficult problem. Instead of using the many measures of physical inputs in the production function, economists often aggregate these inputs by their prices and use their costs as an input measure—this is often the case for measures of capital inputs. Yet, theoretically, there is no way to aggregate such inputs by price and have the resulting measure fit accurately into a production function formulated in terms of physical relation-ships. Moreover, even if there is a willingness to accept cost mea-sures, or even if a physical measure is used, economists have pointed out that it is not the total stock of capital that is relevant; what must be measured is the flow of services that the farmer gets from it during the production period studied (Yotopoulos 1967). Different farmers may get different uses out of animals or tractors, for exam-ple, but in most studies it is usually assumed to be the same for all farmers. Similarly, measures of educational inputs, which are criti-cal to our topic of interest, are poorly specified. The number of years of formal schooling attained, dummy variables to measure at-tendance or nonattendance in a nonformal educational program, and the number of agricultural extension contacts—all are clearly inade-quate measures of whatever aspects it is of education that contribute to productivity.

Furthermore, cross-sectional studies almost always ignore weather. Nor does any agricultural production function study include a measure of the farmer's intelligence or abilities, although omission of them in earnings or educational production functions biases the re-sults. With regard to these input specification problems, it is impor-tant to realize that the mishandling of any one input does not just af-fect the impact measure of that input but can bias some or all of the regression coefficients obtained.

A third general problem is that agricultural production relation-ships are considerably more complex than can be expressed within a single equation. For example, it is likely that the levels of certain types of inputs used, such as fertilizer or capital equipment for which the farmer must go into debt, are influenced by expected production and profit. If Benito's (1976) analysis of farmers' adoption of new techniques is correct, expectations of output affect adoption and prob-ably even the motivation of the farmer. This implies that both recur-sive and simultaneous equation models need to be estimated to get a picture of total effects and accurate measures of impact.

Fourth, it is important to observe that economists' models of agricultural production typically ignore the processes in which farm-ers engage, for example, how to clear the land, how to apply fertiliz-er, and how to dispose of crop residues. Production functions in-clude measures of the amount of inputs—such as land, labor, and capital—but not usually measures of how these inputs are actually combined. It should be clear, however, that aggregate specifications of the number of days of human labor masks differences in how that labor is applied to plowing, seeding, fertilizing, harvesting, and the like.

Fifth, the efficiency and motivational assumptions often made in economic analyses of agricultural activities are likely to be unrealistic. If the technical efficiency assumption usually made in physical production function analysis is untrue, the resulting estimation is based on a mixture of different inefficient utilizations of resources and the results will not likely be a sensible description of anyone's behavior. When inefficiencies are taken into account, their nature must be so specified by theory as to also be an unrealistic model, again yielding inaccurate results. The use of profit functions, assuming a Cobb–Douglas production function and profit maximization as a motive, is just as likely to misspecify reality.

Finally, because many impacts reflect long-term cumulative processes, it is necessary to engage in long-term studies, or to project estimated short-term impacts into the future, to arrive at cost-benefit measures of any possible policy intervention. Long-term studies are expensive and therefore rare, and projections must usually rely on many quite shaky assumptions. For policy recommendations, the need to believe that the future will behave reasonably like the past is essential to the use of almost all research results, but the problems inherent in this assumption should not be overlooked merely because they are common.

The response of researchers, in general, to these types of serious problems with regression analysis by and large has been both to accept and ignore them. For example, it is striking to find that relatively few empirical studies report the sensitivity of their results to alternative specifications of variables and functions, although many reasonable alternatives are almost always possible. It seems likely from casual observation that many researchers do "play around" in this way in their data analysis but only report the final specification used, despite this being considered a quite dubious procedure for hypothesis testing. One response to these problems seems to be a tacit agreement among most social scientists to place less faith in the magnitude of the regression coefficients than in their sign. That is, all that is usually claimed is that one variable has a statistically significant positive or negative (as opposed to no) influence on a dependent variable of interest, rather than claiming that a one-unit change in one variable will cause X units of change in the other. Unfortunately, it is this latter claim that is necessary to judge if a policy is worthwhile or should be implemented, certainly from a cost-effectiveness or cost-benefit view. Furthermore, the problems with regression analysis may lead one to doubt if even the sign of a variable's coefficient is correct. Despite all these problems, the view of most economists and many other social scientists seems to be based on the following premises:

That quantification is necessary for objective, scientific analysis of causal theories;

That experimentation is usually not feasible and, when it is, its results may not be applicable to policy in an uncontrolled environment;

That correlational and analysis of variance approaches suffer from all the faults of regression analysis and some additional ones of their own; and

That, therefore, regression analysis, despite its faults, is essentially "the only game in town."

This view, although dominant, is not uniformly held, and, in recent years, there has been an increasing critique of the basic tenets of quantification and objectivity. Starr (1974) discusses the "ideology of the positivist hedgehogs in social science," who never deviate from a straight and narrow—but distorted, according to Starr—view of empirical science. A view that allows quantitative data to,

> like the shadows in Plato's cave, . . . become more real than the world itself. . . . The repudiation of other forms of discourse, the neglect of validity in pursuit of reliability, the reification of data as things-in-themselves, the illusion of false precision—these are not by any means necessary aspects of empirical science. But they are frequent enough to warrant mention. [Pp. 409-10]

This negative view of common uses of quantitative data is supplemented by the view that most quantitative studies are mechanistic, devoid of context. Barton (1974) argues:

> The survey is a sociological meat-grinder, tearing the individual from his social context and guaranteeing that nobody in the study interacts with anyone else in it. It is a little like a biologist putting his experimental animals through a hamburger machine and looking at every hundredth cell through a microscope: anatomy and physiology get lost; structure and function disappear and one is left with cell biology. [P. 29]

Finally, there are basic questions raised about the objectivity of science in terms of the questions asked, the framework used to research them, and the analysis itself. Beltran (1976) quotes Berlo:

> The scientist's own values inherently are partial determinants of his work, the types of behavior he chooses to study. In that case, it is absurd to argue that scientific activity is value free, or should be. . . . The observer is part of any

observation. That statement should lead the scientist to
protect his observations as much as possible from his own
biases, but it should not cause him to rule out his own experiences and introspective ideas from his conceptual
framing of constructs and hypotheses. [P. 33]

All of these criticisms have combined to yield a growing interest in
more qualitative approaches to research. The human observation approaches that formerly characterized sociological research, and still
are the norm in fields such as anthropology and ethnography, are being discussed more broadly. In particular, the participant observation
approach to studying research problems has enjoyed a resurgence.
Within this methodology, the researcher attempts to suspend precon-
ceptions while participating in a process to be studied yet, at the same
time, maintain the role of outside observer. The dynamic tension
generated by playing these two roles is supposed to allow the researcher to ground theories in the social reality in which the researcher is participating (Glaser and Strauss 1967). Moreover, the
participant role fosters the ability of the researcher to understand
the meanings—from the viewpoint of the participant—of the behaviors
studied, an element usually neglected by quantitative, survey-oriented
research. Finally, it is thought that this method gives the researcher
considerably greater flexibility to study those aspects of the process
that appear critical to its understanding (Wilson 1977).

Other research methods that do not rely on quantitative technique to establish causal impact are available. The process by which
the historian builds up an understanding of why events occurred is essentially a qualitative, judgmental procedure. The approaches of the
psychoanalyst and the clinical psychologist to understanding individual
behavior and problems are, in many ways, similar. In essence,
such methods rely on the individual researcher to build what may be
thought of as a coherent, sensible story out of past events. Clearly,
one may build different stories out of the same events—as evidenced,
for example, by recent "revisionist" histories of education in the
United States (Spring 1971) or by the different interpretations of individual histories by different psychologists. From these perspectives,
proof is almost impossible to achieve, and the degree to which a certain theory is accepted as explanation depends on the judgment of
readers of the strength of its argument.

The major criticism of these more qualitative approaches centers on their supposed lack of objectivity, in that they are often seen
as allowing too great a latitude for the subjective, individual biases
of the researcher to enter. However, the more quantitative methods
may be viewed as also having considerable latitude for the researcher
to formulate the problem, to select which variables to include, how

to interrelate them, and how to interpret the results. If replicability
is what is really meant by objectivity, the endless debates on any
topic studied by quantitative research methods—as well as the inability of anthropologists, historians, and others to concur on particular
theoretical arguments—indicate that quantitative investigations of human behaviors are not necessarily more replicable than qualitative
studies. It seems that most quantitative and qualitative researchers
admit the need for both approaches as complements that may allow a
fuller understanding of complex processes when combined. What
most critics of quantitative research object to is the rigid, formula-
based approach to what one may count as evidence (for example, significant coefficients), and what type of research is considered to count
for professional status (Phillips, Costner, and Fennessey 1974).

In conclusion, although these criticisms of research methods
do not directly follow the neoclassical/Marxist economics debates
discussed earlier, there are important parallels. The dominant
economist, sociologist, communications theorist, and educational researcher perspectives generally focus on quantitative methods as
their sources of evidence to support causal theories. On the other
hand, Marx and Marxist theorists stress a more qualitative, historical, structural analysis, focusing on the analysis of class struggle
and internal system contradictions that are thought to generate social
change. Nonetheless, although Marxist theorists from disciplinary
perspectives other than economics may utilize a more qualitative approach, it is interesting to observe that Marxist economists seem to
have a more difficult time abandoning the dominant quantitative methodology. Many Marxist economists who use such techniques as regression analysis do so more out of the impetus of their initial neoclassical training, the reward structure of the academic world, and
the necessity of using the dominant methodology to have their arguments receive attention than out of any strong belief that such methods
can yield much support for causal hypotheses. At least in economics,
the dialectical, historical, materialist methods of Marxist tradition
are often considered tautological by neoclassicists who often urge
Marxists to develop better and more testable models so that empirics
will be able to establish the "truth" (Poirier 1977).

Summary and Implications

In this section, the authors have reviewed the main methods
social scientists use to gather empirical evidence to support their
theories. They also have examined the strengths and weaknesses of
the quantitative experimental, correlational, and regression analysis
approaches, paying particular attention to economists' uses of the

latter. Also briefly considered were aspects of some qualitative approaches to research. The main points of this section will be an examination of how these methods apply to the evaluation of ECT activities.

Given the discussion in this section, it seems likely that, in the future, considerably more evaluations will use regression analysis, and that most quantitative-oriented researchers would argue that this should be the case. Regression analysis approaches to the evaluation of the effects and benefits of agriculture-oriented ECT activities will probably take several related directions. First, it seems likely that more use will be made of the type of analysis economists have applied to the study of the earnings, productivity, and knowledge generated by education, which was discussed in detail earlier. On the benefits side, the agricultural production function approach seems better than earnings function studies, because the theory of the former is more developed and wage-labor markets are not extensive in rural areas. However, where ECT project participants enter into work for wages, earnings function approaches will be considered more reasonable. It is also likely that the educational production function approach will replace the analysis of partial correlations (or of variance) in looking at how ECT activities affect rural individuals' knowledge, attitudes, and practices. Sociology and communications research perspectives can supplement this approach in that their focus on the adoption process brings into question the usual single equation model of economic theory. It therefore seems likely that more effort will be put into devising simultaneous or recursive equations to model the process being studied.

According to the dominant, quantitative research paradigm, the shift to the regression-analysis-based evaluation hypothesized above will be viewed as an improvement, given the difficulties with experimental and correlational approaches. However, although this is true according to the research methodology considerations discussed in "Methodological Approaches," the problems with regression analysis (as discussed in the section that followed) raise considerable doubts concerning the extent of this improvement. Although, in theory, regression analysis is considerably better than correlational analysis, the conditions required for regression analysis to give accurate results rarely, if ever, hold in practice. Thus, in practice there are usually good reasons to argue that regression coefficient measures of impact are both biased upward and downward, which leads to the conclusion that they are erroneous in an indeterminable fashion. It is therefore not clear whether, in practice, more faith can be put in the regression coefficients of a several-variable, complex equation system derived from theory than in the coefficients of a much simpler linear model with only two or three variables.

More qualitative approaches to ECT evaluation may offer a greater potential for understanding the social system phenomenon. Personal observation or participation by an ECT system researcher may be quite useful in studying such topics as how information spreads in a rural society, how farmers get access to agricultural inputs, or what agricultural processes they actually engage in. Historical and sociological research based on qualitative procedures, such as examining documents or interviewing participants in depth, may increase understanding of effects and benefits by studying the process by which an ECT system was formed or is operating. None of these approaches yields the measures of impact that are needed by the usual economist cost-effectiveness and cost-benefit analysis of policies; but, given the difficulties with quantitative analyses, they may present a more believable story concerning the consequences of an ECT system. Moreover, in concept, the cost-effectiveness and cost-benefit criteria of economics do not necessarily require quantification. Whether intuitive cost-effectiveness and cost-benefit judgments of a decision maker based on qualitative (and perhaps certain types of quantitative) information are more accurate than using the results of explicit impact measures based on regression analysis procedures is an empirical question that may not be possible to answer.

CONCLUSIONS

To evaluate any project, one needs to ask specific questions that direct attention toward potential impacts, to gather data specific to these questions, and to employ methods for analyzing these data that yield impact information. Any evaluation, therefore, must be explicitly or implicitly guided by theoretical and methodological perspectives. This study has examined the main theories and methods that social science—most specifically, economics—would bring to bear in evaluating the use of ECT strategies for agricultural development. In conclusion, the major points of this analysis will be reviewed, and their general implications, as well as their particular import for policy makers who need to make decisions concerning concrete strategy alternatives will be discussed.

The reader's attention is directed toward what the authors have called the "dominant social science perspective," both in theory and method, and the criticisms that have been levied against it. In some ways, of course, this aggregate concept of a dominant perspective masks all the deviations within and between fields of study that are important to the choice of specific hypotheses and methods. However, as has been shown, the commonalities and complementarities of the theories and methods used by mainstream economics, sociology, education, and communications are quite significant. In terms of theory, they have yielded a coherent, interrelated, internally consistent conception of how the development process operates and the role of education and communications system policies within this process. As was discussed extensively in the beginning of this chapter, the focal points of this dominant development paradigm have changed over the last several decades from industrial-based growth to greater emphasis on agriculture; from concern only with the speed of overall growth to more widely stated concerns with equity; and from centrally devised strategies for technology use by traditional, change-resistant farmers to more locally relevant technology designs constructed with the participation and knowledge of farmers who are now thought of as operating quite rationally. Despite shifts in the overall focus, the key facets of the specific theoretical approach the dominant perspective uses to analyze development strategies have remained quite constant: the approach of economists to the efficiency of private and public sector decision making; the centrality of the process of technology transfer to economists, sociologists, and communications researchers; and, for at least the past two decades, the notion that education and communications systems are essential for efficient decision making and rapid, informed technology transfer, through changing the knowledge, attitudes, and behavior of individuals.

To use this dominant perspective to evaluate alternative development strategies and projects, it is necessary to concur in their overall focus, in the sensibility of those constant key facets of their approach summarized above as well as in their ability to direct policies toward desired ends. Most of these beliefs have been criticized extensively by what may also be viewed as a coherent, interrelated, internally consistent, alternative perspective that has developed in the social sciences. The simplicity of the notion that development strategies may be intentionally directed toward more agriculturally oriented, equitable, decentralized, and participatory forms by well-meaning policy makers is called into serious question. To the contrary, the alternative view posited is that the industrial-based, inequitable, and centralized strategies that have, for the most part, characterized development efforts are of primary utility to the logic of a social system in which the interests of those few who control the economic power also control the most political power. Again, this is not to say that the outcomes of these conflicting interests are predetermined in favor of the controlling classes (or of the working class). Indeed, many Marxists would likely argue that the political need now being expressed to pay attention to equity issues has arisen from the increased power and consciousness of the poorer classes. The primary implication is that the absence of power and class conflict in most social scientists' analyses of alternative policies makes their recommendations of dubious value.

More specifically, this alternative paradigm criticizes each of the three constant facets of the dominant paradigm. The examination of efficiency by neoclassical economists (based entirely on assumptions of how a perfectly competitive system operates) is seen as almost totally inapplicable to the power and class realities of the world in which we live. Prices bear no necessary relationship to anything that can be called "social value," and, thus, the monetary analysis of costs and/or benefits offers little, if any, guide to strategies for social betterment. The transfer-of-technology approach to development is seen from this perspective to be largely governed by the motives of economically powerful capitalist organizations and individuals that wish to achieve both greater profits and greater environmental control and stability. Motivating forces do little to ensure the welfare of those at the bottom of the system, and any trickle down is seen as slow, at best, and is usually accompanied by increasing relative differences between the "haves" and the "have nots." Finally, education and communications systems are seen primarily as useful both to transmit the limited technical and behavioral skills relevant to capitalist system production and to reinforce a capitalist system ideology that is based on the individualistic success orientation, associated work ethic, and the nonexistence of broad class interests in the guise of a meritocratic system that rewards individual ability and effort.

Within the dominant social science paradigm, the most appropriate means to discover the applicability of theory—and, consequently, to evaluate alternative strategies—is to utilize quantitative, statistical methodologies. The section on methodological approaches reviewed the experimental, correlational, and regression analysis approaches usually taken, and their limitations. The problems with the first two approaches have led economists—and, more recently, many other social scientists—to concentrate on regression-analysis-based studies. However, economists' use of regression analysis is also problematic in that the conditions necessary for accurate input estimation are rarely, if ever, fulfilled. The discussion of the literature in this chapter casts some doubt on the reliability of the faith in such methods. All regression analysis studies are based on inexact theories, which are operationalized with even greater imprecision. Thus, regression analysis coefficients are likely to be always biased, and there are really no guidelines for how erroneous they are. It should be no surprise, therefore, that almost every issue discussed in the economic development, education, or communications literature (or, for that matter, all social science literature) can be, and often is, endlessly debated with regression-analysis-based evidence being used to support all positions. The few consistent associations observed (such as education or social class background having a positive impact on earnings) are almost always the same observations that could be made from gross correlations between two variables, without "controlling" for other assumed causal factors.

Social scientists who view the world from the perspective of what has been called the alternative paradigm sometimes also use the quantitative methods above, but many place greater reliance on more qualitative methods. The argument they make is, essentially, that human beings can make sense out of relationships from logical and insightful observation of qualitative data (historical records, interviews, knowledge obtained through personal participation, and the like) and that these analyses are as objective, valid, and useful as those of quantitative researchers. Of course, such qualitative studies do not yield the quantitative impact measures so useful for explicit decision analysis, but then the reliability of those that can be obtained are questionable. Fundamentally, it may simply be that the mathematical regularities that science has uncovered in the physical world are not matched by such regularities (that can be expressed quantitatively) in the social world.

Out of this critical analysis come some very basic questions about social science research. For example, regarding conventional economic analysis in particular, Is competitive market theory a reasonable foundation on which to base ECT evaluation analysis, or Is it mostly a reflection of ideological biases? Or, How much can the empirical methods available to social science discriminate among competing cause-effect hypotheses of how the world actually works? Similar questions can be raised concerning the alternative theoretical and methodological perspectives discussed. The individual-oriented theory of the neoclassical economist constitutes a fundamentally different way of perceiving the social world than the more structural, historical view of the Marxist economist. These differences parallel a broader basic split that seems to penetrate all of social science, reflected not only in theory but in the very questions asked and the methodology seen as appropriate to answering them. Basically, the authors view these two perspectives as coherent, alternative, social science paradigms in the sense that Kuhn (1962) described the shared core beliefs held by physical scientists at various times as paradigms. To choose between them by the empirical approach of scientific research seems impossible, both because of the problem within the quantitative methods approach and because such methods are not necessarily agreed upon as reasonable rules for selection by those who hold different paradigmatic perspectives. In the authors' opinion, such choices reflect value and belief systems and associated training and experience, all of which are influenced to a great degree by the prevailing structures of power.

It is, of course, a truism that both paradigms have some validity (both neoclassical and Marxist theories clearly admit that individual characteristics and systemic properties are interrelated), but the differences are significant in terms of how each sees the focal points for societal change. It is possible that a resolution of such different perspectives will be forthcoming. Perhaps some beginning fields of study may eventually shed more light on such paradigmatic interconnections. For example, general systems theory (not to be confused with its more restricted relative, systems analysis) with its emphasis on viewing systems as organic, circuitous sets of relationships (whether stable or runaway), and its sensitivity to the telling question of where one draws the boundaries around the system one views, attempts to bridge the gap between individual and systemic behavior (Bateson 1972; Ollman 1973).

For the present, however, it would seem that policy makers will have to make serious choices about development strategies and various possible ECT activities with little in the way of clear guidance from economics or other social sciences. In many ways, it seems a matter of faith and philosophical commitment whether to view education and communications activities as a means to the formation of human capital, and trust in the resultant quantitative impact measures derived from empirics, or, alternatively, to view education and communications systems as fundamentally system conserving and inequitable, and to attempt to counter this with policies directed toward those education and communications activities that can increase working-class consciousness, worker control and organization, and their associated political and economic power. Perhaps the most important aspect of economics for decision makers is its ability to provide coherent alternative perspectives from which to decide what the potential alternatives are, how they are to be valued, and, even, what the most important issues are to be considered. Although this may be less guidance than policy makers might like, in many respects the definition of what are the most relevant alternative choices, concerning which both paradigms have much to say, may be the most important component of policy making. Perhaps the greatest social waste is engendered by the forgone opportunities of alternatives that are never even considered.

The intention of this chapter has been neither to berate social science nor to despair of human progress. The intention has been primarily to stimulate, broaden, and expand access to the discussion of what seem to be the most basic issues of economic analysis applied to social policy evaluation. In concluding, there are several recommendations that, at least tentatively, grow out of the analysis in this chapter. First, perhaps research activities should be carried on and used at a much more micro level than is the case. That is, part of the reason for insignificant or inconsistent research results may possibly be the result of trying to generalize relationships that cannot be generalized. For example, the way in which factors affect learning within one particular agricultural environment may not be relevant to other environments. If this were true, it would imply that decision-making power and research and decision analysis capabilities would be much more decentralized than they are now.

Second, within each paradigm there would seem to be possibilities for significant improvement through the promotion of interdisciplinary dialogue and research. Economics, sociology, education, and communications researchers complement each other's analysis, and the authors have discussed the directions that some interdisciplinary combinations might take relevant to the analysis of ECT strategies.

However, the third point is that the essential divisions are even greater within disciplines than they are between them. It seems likely that interdisciplinary research will do little to resolve the fundamental paradigmatic differences discussed. An alternative or additional strategy for policy makers may therefore be to fund competing studies of the same issue or project in order to open these evaluations to different views. This strategy has already been adopted—at least in a few policy-research endeavors of which the authors are aware, and it is being suggested by other researchers as well (Cohen and Garet 1975). Although it likely will increase the cost of evaluation, it may not do so substantially if the separate evaluators can agree on what data should be gathered.

Fourth, based on the authors' analysis of the dominant economics paradigm, it seems important that policy makers do not get too easily seduced by the current fervor with terms such as efficiency, optimize, maximize, cost-effectiveness analysis, and cost-benefit analysis. Furthermore, it seems likely that research and evaluation that takes a more historical, structural, qualitative perspective has been considerably underemphasized and underfunded, and that decision making would benefit from at least a more balanced approach to empirical observation. (Clearly, this state of affairs would come as no surprise to a Marxist, who sees research, like any other social endeavor, as strongly influenced by monopolistic, capitalist interests.)

Fifth, to the extent that the authors believe that scientific analysis will not yield unequivocal or even unidirectional guides to social policy, more attention should be focused on the process by which decisions are made. For example, within neoclassical economic theory, who is making public sector decisions is almost irrelevant if they use the proper social criteria for choosing among competing alternatives. However, if the criteria posited are ambiguous or debatable, then it would seem that much more care needs to be taken to ensure the openness and legitimacy of the decision-making processes. This would seem to require considerably more than the current vogue with "needs assessments," implying a basic need for widespread participation in decision formulation, analysis, and choice.

Finally, all of the above points emphasize the need for moving beyond an ill-informed dependency on specialization to examine the issues of the day. In the authors' opinion, decision makers must place less reliance on the judgments of expertise and greater reliance on understanding the frameworks of such expertise. This seems essential if the debates on issues are going to be opened to different perspectives and broader participation, or even if a policy maker merely wants to understand the multitudinous and often conflicting recommendations of the experts now hired. To argue that specialization may be necessary for understanding and functioning in a complex world may be quite true, but this does not mean that the conceptual foundations of competing approaches cannot be widely understood, as the authors hope to have demonstrated.

BIBLIOGRAPHY

Academy for Educational Development. 1978. The Basic Village Education Project, Guatemala: Final Report. Washington, D.C.: AED.

Amsellem, J., and E. Bouchet. 1975. "Reseaux d'écoute en espace urbain." Abidjan: Centre de Recherches Architecturales et Urbaines.

Arndt, T., D. Dalrymple, and V. Ruttan, eds. 1977. Resource Allocation and Productivity in National and International Agricultural Research. Minneapolis: University of Minnesota Press.

Arrow, K. 1973. "Higher Education as a Filter." Journal of Political Economy 2: 193-216.

Ashby, J., S. Klees, D. Pachico, and S. Wells. 1977. Agricultural Development and Human Capital: The Impact of Education and Communications. Palo Alto, Calif.: EDUTEL.

Baran, P., and P. Sweezy. 1966. Monopoly Capital. New York: Monthly Review Press.

Barghouti, S. 1974. "The Role of Communication in Jordan's Rural Development." Journalism Quarterly 51: 418-24.

Barnet, D. 1973. Peasant Types and Revolutionary Potential in Colonial Africa. Richmond, B.C.: LSM Information Center.

Barraclough, S. 1972. "Estratégia de desarrollo rural y reforma agraria." Desarrollo rural en las Américas (Colombia) 4: 61-79.

Barton, A. 1968. "Bringing Society Back in: Survey Research and Macromethodology." American Behavioral Scientist 12: 1-9.

Bartra, R. 1974. Estructura agraria y clases sociales en México. Mexico: Ediciones ERA.

Bateson, G. 1972. Step to an Ecology of Mind. New York: Ballantine Books.

Baumol, W. 1972. Economic Theory and Operations Analysis. Englewood Cliffs, N.J.: Prentice-Hall.

Becker, G. 1964. Human Capital. New York: National Bureau of Economic Research.

Beltran, L. 1976a. "Alien Premises, Objects, Methods." Communication Research 3, no. 2: 107-37.

_____. 1976b. "TV Etchings in the Minds of Latin Americans: Conservatism, Materialism and Communism." Paper read at the conference of the International Association of Mass Communication Research, Leicester, United Kingdom.

_____. 1974. "Rural Development and Social Communication: Relationships and Strategies." In Communication Strategies for Rural Development: Proceedings of the Cornell-CIAT International Symposium. Ithaca, N.Y.: Cornell University Press.

_____. 1971. "Communication and Domination: The Case of Latin America." Paper read at the Seminario Interamericano de Educación y Comunicación Social, Mexico City.

Benito, C. A. 1976. "Peasants' Response to Modernization Projects in Minifundia Economies." American Journal of Agricultural Economics 58, no. 2: 143-51.

Berg, I. 1971. Education and Jobs: The Great Training Robbery. New York: Beacon Press.

Bibliowicz, A. 1973. "La TV, un nuevo abuelo: Alegrate porque tu padre no es tu padre." El tiempo, Lecturas Dominicales, Bogotá.

Blair, T. 1960. "Social Structures and Information Exposure in Rural Brazil." Rural Sociology 25, no. 1: 65-75.

Blaug, M. 1973. Education and the Employment Problem in Developing Countries. Geneva: International Labour Office.

_____. 1970. An Introduction to the Economics of Education. Baltimore: Penguin Books.

Bostian, L., and F. Oliveira. 1965. "Relationships of Literacy and Education to Communication and to Social Conditions on Small

farms in Two Municipios in Southern Brazil." Paper read at
the Rural Sociological Society meeting, Chicago.

Bowles, S., and H. Gintis. 1976. Schooling in Capitalist America.
New York: Basic Books.

Bowman, M., and C. Anderson. 1965. Education and Economic Development. Chicago: Aldine.

Brown, L. 1970. Seeds of Change: The Green Revolution and Development in the 1970's. New York: Praeger.

Brown, M., and B. Kearl. 1967. "Mass Communication and Devel-
opment: The Problem of Local and Functional Relevance."
Paper no. 38. Madison: University of Wisconsin, Land Tenure
Center.

Canizales, J., and D. Myren. 1967. "Difusión de la información
agrícola en la valle del Yaqui." Technical Pamphlet no. 51.
Mexico City: Instituto Nacional de Investigaciones Agrícolas.

Cardoso, F. 1972. "Dependency and Development in Latin America."
New Left Review 74: 193-226.

Carnoy, M. 1974. Education as Cultural Imperialism. New York:
David McKay.

Carnoy, M., and H. Levin, eds. 1976. The Limits of Educational
Reform. New York: David McKay.

Chilcote, R. 1974. "Dependency: A Critical Synthesis of the Literature." Latin American Perspective 1: 4-29.

Chu, G., S. Rahim, L. Kincaid, eds. 1976. Communication for
Group Transformation in Development. Communications Monographs no. 2. Honolulu: East-West Center.

Coates, H. 1973. "The Marketplace of Ideas." American Economic
Association Papers and Proceedings.

Cohen, D., and M. Garet. 1975. "Reforming Educational Policy
with Applied Social Research." Harvard Educational Review 45:
17-43.

Colomina de Rivera, M. 1968. "El huesped alienante: Un estudio
sobre audiencia y effectos de las radio-telenovelas en Vene-

zuela." Colección de ensayos, no. 1. Maracaibo: Universidad de Zulia, Faculdad de Humanidades y Educación.

Contreras, E. 1979. "Communication, Rural Modernity and Structural Constraints." Ph.D. dissertation, Stanford University.

Cooke, T., and S. Romweber. 1977. Radio Advertising Techniques and Nutrition Education: A Summary of a Field Experiment in the Philippines and Nicaragua. New York: Manoff International.

Coombs, P., and M. Ahmed. 1974. Attacking Rural Poverty: How Nonformal Education Can Help. Baltimore: Johns Hopkins University Press.

Cordera, R. 1973. "Análisis de contenido de los suplementos agropecuarios de los periódicos de Costa Rica." Thesis, Universidad de Costa Rica, Escuela de Periodismo, San José, Costa Rica.

Daines, S., and H. Howell. 1975. Guatemala Farm Policy Analysis. Washington, D.C.: Agency for International Development, Latin American Bureau.

De Janvry, A. 1975. "The Political Economy of Rural Development in Latin America: An Interpretation." American Journal of Agricultural Economics 57, no. 3: 490-99.

Denison, E. 1962. Why Growth Rates Differ. Washington, D.C.: Brookings Institution.

Dervin, B. 1978. "Communicating with the Urban Poor: An Alternative Perspective." Paper presented at the meeting of the International Communication Association, Chicago.

Deutchman, P., J. McNelly, and H. Ellingworth. 1961. "Mass Media Use by Sub-Elites in Latin American Countries." Journalism Quarterly 38: 460-72.

De Vries, E., and M. Echevarría. 1967. Social Aspects of Economic Development in Latin America. 2 vols. Tournai, Belgium: United Nations Educational, Scientific and Cultural Organization.

Diawara, M. "Le plan 1976-1980." Revenue française d'etudes politiques africaines 11: 22-39.

Diaz Bordenave, J. 1976. "Communication of Agricultural Innovations in Latin America: The Need for New Models." Communication Research 3, no. 2: 135-54.

_____. 1964. "A Survey of Educational and Informational Institutions in Pernambuco: Case Studies of Selected Services Agencies in Northeastern Brazil." Madison: University of Wisconsin, Land Tenure Center.

Diaz-Guerrero, R., I. Reyes-Lagunes, D. Witzke, and W. Holtzman. 1976. "Plaza Sesamo in Mexico: An Evaluation." Journal of Communication 26, no. 2: 145-54.

Diaz Rangel, E. 1967. "Pueblos subinformados: Las agencias de noticias y América Latina." Caracas: Universidad Central de Venezuela.

Dirección General de Estadística. 1973. "Resultados de tabulación por muestreo del VIII censo de población." Guatemala City: Dirección General de Estadística.

Donohue, G. A., T. Tichneor, and C. Olien. 1975. "Mass Media and the Knowledge Gap: A Hypothesis Reconsidered." Communication Research 1, no. 2: 3-23.

Dos Santos, T. 1970. "The Structure of Dependence." American Economic Review 60: 231-36.

Eicher, J. C., and F. Orivel. 1977. Analyses des coûts de l'enseignement primaire télévisuel en Côte d'Ivoire. Washington, D.C.: Academy for Educational Development.

Elliot, H. 1974. "Animation Rurale and Encadrement Technique in the Ivory Coast." Discussion Paper no. 40. Ann Arbor: University of Michigan, Center for Research on Economic Development.

Elliott, P. 1974. Uses and Gratifications Research: A Critique and a Sociological Alternative." In The Uses of Mass Communication: Current Perspectives on Gratifications Research, edited by J. Blumler and E. Katz. Beverly Hills, Calif.: Sage.

Esman, M. 1974. "Popular Participation and Feedback Systems in Rural Development." In Communication Strategies for Rural Development: Proceedings of the Cornell-CIAT Symposium. Ithaca, N.Y.: Cornell University Press.

Etaix, M., and F. Lenglet. 1977. "Tel pour Tous" in Rural Ivory Coast: Audience, Impact, Perceptions. Washington, D.C.: Academy for Educational Development.

Fagen, R. 1969. The Transformation of Political Culture in Cuba. Stanford, Calif.: Stanford University Press.

Fanon, F. 1963. Los condenados de la tierra. Mexico City: Fondo de Cultura Económica.

Felstehausen, H. 1968. "Economic Knowledge, Participation and Farmer Decision Making in a Developed and an Underdeveloped Country." International Journal of Agrarian Affairs 5, no. 4: 263-81.

Frankel, F. 1971. India's Green Revolution: Economic Gains and Political Costs. Princeton, N.J.: Princeton University Press.

Frapier, J. 1969. "U.S. Media Empire: Latin America." North American Congress of Latin America Newsletter, vol. 11, no. 9.

Freebairn, D. 1973. "Income Disparities in the Agricultural Sector: Regional and Institutional Stresses." In Food, Population and Employment: The Impact of the Green Revolution, edited by T. Poleman and D. Freebairn. New York: Praeger.

Freire, P. 1973. Education for Critical Consciousness. New York: Seabury Press.

Frey, F. 1966. The Mass Media and Rural Development in Turkey. Report no. 3. Cambridge, Mass.: MIT Center for International Studies.

Galjart, B. 1971. "Rural Development and Sociological Concepts: A Critique." Rural Sociology 36, no. 1: 31-41.

Garcia, A. 1966. "El problema agrario en América Latina y los medios de información collectiva." Quito, Ecuador: Centro Internacional de Estudios Superiores en Periodismo para América Latina.

Germani, G. 1973. El concepto de marginalidad. Buenos Aires: Ediciones Nueva Visión.

Gillette, C., and N. Uphoff. 1973. "Cultural and Social Factors Affecting Small Farmers' Participation in Formal Credit Programs." Occasional Paper no. 3. Ithaca, N.Y.: Cornell University, Center for International Studies.

Gintis, H. 1976. "The Nature of Labor Exchange and the Theory of Capitalist Production." Review of Radical Political Economy 8: 36-54.

_____. 1974. "Welfare Criteria with Endogenous Preferences: The Economics of Education." International Economic Review 15: 415-30.

Glaser, B., and A. Strauss. 1967. The Discovery of Grounded Theory: Strategies for Qualitative Research. Chicago: Aldine.

Golding, P. 1974. "Media Role in National Development: Critique of a Theoretical Orthodoxy." Journal of Communication 24: 39-53.

Golding, P., and M. Murdock. 1976. "Theories of Communication and Theories of Society." Paper read at the meeting of the International Association of Mass Communication Research, Leicester, United Kingdom.

Gotsch, C. 1972. "Technical Change and the Distribution of Income in Rural Areas." American Journal of Agricultural Economics 45: 326-41.

Goulet, D. 1977. The Uncertain Promise: Value Conflicts in Technology Transfer. New York: IDOC/North America.

Goussault, Y. 1976. "L'état et le dévelopment de l'agriculture: Le concept d'intervention." Revue tiers-monde 17: 615-33.

Grant, S., and P. Seya. 1976. "Visits to Twenty-Three Villages to Determine the Impact of the Water Series Produced by the Out-of-School Department." Abidjan, Ivory Coast: Service d'Evaluation; Washington, D.C.: Academy for Educational Development.

Grant, S., S. Klees, F. Lenglet, and E. McAnany. 1978. Final Report: Economic Studies and Out-of-School Education Program Evaluation for the Ivory Coast. Washington, D.C.: Academy for Educational Development.

Griffin, K. 1974. The Political Economy of Agrarian Change. New York: Macmillan.

_____. 1973. "Policy Options for Rural Development." Paper prepared for the Ford Foundation Seminar in Rural Development, Ibadan, Nigeria.

Grunig, J. 1971. "Communication and Economic Decision Making of Colombian Peasants." Economic Development and Cultural Change 18: 580-97.

_____. 1969. "Information and Decision Making in Economic Development." Journalism Quarterly 46: 565-75.

Gutierrez Sanchez, J. 1966. "Content Analysis and Readability Study of Agricultural Pages in Five Colombian Newspapers." Thesis, University of Wisconsin-Madison, Department of Agricultural Journalism.

Gutierrez Sanchez, J., and R. McNamara. 1968. "Algunos factores que afectan el proceso de comunicación en Venezuela y Colombia." Revista ICA (Colombia), vol. 3.

Hall, B. 1978. Mtu Ni Afya: Tanzania's Health Campaign. Washington, D.C.: Academy for Educational Development.

Hall, B., and A. Dodds. 1977. "Voices for Development: The Tanzanian Radio Study Campaigns." In Radio for Education and Development: Case Studies, edited by P. Spain, D. Jamison, and E. McAnany. Working Paper no. 266, 2 vols. Washington, D.C.: World Bank.

Harker, B. 1973. "The Contribution of Schooling to Agricultural Modernization: An Empirical Analysis." In Education and Rural Development, edited by P. Foster and J. Sheffield. London: Evans Brothers, World Yearbook of Education.

Henderson, J., and R. E. Quandt. 1971. Microeconomic Theory: A Mathematical Approach. New York: McGraw-Hill.

Hirschman, A. O. 1958. The Strategy of Economic Development. New Haven, Conn.: Yale University Press.

Hyami, Y., and V. Ruttan. 1971. Agricultural Development: An International Perspective. Baltimore: Johns Hopkins University Press.

Inkeles, A., and D. Smith. 1974. Becoming Modern: Individual Change in Six Developing Countries. Cambridge, Mass.: Harvard University Press.

Institut Ivoirien d'Opinion Publique (IIOP). 1975. Untitled results of a national survey among urban and rural populations.

Ivory Coast Republic. 1976a. La Côte d'Ivoire en chiffres, 1976-77. Abidjan: Ministére du Plan.

_____. 1976b. Untitled document. Abidjan: Ministére de l'Information, Comité Permanent pour la Mise au Travail des Populations, Sous Comité de Presse.

_____. 1976c. "Preparation au comité internationale de programmation de Télé pour Tous." Abidjan: Sous-Direction de l'Education Extra-Scolaire.

_____. 1975. "La télévision educative au service du développement: L'extra-Scolaire et Télé pour Tous." Abidjan: Sous-Direction de L'Education Extra-Scolaire.

Jamison, D., and L. Lau. 1978. Farmer Education and Farm Efficiency. Washington, D.C.: World Bank.

Jamison, D., and E. McAnany. 1978. Radio for Education and Development. Beverly Hills, Calif.: Sage.

Jouët, J. 1977. "Communication Media and Development: Problems of Adaptation." Paper read at the United Nations Educational, Scientific and Cultural Organization meeting on Self-Management, Access and Participation in Communication, Belgrade, Yugoslavia.

_____. 1976. "Rapport d'enquête sur la compréhension de l'emission et de l'affiche sur le ver du Guinée." Abidjan: Sous-Direction de l'Education Extra-Scolaire.

Kahl, J. 1968. The Measurement of Modernism: A Study of Values in Brazil and Mexico. Austin: University of Texas Press.

Kao, C., K. Anschell, and C. Eicher. 1964. "Disguised Unemployment in Agriculture: A Survey." In Agriculture in Economic Development, edited by C. Eicher and L. Witt. New York: McGraw-Hill.

Kearl, B. 1978. "An Overview of Communication in Agriculture Projects." Development Communication Report (Academy for Educational Development, Washington, D.C.) 22: 1-3.

Kiray, M. 1964. Ereğli, a Coastal Town before Heavy Development. Ankara: T. C. Devlet Plolama.

Klees, S., and S. Wells. Forthcoming. "Economic Analysis for Communications and Development." In Communication Planning for Development, edited by A. Hancock. Paris: United Nations Educational, Scientific and Cultural Organization.

_____. 1978. Cost Benefit Analysis of Non-Formal Educational Techniques for Agricultural Development: A Case Study of the Basic Village Education Project of Guatemala. Washington, D.C.: Academy for Educational Development.

_____. 1977. Cost-Effectiveness and Cost-Benefit Analysis for Educational Planning and Evaluation: Methodology and Application to Instructional Technology. Washington, D.C.: U.S. Agency for International Development.

Kochner, J. 1973. Rural Development, Income Distribution and Fertility Decline. New York: Population Council.

Kuhn, T. 1962. The Structure of Scientific Revolutions. Chicago: University of Chicago Press.

Lamberton, D., ed. 1971. Economics of Information and Knowledge. New York: Penguin Books.

Lange, O. 1965. Problems of the Political Economy of Socialism. New Delhi: Peoples Publishing House.

Lau, L., and P. Yotopoulos. 1971. "A Test for Relative Efficiency and Application to Indian Agriculture." American Economic Review 56: 94-109.

Leibenstein, H. 1966. "Allocative Efficiency versus X-Efficiency." American Economic Review 66: 392-415.

Lele, U. 1975. The Design of Rural Development: Lessons from Africa. Baltimore: Johns Hopkins University Press.

Lenglet, F. 1978. Out-of-School Educational Television in the Ivory Coast: Its Effectiveness in Rural Development. Ph.D. dissertation, Stanford University.

_____. 1976. "The Impact of 25 Television Programs on 'Water' Produced and Broadcast by the Ivorian Out-of-School Education Project." Washington, D.C.: Academy for Educational Development.

Lenglet, F., and E. McAnany. 1977. Rural Adult Education and the Role of the Mass Media: A Comparative Analysis of Four Projects. Washington, D.C.: Academy for Educational Development.

Lerner, D. 1958. The Passing of Traditional Society. Glencoe, Ill.: Free Press.

Lessa, C. 1975. "Marginalidad y proceso de marginalización." In América Latina: Dependencia y subdesarrollo. San José, Costa Rica: EDUCA.

Lockheed, M., D. Jamison, and L. Lau. Forthcoming. "Farmer Education and Farm Efficiency: A Survey." Economic Development and Cultural Change.

Lopez, T. 1971. "Discurso." El tiempo, March 5.

Ma Ekonzo, E., and T. Basri. 1976. "Final Report of the Second Committee: Role of Information in Consolidating Economic and Social Cooperation among Nonaligned Nations." Report of the Symposium of the Nonaligned Nations on Information, Tunis, March.

Marques de Melo, J. 1969. "Communicação social no Brasil." Vozes 63: 1.

Mattelart, A. 1970. "Los medios de comunicación de massas: La ideología de la prensa liberal en Chile." Cuadernos de la realidad nacional (Special 2d ed.), no. 3.

McAnany, E. 1978a. "Does Information Really Work?" Journal of Communication 28, no. 1: 84-90.

_____. 1978b. "Success or Failure of Communication Technology in the Third World: By What Criteria Shall We Judge?" Paper read at the United Nations Educational, Scientific and Cultural Organization conference on Economic Analysis for Educational Technology Decisions, Dijon, France.

_____. 1973. Radio's Role in Development: Five Strategies for Use. Information Bulletin no. 4. Washington, D.C.: Information Center for Instructional Technology, Academy for Educational Development.

McAnany, E., and J. Oliveira. Forthcoming. The SACI/EXERN Project in Brazil: An Analytical Case Study. Paris: United Nations Educational, Scientific and Cultural Organization, Reports and Papers on Mass Communication.

McClelland, D. 1961. The Achieving Society. New York: Van Nostrand.

McNelly, J. 1966. "Mass Communication and the Climate for Modernization in Latin America." Journal of Inter-American Studies 8: 345-57.

Mayo, J., R. Hornik, and E. McAnany. 1976. Educational Reform with Television: The El Salvador Experience. Stanford, Calif.: Stanford University Press.

Mayo, J., McAnany, E., and S. Klees. 1975. "The Mexican Telesecundaria: A Cost-Effectiveness Analysis." Instructional Science 4: 193-236.

Mejia, P. 1971. "El poder y reacciones a la reforma agraria." Master's thesis, Universidad Agraria la Molina, Lima.

Mellor, J. 1976. The New Economics of Growth: A Strategy for India and the Developing World. Ithaca, N.Y.: Cornell University Press.

Melody, W. 1973. "The Role of Advocacy in Public Policy Planning." In Communications Technology and Social Policy, edited by G. Gerbner, L. Gross, and W. Melody. New York: John Wiley & Sons.

Moulton, Jeanne. 1977. "Animation Rurale: Education for Rural Development." Ph.D. dissertation, University of Massachusetts, Amherst.

Myrdal, G. 1968. Asian Drama: An Inquiry into the Poverty of Nations. New York: Twentieth Century Fund.

Myren, D., ed. 1970. Strategies for Increasing Agricultural Productivity on Small Holdings. Mexico City: International Maize and Wheat Improvement Center.

_____. 1964. "The Role of Information in Farm Decisions under Conditions of High Risk and Uncertainty." In International Research Symposium on the Role of Communications in Agricultural Development, edited by D. Myren. Mexico City: Mexican Agricultural Program, Rockefeller Foundation.

Nordenstreng, K., and T. Varis. 1973. Television Traffic: One Way Street? Papers and Reports on Mass Communication no. 70. Paris: United Nations Educational, Scientific and Cultural Organization.

Oettinger, A., and J. Legates. 1977. "International Information and Communication Issues: An Overview and International Security." In Congressional Record, vol. 123, no. 101, S. 9534-9537, June 13, 1977.

Ollman, B. 1973. Alienation: Marx's Conception of Man in Capitalist Society. New York: Cambridge University Press.

O'Sullivan, J. 1978a. Rural Development Programs among Marginal Farmers in the Western Highlands of Guatemala. Stanford, Calif.: Stanford University, Institute for Communication Research.

_____. 1978b. "Rural Development Programs and the Problem of Marginality in the Western Highlands of Guatemala." Ph.D. dissertation, Stanford University.

_____. 1977. Personal communication.

O'Sullivan, J., and M. Kaplun. Forthcoming. "Communication Methods to Promote Grass-Roots Participation for an Endogenous Development." Paris: United Nations Educational, Scientific and Cultural Organization.

Papagiannis, G. 1977. "Nonformal Education and National Development: A Study of the Thai Mobile Training School and Its Effects on Adult Participants." Ph.D. dissertation, Stanford University.

Parker, E. 1978. "An Information-Based Hypothesis." Journal of Communication 28: 81-83.

_____. 1976. "Social Implications of Computer/Telecommunications Systems." In OECD Informatics Study: Conference on Computer/Telecommunications. Paris: Organization for Economic Cooperation and Development.

Pasquali, A. 1967. "El aparato singular: Un día de televisión en Caracas." Mimeographed. Caracas: Universidad Central de Venezuela, Faculdad de Economía.

_____. 1963. Comunicación y cultura de masas. Caracas: EDUC.

Phillips, D., H. Costner, and J. Fennessey. 1974. "The Madness of Our Methods: A Three Author Exchange in Four Parts." Sociology and Social Research 58: 225-36.

Poirier, D. 1977. "Econometric Methodology in Radical Economics." American Economic Review 62: 393-99.

Polpatanarithi, S. 1970. "Villagers' Media Habits and General Interest Survey in Amphoe Seat, Supanburi Province." Washington, D.C.: U.S. International Communication Agency.

Prebisch, R. 1959. "Commercial Policy in Underdeveloped Countries." American Economic Review 44: 251-73.

Pye, L., ed. 1963. Communications and Political Development. Princeton, N.J.: Princeton University Press.

Quijano, A. 1971. "La formación de un universo marginal en las cuidades de América Latina." Espaces et societes, vol. 3.

Quijano, A., and F. Weffort. 1973. Populismo, marginalización y dependencia. San José, Costa Rica: EDUCA.

Ranis, G. 1968. "Economic Growth Theory." In International Encyclopedia of the Social Sciences, edited by D. Sills, vol. 4. New York: Macmillan.

Reynolds, L. 1969. "The Content of Development Economics." American Economic Review 59: 401-8.

Rincon, C. 1968. "Notas sobre el contenido de las tele-radionovelas." In El huesped alienante: Un estudio sobre audiencia y efectos de la radio-telenovelas en Venezuela, edited by M. Colomina de Rivera. Colección de Ensayos no. 1. Maracaibo: Universidad de Zulia, Faculdad de Humanidades y Educación.

Roca, L. 1969. "Los intereses económicos y la orientación de noticias sobre el movimiento campesino." Campesino (Peru), vol. 1.

Rogers, E. 1977. "Network Analysis of the Diffusion of Family Planning Innovations." In Social Networks: Surveys, Advances and Commentaries, edited by P. W. Holland and S. Leinhardt. New York: Academic Press.

_____. 1976. "Communication and Development: The Passing of the Dominant Paradigm. Communication Research 3, no. 2: 213-40.

_____. 1964. "Information Sources in the Adoption Process for 2-4-D Weed Spray in Three Colombian Neighborhoods." In International Research Symposium on the Role of Communication in Agricultural Development, edited by D. Myren. Mexico City: Mexican Agricultural Program, Rockefeller Foundation.

_____. 1962. Diffusion of Innovations. New York: Free Press.

Rogers, E., and L. Shoemaker. 1971. Communications of Innovations: A Cross-Cultural Approach. New York: Free Press.

Rogers, E., and L. Svenning. 1969. Modernization among Peasants: The Impact of Communication. New York: Holt, Rinehart and Winston.

Rogers, E., J. Ascroft, and N. Röling. 1970. Diffusion of Innovations in Brazil, Nigeria and India. Report no. 24. East Lansing: Michigan State University, Department of Communication.

Röling, N., J. Ascroft, and F. Chege. 1976. "The Diffusion of Innovations and the Issue of Equity in Rural Development." Communication Research 3, no. 2: 155-70.

_____. 1974. "Innovation and Equity in Rural Development." Paper read at the Eighth World Congress of Sociology, Toronto.

Ruanova, H. 1958. "Content and Readability of Some Latin American Agricultural Magazines." Master's thesis, University of Wisconsin-Madison, Department of Agricultural Journalism.

Salazar, J. 1962. "Televisión, actitudes y propaganda." Mimeographed. Caracas: Universidad Central de Venezuela.

Schramm, W. 1976a. "An Overview of the Past Decade." In Communication and Change: The Last Ten Years and the Next, edited by W. Schramm and D. Lerner. Honolulu: University of Hawaii Press.

_____. 1976b. "Data on Communication Systems in Three Developing Regions." In Communication and Change: The Last Ten Years and the Next, edited by W. Schramm and D. Lerner. Honolulu: University of Hawaii Press.

_____. 1964. Mass Media and National Development. Stanford, Calif.: Stanford University Press.

Schramm, W. and D. Lerner, eds. 1976. Communication and Change: The Last Ten Years and the Next. Honolulu: University of Hawaii Press.

Schultz, T. 1975. "The Value of the Ability to Deal with Disequilibria." Journal of Economic Literature 13, no. 3: 827-45.

_____. 1965. Economic Crises in World Agriculture. Ann Arbor: University of Michigan Press.

_____. 1964. Transforming Traditional Agriculture. New Haven, Conn.: Yale University Press.

Secretaría General del Consejo Nacional de Planificación Económica. 1975a. Plan de Desarrollo Agrícola, 1975/79. 14 vols. Guatemala: Government of Guatemala.

_____. 1975b. Plan nacional de educación, ciencia y tecnología, 1975/79. Guatemala: Government of Guatemala.

Sewell, G. 1964. "Squatter Settlements in Turkey." Ph.D. dissertation, Massachusetts Institute of Technology.

Seya, P., and F. Yao. 1977. Television for the Rural African Village: Studies of Audiences and Impact in the Ivory Coast. Washington, D.C.: Academy for Educational Development.

Shingi, P., and B. Mody. 1976. "The Communication Effects Gap: A Field Experiment on Television and Agricultural Ignorance in India." Communication Research 3, no. 2: 171-90.

Shore, L. 1978. "Mass Media for Development: A Reexamination of Access, Exposure and Impact." In Communication with the Rural Poor of the Third World: Does Information Make a Difference?, edited by E. McAnany. Stanford, Calif.: Stanford University, Institute for Communication Research.

Silva, M., et al. 1964. "Study of Conflict in Consensus." Mimeographed. Caracas: Universidad Central de Venezuela.

Simmons, R., K. Kent, and V. Misgra. 1968. "Media Development and News in the Slums of Ecuador and India." Journalism Quarterly 45: 698-705.

Spain, P. 1977. "The Mexican Radioprimaria Project." In Radio for Education and Development: Case Studies, edited by P. Spain, D. Jamison, and E. McAnany. Working Paper no. 266. 2 vols. Washington, D.C.: World Bank.

_____. 1971. "A Survey of Radio Listenership in the Davao Province of Mindinao, the Philippines." Mimeographed. Stanford, Calif.: Stanford University, Institute for Communication Research.

Spain, P., D. Jamison, and E. McAnany, eds. 1977. Radio for Education and Development: Case Studies. Working Paper 266. 2 vols. Washington, D.C.: World Bank.

Spring, J. 1972. Education and the Rise of the Corporate State. Boston: Beacon Press.

Starr, P. 1974. "The Edge of Social Science." Harvard Educational Review 44: 393-415.

Story, J., and J. Story. 1969. "Hill Tribes, the Target Audience." Washington, D.C.: U.S. International Communications Agency.

Sunkel, O., and P. Paz. 1970. El subdesarrollo Latino-americano y la teoría del desarrollo. Mexico City: Siglo XXI.

Suppes, P., B. Searle, and J. Friend. 1979. The Radio Mathematics Project: Nicaragua 1976-77. Stanford, Calif.: Stanford University, Institute for Mathematical Studies in the Social Sciences.

Sweeney, W. 1977. Population Reports: Family Planning Programs. Series J, no. 16. Washington, D.C.: George Washington University, Department of Medical and Public Affairs.

Tichenor, P., G. Donahue, and C. Oline. 1970. "Mass Media and Differential Growth in Knowledge." Public Opinion Quarterly 34: 158-70.

University of California at Los Angeles. 1976. Statistical Abstract of Latin America. Los Angeles: UCLA, Center of Latin American Studies.

United Nations Educational, Scientific and Cultural Organization. 1978a. Interim Report on Communication Problems in Modern Society. Paris: UNESCO.

_____. 1978b. UNESCO Statistical Yearbook, 1976. Paris: UNESCO.

_____. 1976. The Experimental World Literacy Programme: A Critical Assessment. Paris: UNESCO.

U.S., Congress. Committee on International Relations. 1975. Implementation of "New Directions" in Development Assistance. Report prepared by the Agency for International Development, 94th Cong., 1st sess., July 22, 1975.

Vanek, J. 1970. The General Theory of Labor-Managed Market Economies. Ithaca, N.Y.: Cornell University Press.

Welch, F. 1970. "Education in Production." Journal of Political Economy 78: 35-59.

Wells, A. 1972. Picture-Tube Imperialism? The Impact of U.S. Television in Latin America. Maryknoll, N.Y.: Orbis Books.

Wharton, C. 1976. "Risk, Uncertainty and the Subsistence Farmer: Technological Innovation and the Resistance to Change in the Context of Survival." Studies in Economic Anthropology 7: 151-78.

White, R. 1977. "Mass Communication and the Popular Promotion Strategy of Rural Development in Honduras." In Radio for Education and Development: Case Studies, edited by P. Spain, D. Jamison, and E. McAnany. Working Paper 266. 2 vols. Washington, D.C.: World Bank.

_____. 1976. An Alternative Pattern of Basic Education: Radio Santa Maria. Series no. 30. Hamburg: United Nations Educational, Scientific and Cultural Organization, Institute for Education, Experiments and Innovations in Education.

Whiting, G., and J. Stanfield. 1972. "Mass Media Use and Opportunity Structure in Rural Brazil." Public Opinion Quarterly 36: 56–68.

Whyte, W. 1977. "Toward a New Strategy for Research and Development in Agriculture: Helping Small Farmers in Developing Countries." Desarrollo rural en las Américas 9, no. 1/2: 51–61.

Williams, R. 1973. "Base and Superstructure in Marxist Cultural Theory." New Left Review 82: 3–16.

Wilson, S. 1977. "The Use of Ethnographic Techniques in Educational Research." Review of Educational Research 47, no. 1: 245–65.

World Bank. 1978. Annual Report, 1978. Washington, D.C.: World Bank.

_____. 1975. Rural Development: Sector Policy Paper. Washington, D.C.: World Bank.

Yotopoulos, P. 1967. "From Stock to Flow Capital Inputs for Agricultural Production Functions: A Microanalytical Approach." Journal of Farm Economics 49, no. 1, 476–91.

INDEX

ABOUT THE EDITOR
AND CONTRIBUTORS

EMILE G. McANANY, associate professor of international communication, School of Communication, University of Texas-at-Austin, has spent the last ten years studying the role of communications in social change and development. Previously, he spent a number of years doing research and teaching at the Institute for Communication Research, Stanford University, and has conducted field research in Brazil, El Salvador, Guatemala, and the Ivory Coast. He is coauthor of a number of books, including Educational Reform with Television: The El Salvador Experience (Stanford University Press) and Radio for Education and Development (Sage), and his numerous articles and monographs have appeared in such publications as Journal of Communication, Prospects, Instructional Science, and Society.

JACQUELINE ASHBY is a research associate and specialist in rural sociology for the International Fertilizer Center at the agricultural research center, CIAT, in Cali, Colombia.

EDUARDO CONTRERAS is director of research for the Latin American Association of Radio Schools in Buenos Aires, Argentina.

STEVEN KLEES is currently visiting professor of economics, School of Administration, Federal University of Rio Grande do Norte, Natal, Brazil.

FRANS LENGLET is senior technical adviser to the Zambian government for its agricultural education program in Kabwe, Zambia.

JEREMIAH O'SULLIVAN is director of the nonformal and technical education sector for the church/government-sponsored public corporation, INCE, in Caracas, Venezuela.

DOUGLAS PACHICO is a Rockefeller postdoctoral fellow at the agricultural research center, CIAT, in Cali, Colombia.

LARRY SHORE is on the faculty of the Department of Communication, Hunter College, New York.

STUART WELLS is an associate professor of management, School of Business, California State University, San Jose.